CORPORATE SOCIAL DEVELOPMENT
A PARADIGM SHIFT

About the Author

Debasis Bhattacharya, Ph.D. on Corporate Social Development from University of Pune, and graduated from Visva-Bharati University, Santiniketan. Born and brought up in Kolkata, he is 38.

His interest spans across a widerange of areas such as Corporate Social Development, Public-Private Partnership, Strategic-Planning, Welfare-Business and Participatory Research. He is a rare blend of an academician and a practitioner, having good knowledge base, hands-on-experience and a strong commitment towards working for the community.

He is credited with conceptualisation, articulation and administration of innovative National Projects, Studies and Seminars in the area of Corporate Social Development. His quality of relating micro aspects of a problem with macro issues comes from his working with organisations entirely different in character, structure and approach—gained over one and half a decade diverse organisational experience from grassroots level NGO, International. Organisation, Government on one hand and CII, an apex and premier industry associaltion on the other. This rich and diverse experience and exposure helps him venture into new areas.

CORPORATE SOCIAL DEVELOPMENT
A PARADIGM SHIFT

Debasis Bhattacharya

CONCEPT PUBLISHING COMPANY, NEW DELHI-110059

Cataloging in Publication Data—DK
Courtesy: D.K. Agencies (P) Ltd. <docinfo@dkagencies.com>

Bhattacharya, Debasis, 1967-
Corporate social development : a paradigm shift / Debasis Bhattacharya.
p. cm.
In Indian context.
Includes bibliographical references (p.)
Includes index.
ISBN 8180693244

1. Social responsibility of business—India. I. Title.

DDC 658.408 095 4 22

ISBN : 81-8069-324-4

First Published 2006

Published and Printed by
Ashok Kumar Mittal
Concept Publishing Company
A/15-16, Commercial Block, Mohan Garden,
New Delhi-110059 (India)

Phones : 25351460, 25351794
Fax : 091-11-25357103
Email : publishing@conceptpub.com

Dedicated
to
My Beloved Mother
Sova Bhattacharya

PREFACE

The socio-economic history of '90s had shown us and also its been realised in contemporary Indian context that the government and business are two sides of the same coin. The third link to this pair is the people of the Nation. After the onslaught of Liberation, Privatisation and Globalisation (LPG), bird's view from the study manifest about the Government's standing for the Social sector programmes, which are electorally sensitive, have remained fluid and unstandardised.

With tremendous heterogeneous constraining factors, India has a vision of being the fourth largest economy and the second largest vibrant market. But this vision can be realised only when 'Social Capital' in India keeps pace with the demand of development and growth. To justifying the real picture, thirty-five diverse sectors cases had selected for the study, these had given a broader look into the creative and positive approaches of corporate social development specially in consonance with the present context. It has been found from the study that the recent years have witnessed a growing shift in the corporate involvement in social development. It's a major paradigm shift in the recent trend and contemporary history of social development—for both the sectors of India.

In light of above, it analysed and intervened various pertinent and broader issues regarding the determinants of social development and its funding. Its being well reflected from the study that the government sector is the single largest financier for social development, and at the same time trend in multilateral and bilateral grants to India is declining. A parallel exploration was also carried out through e-mail to have a better understanding of the perception of social development among the corporates. Finally, in order to explore the implications of the different determinants of social development, the beneficiaries' viewpoint is taken into consideration to have a better understanding of the effectiveness of development programmes undertaken by the Corporate and NGO sectors towards a synergetic and strategic partnership to achieve the mutual goal for sustainable development.

Through this research, another future dimension is being realised that a national level consorted effort is essential for Corporate Social Developer, basically it would create a culture and broader understandability among the corporate sector to invest in social sector. After LPG, the State Governments are running out of money. Contrary to this, still there are tremendous in-house untapped resources are existing. So, in this juncture, to name a few, corporate sector and its respective associations can act as a catalyst and as partner to empower the people, artisans, producers groups and NGOs towards a win-win situation for 'sustainability'.

Acknowledgements

Many people and organisations have helped and contributed immensely, albeit in different ways, to complete my assignment. Most importantly, I express my deep sense of gratitude to Dr. S.D. Gokhale, who, as a visionary, motivated me to aspire for more academic insights and to seek to their practical applications in professional social development practice. Simply it is impossible to equate the fastidious and valuable guidance according to me by him. Without his continuous support, I could not even imagine that I have completed this book.

I have benefited greatly from candid discussion with many academicians, corporate and NGO leaders particularly the then Director of Centre for Workers' Management Mr. D. Thankappan; former Director General of Central Statistical Organisation, Government of India, Dr. S. Srivastava; former Vice-Chancellor of Himachal Pradesh University and Advisor of Rehabilitation Council of India, Government of India, Prof. C.L. Kundu; former Principal Advisor, Social Sector, Planning Commission, Government of India, Dr. K.G. Krishnamurty; Development Economist, Dr. Pratap Sisodia; Bureau Manager of 'The New York Times', Mr. P.J. Anthony; Executive Director of Lupin Human Welfare & Research Foundation, Mr. S.R. Gupta; the Tata Institute of Social Sciences former Director, Prof. R.R. Singh; the then President of Partners in Change Mr. S.V. Sista; Senior Advisor of Mahindra and Mahindra Mr. M. Raghuram; Advisor of DCM Ltd. Mr. D.R. Sen; the then Professor and Head of the Department of Social Science at National Institute of Health & Family Welfare, Government of India, Prof. S. Rath; Deputy Director General of CII, Mr. S. Sen; Managing Director of BASIX, Mr. Vijay Mahajan and Ex-Chairman, C.M.A.—Indian Institute of Management, Ahmedabad, Prof. S.K. Datta.

I am also indebted to sixteen corporates and sixteen NGOs where I have done the case studies. Without their support and cooperation it would have been extremely difficult to complete this endeavour. And I owe my special thanks to all the study respondents for their valuable time and assistance during the data collection exercise.

Finally, it would be unfair to forget the moral support and continuous encouragements from my close friends and special thanks to my dear parents, wife Vandana Bhattacharya and son Deekhit Bhattacharya. They constantly stood with me during the turbulent as well as good moments experienced in the course of the study.

Last but not the least, I am grateful to Mrs. Meghna Kher and Dr. M.B. Konnur for their cooperation. For meticulously setting and typing I am thankful to Mr. N. Rajput.

Debasis Bhattacharya

Contents

Abbreviations

AAA	Analytic and Advisory Activity
ADB	Asian Development Bank
BCF	Business and Community Foundation
CBOs	Community-Based Organizations
CAE	Country Assistance Evaluation
CAS	Country Assistance Strategy
CDF	Comprehensive Development Framework
CGAP	Consultative Group to Assist the Poorest
CII	Confederation of Indian Industry
CINI	Children in Need Institute
CSD	Corporate Social Development
CSOs	Civil Society Organizations
CSP	Corporate Social Performance
CSR	Corporate Social Responsibility
CSWB	Central Social Welfare Board
DRDA	District Rural Development Agency
EBRD	European Bank for Reconstruction and Development
ESW	Economic Sector Work
FAO	Food and Agriculture Organization
FICCI	Federation of Indian Chambers of Commerce and Industry
FIAS	Foreign Investment Advisory Service
FSAP	Finance Sector Adjustment Programme
FSE	Financial Sector
GDI	Gender Development Index
GDP	Gross Domestic Product
HD	Human Development
HNP	Health, Nutrition and Population
HDR	Human Development Report
HDI	Human Development Index

IBRD	International Bank for Reconstruction and Development
IDA	International Development Association
IFC	International Finance Corporation
IMS	Investment Marketing Service (MIGA)
ILO	International Labour Organization
IT	Information Technology
LPG	Liberalization, Privatization and Globalization
MNCs	Multinational Corporations
MFI	Micro Finance Institution
NGO	Non-Government Organization
OBA	Output Based Aid
OD	Operational Directive
ODA	Overseas Development Assistance
OECD	Organization for Economic Cooperation and Development
OED	Operations Evaluation Department
OEG	Operations Evaluation Group (IFC)
OP	Operational Policy
PPP	People's Participation Programme
PRIs	Panchayati Raj Institutions
PRG	Partial Risk Guarantee
PRSP	Poverty Reduction Strategy Paper
PPI	Private Participation in Infrastructure
PPIAF	Public-Private Infrastructure Advisory Facility
PSAS	Private Sector Advisory Service
PSD	Private Sector Development
PSI	Private Sector Development and Infrastructure
QAG	Quality Assurance Group
RD	Rural Development
ROSC	Review of the Observance of Standards and Codes
SMEs	Small and Medium Enterprises
SC/ST	Scheduled Caste/ Scheduled Tribe
SDCA	Social Development and Community Affairs Council
SHGs	Self Help Groups
UNDP	United Nations Development Programme
UNICEF	United Nations Children's Fund
UNO	United Nations Organization
WHO	World Health Organization
WBG	World Bank Group

WBES	World Business Environment Survey
WBCSD	World Business Council for Sustainable Development
WBI	World Bank Institute

List of Tables and Figures

1 INTRODUCTION

Backdrop

Development[1] is a multidimensional[2] concept. It is a process. At any given time it is a dynamics between creation of new problems and solution of old ones. Development stands for bringing about a transformation[3] in the social, political, cultural, economic, environmental and health profiles of people in a positive direction. Development implies a progressive change from an existing situation to a new one. A balanced development strategy has to pay adequate attention to both acceleration of the growth process and a more direct attack on problems of mass poverty, illiteracy, health, unemployment, population growth, etc. Social justice[4] should be the guiding principle of developmental process, so that social imbalance will be eradicated. Many a factors i.e., political, economic, cultural, scientific, social, legal, religious, etc. have definite presence in the process of development. It is a web of network of relations against which social development[5] takes place. A balanced relation between the different forces or currents of the web of network is necessary for the development process to be ideal. But there is no true democracy[6] among these social, political and economic forces. Three forces are powerful in their own right and combined together they can give justice to the process of social development. These three forces are—the Government, Non-governmental-Non-profit development organizations (NGOs[7] and CBOs[8]), and the Industry (Corporate sector). *Though the government and the business sector are indispensable to the development needs of the nation, the integration of the civil society is necessary to enhance the sensitization and understanding of the complex and deep-rooted problems of the people.*

In South Asia, companies have made significant contributions to community development. With many civil society organizations like South Asian Partnership in Sri Lanka, Bangladesh Freedom Foundation and PRIP Trust in Bangladesh and Action Aid in Pakistan, Nepal and Bangladesh along with the business chambers, corporate social responsibility appears vibrant in the region.

This study is an attempt to generate and analyse data on a substantial part of corporate and social sector relationships. It has a national flavour since corporates and NGOs from the 'five zones of the country' have been covered.

Growing Trends of Social Imbalance

The central problems of the Indian economy continue to be widespread and extreme poverty, low productivity and ever increasing disparities.[9] The growing socio-economic[10] imbalances have resulted in diversified problems in the economy. As far as India's social development is concerned, there is a big question whether with the existing socio-economic situation can we achieve happiness (minimum livelihood)[11] for the largest number? This is not possible as long as there is a large-scale social imbalance. Economic growth does not lead to the removal of poverty, since the poor are not in a position to grasp opportunities in the market. Poverty estimates concentrate on the calorie intake and do not include dimensions such as social vulnerability[12] health, etc.

Differences among regions are particularly marked in economic growth that generates public resources to invest in education and health services and increases the resources people have to enjoy a decent standard of living and improve many other aspects of their lives. Whether and why inequality matters is an old issue. For development economist concerned primarily with world's poor countries, the central issues have been growth and poverty reduction, not inequality. And for mainstream economists inequality was at worst a necessary evil—helping to enhance growth by concentrating income among the rich. Concentration of income at the top can undermine the kinds of public policies such as support for high-quality universal public education, that are likely to advance human development. Developing and implementing good social policies is especially difficult where inequality takes the form of concentration at the top combined with substantial poverty at the bottom. Inequality can erode social capital,[13] including the sense of trust and citizen responsibility that is key to the formation of sustainability of sound public institutions. It can undermine participation in such common spheres of community life. If inequality matters for any of the reasons above, the possibility that it can worsen matters too (UNDP Report, 2001).

India is undergoing a rapid socio-economic transformation. The forces of modernization, technological changes and industrialization have been affecting the lifestyle[14] and the social structures.[15] There is fast loosening of the methods of social control and breakdown of social and familial[16] relationships. These social forces have aggravated many social problems. The problems of women and children, youth, urban slum dwellers, aged and infirm etc. have increased manifold and thus call for massive development and welfare services to these target groups. *The Government's initiatives to social sector programmes have had a feeling of being electorally motivated and lacunas like lack of transparency and accountability persist.*

The ultimate goal of social development is to improve and enhance the quality of life of one and all in the community, *it is essential to promote shared growth in the sense of ensuring that the benefits of growth percolate to all sections rather than being the exclusive prerogative of some pockets,* making economic growth and the interaction of the market forces to be more conducive to social development requires implementation of open market opportunities for all. The central issue in economic development is to expand the social opportunities open to the people. The expansion of markets has crucial role to play in this transformation. The creation and use of social opportunities on a wide basis requires much more than the "freeing" of markets. They call emphatically for an active public policy that could enable people to use the opportunities that the possibility of more trade—domestic and international—offers. It calls for a rapid expansion of basic education, overcoming the massive illiteracy and educational backwardness that characterize India. There are also other expansions of social opportunity that need urgent attention. These include the need for more widespread and better healthcare, greater access to provisions of social security and a more effective and sweeping land reform system. To tackle these problems, there is an urgent need for various sectors to cooperate and coordinate to come up with solutions.

It is difficult to understand that even though this issue is of utmost importance not much participatory action has been carried out with the joint effort of private sector involvement.

Support by the Government

The Government of India has been a major player in social development over the past decades through its plan programmes. The delivery mechanism[17] of government programmes is very diverse and complex with many departments and agencies engaged in the task. Apart form the central and state governments, the Panchayati Raj Institution[18] are important parts of the delivery mechanism.

The productivity of government is critical for economic growth. There are vital functions a government ought to perform to promote growth. Public order, justice and rule of law are the three most important monopoly functions of the government. Then we have school education and primary healthcare. An illiterate and unskilled population cannot be productive in a modern economy. Private sector can certainly acquire dominance in hospital care; but primary healthcare[19] burden has to be borne by the state in any civilized society. *Even though the government is the dominant player in social development, the spending in social sectors have remained more or less stagnant, hence the resources from the business and civil society[20] need to be mobilized to expand the domain of development activities to different fields like education, community development, health, women's development, infrastructure, environment and rural development.*

The study is designed to provide an evidence of the amount of resources available with the corporate sector. A participatory[21] approach is taken so as to get a view of all the stakeholders[22] at different levels to have a better understanding of the efficacy of development programmes.

Role of Non-Government Organizations

Over the last 50 years NGOs have been playing important role in the society. The size of this sector has also gone up massively. This explosion of NGOs has been characterized by rapid, complex and often unpredictable political, institutional, environmental, demographic, social and economic changes. NGOs are also an expression of people's belief that through their own initiative they can better fulfil their potential by working together, and is so, doing reduce the opportunity gap which exists between the advantaged and disadvantaged in the society. Some NGOs have contractual relationships to deliver services on behalf of government departments, some mobilize resources in support of government policies and programmes, in diverse fields such as literacy, unemployment adult education, and commonunity development. NGOs are almost totally dependent on donors[23] for project grants. Overtly 'political' activities like advocacy, networking, community mobilization, formation of people's organizations, building pressure groups[24] are supported as projects. Given the changing international scenario, donor priorities change every few years. Changes in what NGOs do, and in the political, economic, social and institutional environments in which they operate, have considerably changed the nature and extent of the relationships which NGOs have with other. These relationships are with (Ball & Dunn, 1995) :

(i) A variety of central, state regional and local government ministries. The relationships may be at both political and official levels;
(ii) Funding and donor agencies, which may include government departments, trusts, foundations, private sector donors, the general public, external (overseas) governmental, non-governmental, international, bilateral and multilateral aid and development agencies;
(iii) The private sector. Relationships with this sector will partly be about funding, where companies act as donors, but also about other ways in which the private sector supports and works with NGOs. While funding and other relationships with the private sector are not common in all countries, 'corporate social responsibility' in the private sector is growing;
(iv) Other NGOs (locally, nationally, originally and internationally);
(v) Individual and organizational members;
(vi) Beneficiary groups[28], communities and individuals who are disadvantaged; and
(vii) The general public.

NGOs' today are under tremendous pressure to become service providers over a wide territory. In order to do so, they have to either form networks or expand their scale of operation. Their unique ability to be in touch with the people and respond to their needs is dependent on their proximity to the ground. Territorial expansion coupled with diversification into multiple sectors in order to service frequent change in donor priorities have robbed many NGOs of their unique selling proposition—accountability, quality, cost-effectiveness and closeness to ground realities. They are also prey to the danger of being over-funded. They gradually become big and hierarchical.[26]

The stakes increase rapidly. Having employed so many people, organizational heads are forever busy generating resources to maintain their staff. Power, scale, organizational assets, visibility, take over—Organizational heads are increasingly alienated from the people. Finally, they become incapable of working towards genuine 'empowerment'[27] of the people and slip into the role of a service provider.

We can talk of NGOs in three categories. First are those which have been inspired by great individuals in the wake of India's freedom movement. The second lot is motivated by the need for voluntary action in view of the inability of the state to cover a holistic development paradigm.[28] This group can be characterized essentially as developmentalists who attempt to improve the socio-economic conditions of the people. The third category can be those engaged in empowerment, advocacy and sensitization[29] actions. NGOs can provide the inspiration underlying the freedom movement which fought for justice, equality and solidarity. Secondly, they can also make inputs in terms of providing services to the poor in the marginalized[30] community. The services could be direct or state and donor sponsored projects in the areas of health, education, sanitation, appropriate technology and so on. The need may differ from area to area; but the NGOs are flexible, locally grounded and responsive to the needs of the people.

On the other hand, the growth civil society has corresponded to the decline of the role of state in delivering public goods and social services and overall in development. Civil society is composed of groups and associations organized voluntarily, devoted to the cause of collective good, independent of state and of any other vested interest. Civil society should compliment the state if desirable, collaborate if possible, and confront it if necessary. In normative[31] terms, the civil society is widely seen as empowering the people, mobilizing them for participation, enforcing accountability, moderating both state and market, and helping in the supply of public goods and social services.

A structured and long-term partnership[32] with the civil society and the state is perhaps the need of the hour, in order to promote development. Business community involvement has been characterized as ABC of corporate responsibility by a Delhi based organization called Business and Community Foundation. 'A' stands of advocacy for social development with key decision makers and donor agencies; 'B' means building partnership between business, state and civil society and bringing together the complementary skills and experience in these sectors; and 'C' is the capacity building of individual organization.

Another aspect is dissemination[33] of appropriate knowledge, rather than giving funds or goods, and this one is a difficult task in which administrators, businessmen and communicators should work in partnership, is in tune with the contemporary approaches.

The state with its huge resources, bureaucracy and legitimacy with elected governments should be repositioned into more of a facilitatory[34] role, from that of a regulatory[35] one in the development process. Here the argument is that state, market and the civil society should operate in a conjoined[36] relationship. In this, the state empowers the civil society withdrawing from large areas and moderates the market, in keeping with its philosophy of governance. The market in partnership with the civil society supports the state in the gigantic task of development. And civil society watches both the market and the state.

Having Welfare State through Partnership

The concept of welfare state[37] is very well represented in the Preamble and the Directive Principles of State Policy of the Constitution of India. Articles 38, 39 and 46 of the Constitution envisage a very positive role for the state in bringing about welfare and development of disadvantaged and marginalized groups of the society. Towards concretizing the goals and objectives of the welfare state, the earlier Ministry of Welfare, renamed as the Ministry of Social Justice and Empowerment in May 1998, has been pursuing policies, strategies and programmes for the welfare and development of the disadvantaged and marginalized sections of the society, viz. SCs, STs, backward classes, minorities, disabled, aged persons, street children. The basic objective of the policies and programmes of the Ministry is to bring these target groups into the mainstream of development by making them self-reliant. A holistic and integrated[38] approach covering social and economic empowerment and social justice to weaker sections is the main thrust of the Ministry to accomplish an all around development of these groups.

The policy of the Ministry is to encourage participation of the community and maximum utilization of existing infrastructure and voluntary action in its programme interventions. The Ministry promotes and assists voluntary organizations and NGOs in implementing its various programmes which broadly fall under the Ministry to accomplish an all-round development of these groups.

One of major roles of the government is to carry out social welfare spending. *It is imperative for social capital to increase to keep in pace with demand of economic growth, a fact which is acknowledged by the corporate sector.* The greater the level of economic development, the more extensive is the government's provision of social welfare services, the smaller the non-profit sector (Weisbrod, 1975). However, in developing countries where social welfare spending has usually been low, growth of non-profit sector has been influenced by other government policies. In most developing countries, governments have not been able to bring about equitable economic development. As a result, to promote both economic development and more participatory, viz. democratic societies is now being recognized that governments can no longer cope with the growing social needs.

In Asian countries like Japan and Thailand, there have been major changes in the law, recognizing the importance of civil society. There is growing recognition that NGOs are effective because they are independent of the government, also NGOs are becoming confident and forging partnership with government and business. In general, the idea of tripartite agreements between government, NGOs and business is one way of resolving or mitigating[39] social problems, and the multilateral agencies can also play a constructive role in this. Social justice has to be looked at from the ground level, where the poor live.

Business has started to prove itself the most dynamic force for growth and development. Unable to meet the growing demands and expectations of its citizens, governments have had to consider new ways of working. NGOs are also beginning to recognize that some of their goals may be more easily achievable by learning how to work alongside business. This partnership approach may offer the best chance of prosperity and opportunity for the greatest number of people. The key to partnership is learning to recognize where and when the roles of the sectors most usefully intersect, and that comes from learning to analyse local conditions and assessing the potential for collaborative[40] action. *A recent CII study on cost benefit analysis on land have shown the income and employment generation potential of public private partnership.*

This "coming together for sustainable development" within which all nations make cultural, political, social and economic comments, individually and collectively, will ensure the allocations of essential means for a viable and sustainable human future. This intersectoral[41] approach accesses resources unique to each organization or each sector to be productive and creates new options that neither sector or organization can develop on its own. This new stage of relationships can be aptly termed as 'partnership.' For example, Hindustan Machine Tools Limited and Amarjyoti, an Indian NGO, are working together to provide economic independence to physically challenged people. Similarly, Balmer Lawrie, a business house based at Kolkata and Togore Society for Rural Development, an NGO working together in the field of safe drinking water, relief and education. Hindustan Thomson Associate, an internationally known advertising house has worked with the government in spreading the message of importance of family planning. Government in its programme of providing safe drinking water to villages has worked together with Eicher Group for success of its programme. Modi Group have provided school uniforms to the students of some selected government schools in India. In the Indian context, over a decade, government and NGOs are involved in National Literacy Mission aimed to provide basic education to all as part of their total literacy campaign. Similarly, in area of health, CINI and Chetna, two leading NGOs in India are involved with government.

Even though corporates have been participating in social development activities, these have remained miscellaneous. There is no organized channelization of the resources through a well defined media.

India's Social Development Problems Ahead

Economic growth cannot be the only objective for national planning and indeed over the years, development objectives are being defined not just in terms of increase in GDP or per capita income but more broader in terms of enhancement of human well-being. This includes not only an adequate level of consumption of food and other types of consumer goods but also access to basic social services, especially education, health availability of drinking water and basic sanitation. It also includes the expansion of economic and social opportunities for all individuals and groups, and greater participation in decision-making.

The concept of human development according to the Human Development Report (HDR), 1997 is, "The process of widening people's choices and the level of well-being they achieve are at the core of the notion of human development. Regardless of the level of development, the three essential choices for people are: to lead a long and healthy life; to acquire knowledge, and to have access to the resources needed for a decent standard of living." The human problem of developing countries is not just poverty. It includes high unemployment and a skewed[42] distribution of wealth and opportunity. Standards of health, education and nutrition are also low. The provision of basic needs and rapid economic growths are, therefore, simultaneous requirements. Some argue that economic growth (measured in terms of GNP[43]) is the end. Human development is essential for this and is, hence, the means. It is now being recognized that the bettering of human life must be the end.

At present, India has a disappointing human development profile. There are also striking disparities. Certain states and districts report levels of human development similar to those of leading industrialized countries; others report achievement levels that are worse than the average of the poorest countries. As per the HDR 2000, 34.6 per cent of India's population was poor in 1998. A recent measure of socio-economic development is the Human Development Index (HDI). It is computed yearly by the UNDP. HDI is a composite index of three elements of human development—life expectancy, literacy and standard of living. It is a more comprehensive measure than per capita income. According to the index, India's rank of 1998 is 138 among 175 countries of the world, lower than Russia, Sri Lanka, China, and Myanmar. India's rank on the Gender Development Index (GDI), which combines the HDI with a measure of inequality of achievement between women and men, is also abysmally low. It ranked 108 out of 143 countries in 1998. Given any socio-economic indicator of the well-being, e.g., adult literacy, infant mortality, maternal mortality, life expectancy, or gender bias, India ranked among the bottom one-third of countries.

The recently released HDR 2001 gives India's rank at 115 which is significantly higher than the 128 rank given in HDR 2000. This rank elevation has been simply a result of a removal of 12 countries from its main list because of non-availability of reliable data. There is in fact, no significant improvement in the living standards during the last one year in our country. Human Development Index (HDI) measures the average achievements in a country in three basic dimensions of human development : health (measured by life expectancy at birth), education (measured by the adult literacy rate and the combined primary, secondary and tertiary gross enrolment ratio), and income level (measured by estimated earned income in purchasing power parity US dollars).

India scores poorly in all the three components and during the last one year there has only been a marginal improvement : life expectancy[44] index remained unchanged at 0. 63; education index increased from 0.55 to 0.56; and income index increased from 0.51 to 0.52. As result, India's HDI value has increased only marginally in 2001 to 0.571 from last year's level of 0.563, reflecting only a marginal improvement in the living standards.

Participatory Bottom-up Planning

Traditional development planning has too often been "top-down"[45]. Over the past two decades, programmes designed with little reference to the perceptions and capacities of local people have often failed. Local communities have valuable experience and a special understanding of their own environment. When the responsibility for natural resource management is taken away from them, their use of land and other natural resources can become highly inefficient. The result is often land degradation. Participatory development recognizes the rights of local communities over their resources. They have a greater stake than anyone else in improving agricultural productivity while ensuring the long-term ecological balance. In addition, local participation in planning and decision-making is essential for building local capacity. Those most directly involved in the management, use and benefits of a particular resource must be active participants. Participation starts at the very inception of a development initiative. A participatory development process implies that all sections of a community have equal access to, and take part in equal measure in the decision-making process. Empowerment is a process that enables disadvantaged people to become aware of their rights, their potential and the availability of opportunities to improve their status. It also creates an environment in which people can improve their social, political and economic conditions through their own efforts and by demanding better conditions for themselves. This is the 'putting the last first' or 'bottom-up'[46] approach. It focuses on the process and it involves the people as central to the process, thus leading to long-term and sustainable development solutions, where the people can take control of their own lives.

The unique culture of each society shapes its patterns of decision-making and communication. Activities must originate at the local level, but sometimes additional encouragement may be needed to make people feel that they truly own the process of participatory development. NGOs may have a key role to play here. It may also be necessary for the government to delegate more decision-making authority to the local grassroots level.[47] The participatory process is time-consuming and labour-intensive. NGOs can help to build up the community's capacity for "participatory programming". Due attention should also be paid to involving the more marginalized social groups. Unless the rural poor are given the means to participate fully in development, they will continue to be excluded from its benefits. The Food and Agriculture Organization's (FAO, 1996) People's Participation Programme (PPP) has demonstrated that participation is possible when the poor form small self-help groups that allow them to pool resources in pursuit of their own objectives.

PPP projects have been implemented in 12 countries of Africa (Kenya, Ghana, Swaziland, Zimbabwe and Sierra Leone), Asia (Sri Lanka) and Latin America. Some 13,200 people have actively participated in PPP, while there were a total of 80,000 beneficiaries. The central element in PPP is the formation of self-help groups of the rural poor as the first step in a long-term institution building process. Participatory rural development projects seek to improve the economic, social and political conditions and capacities of the rural poor.

Although the need for a participatory approach is now widely accepted by international development agencies, but it is difficult to implement. Obstacles include existing national policy and legislative frameworks, widespread prejudices, a tendency on the part of outside NGOs to control rather than facilitate, and a lack of development planning and management skills on the part of indigenous peoples themselves (The World Bank Group, 2000). *An institutional linkage is very much required towards institutionalising*[48] *the corporate social development.*

Many donors and government organizations now realize the importance of participation and want NGOs to be involved in the formulation and implementation of development projects. One of the most important ways large multilateral and bilateral donor agencies can support development projects that the involvement of communities by conducting discussions with national governments, on what types of support they require to initiate such projects, both on a pilot basis and more broadly. The contribution of additional resources for such undertakings will be an important stimulus to their wider trial and adoption. Multilateral and bilateral donors, as well as private donors, can stimulate widespread learning and thinking about participatory, collaborative approaches and can lend increased credibility to such approaches by supporting research and disseminating the findings through policy conferences, publications, etc.

Furthermore, voluntary organizations have been playing a pioneering role in rural development in recent decades in India. Since the problems of rural development are many and multifaceted,[49] the success of rural development depends on the active participation of the rural people. Today, it is widely believed that the state alone cannot tackle the problems of rural community and the state needs the support of voluntary bodies to supplement its efforts, as the problems of rural communities are vast and varied. The programme areas, in which the participation of voluntary bodies can be of great help for better implementation of anti-poverty and minimum needs programmes, include the following (Srivenkataramana and Raj, 1997) :

(i) Enforcement of minimum wages for agricultural labourers;

(ii) Identification and rehabilitation[50] of bonded labourers;
(iii) Improving living conditions of SC/ST and weaker sections;
(iv) Providing safe drinking water and sanitation facilities;
(v) Promoting social forestry and alternative energy programme;
(vi) Promotion of handicrafts and cottage industries;
(vii) Health services to the community; and
(viii) Primary education and skill development.

Though there are thousands of voluntary organizations, not many of them are affluent. They are neither self-sustaining nor they have ability to mobilize resources for their activities. NGOs are generally financed by different sources : government, non-government, foreign government, foreign non-government and own resources/donations. NGOs cannot by itself make a serious difference to social and economic problems. Corporations are one player willing and able to play a role in development, and have non-monetary resources to offer also. The desired results are somewhat better achieved wherever NGOs are implementing the programmes, possibly because of the following reasons :

(i) Voluntary organizations have flexibility in day-to-day functioning;
(ii) A high degree of commitment and dedication is observed among the field workers of such organizations;
(iii) Closeness to the client groups, innovativeness and ability to stimulate interest in the community is high in NGOs; and
(iv) They involve people right from planning to implementation levels.

It may be noted that India has a long tradition of participatory developmental approaches propounded be great thinkers like Mahatma Gandhi, Rabindranath Tagore and Vinoba Bhave. Brief descriptions about their approaches are given in the following sections to substantiate its relevance in the contemporary phases of social development.

Help to Help Themselves by Rabindranath Tagore

Much earlier than Gandhiji, Tagore had been giving serious thought to the problems besetting Indian society. In 1904, he delivered a speech from an open platform outlining a comprehensive programme for the reorganization of rural Bengal, on the basis of self-help and total development of its rural areas. Owing to insufficient response, he decided to do something by himself. Tagore established the Institute of Rural Reconstruction at Sriniketan in 1922, as an integral part of Santiniketan. The purpose of the institute was to initiate a programme of rural welfare and reconstruction in the villages of the surrounding areas in order to bring 'back life in all its completeness'.

In developing the rural community, Tagore emphasized on the processes rather than on the product. Though the various activities, Tagore wanted to create processes by which the villages could tackle their own problems. Based on observations and experiences, a number of principles were evolved. Primacy[51] of economic factors in the village life led him to agricultural development work. Workers were encouraged not to impose decisions and place their estimate of the problem before the villagers and a likely strategy of work. Individuals were motivated to bank together and existing organizations were strengthened. Tagore's institute manifested in three different types of activities, namely, research, education and extension. Needless to mention here that in the present scenario, there are the entire gamut[52] of development organizations which are involved in these three activities these are nothing but an extension of Tagore's theory.

Gandhian Voluntarism

Mahatma Gandhi stimulated the voluntary movement at turn of the century. He introduced a "constructive programme" to make villages self-sufficient by encouraging people to use the spinning wheel (*charkha*), hand-woven cloth (*khadi*), and village industries (*gramodyog*), which aimed at solving the problems of rural India. From 1920, his concept of Sarvodaya was formally embedded in this programme, of which the initial elements were community cooperation and unity, removal of untouchability[53] and the promotion of village industries. Constructive workers lived in villages and introduced a social reconstruction programme based on self-help and self-reliance. The training of workers emphasized an austere personal life, development of attitudes and pursuit of skills suitable to the local industry.

A little known fact is Gandhi's sojourn at Santiniketan, where he worked as a Sarbadhyaksha in spite of Tagore's reservation on some aspects of Gandhi's work. Gandhian philosophy is based on the philosophy of *Swadeshi.* Swadeshi[54] is the spirit of regeneration, a method of creative reconstruction in period of dependency and colonization. Swadeshi for Gandhi was a positive concept based on building what a community has in terms of resources, skills, institutions and transforming them, where they were inadequate. And also it was central to the creation of peace, freedom and sustainable development. Swadeshi is based on people's economies and their ability to organized themselves. Swadeshi or self-organization in economic affairs is the basis of economic freedom, and without economic freedom, there can be no political freedom, or self-governance and self-rule. For Gandhi, self-rule did not imply governance by a centralized state, but decentralized self-governance by local communities through Gram Swaraj (local self-government), and the present form of 73rd and 74th Amendments[55] of the Constitution is an extension and reflection of Gram Swaraj in the name of 'Panchayat Raj'. Gandhian philosophy is not antithetical to the philosophy of liberalization, privatization and globalization (LPG). A quotation of Gandhi will clear this doubt : "I do not want my house to be walled in on all sides and my windows to be stuffed. I want the cultures of all the lands to be blown about my house as freely as possible. But I refuse to be blown off my feet by any."

Paradigm Shift of Development

There has been noteworthy methodological need based change in consonance with the liberalisation, privatisation and globalization that refers as paradigm shifts in social developoment in India. Intitially, the government was primarily concerned with promoting economic development and the voluntary organizations with welfare of the needy and social reforms; today, people's own organizations are promoting integrated development and empowerment with considerations of social justice by conscientising,[56] organizing and mobilizing people. Development implies a progressive change from an existing situation to a new one. Although, in the ultimate analysis, development has to do with changing the personality traits of the individuals insofar as the basic personality structure is, it is, interrelated with society, culture and economy. Development also stands for bringing about a transformation in the social, political, cultural and economic structures to a community, viz. people in a given direction.

The Indian economic development plans have emphasized the need to achieve the goals of social and economic justice, with emphasis differing from one plan to the other. The First Five Year Plan spelt out three interrelated objectives, viz., maximum production, full employment and attainment of economic equality and justice, and observed that "none of these objectives can be pursued to the exclusion of others." The Second Plan lists, among others, the following objectives : achieving a rapid growth of the national economy and increasing the country's productive potential, a large expansion of employment opportunities and reduction of inequalities of income and wealth and more even distribution of economic power. The Second Plan emphasized the need to progressively reduce concentration of income, wealth and economic power and ensure the accrual of the benefits of economic development to the relatively less privileged classes of society.

The Third Five Year Plan specifically recognizes the basic objective of India's development to be "to provide the masses of the Indian people the opportunity to lead a good life." The objectives enumerated in the Plan document include utilization to the fullest possible extent the manpower resources of the country and ensuring a substantial expansion in employment opportunities. The Plan also underlines the need to establish "progressively greater equality of opportunity and bring about reduction in disparities in income and welfare and a more even distribution of economic power." The Fourth Plan, by and large, repeats the objectives of the earlier three Plans. It pointedly emphasizes the necessity of "acceleration of the tempo of development." It also talks of the monopoly legislation and appropriate fiscal policy to reduce concentration of economic power. Removal of poverty and attainment of self-reliance were declared to be the two main objectives of the Fifth Five Year Plan. The Plan recognized that as necessary corollaries of the twin aims, there was a need for higher growth, better distribution of incomes and a "very significant step-up" in the domestic rate of saving. It was also recognized that attainment of these objectives require coordinated employment of all the instruments of economic policy available to the government.

Removal of poverty was given primacy in the Sixth Plan even

though it recognized that it could not be accomplished in a five-year period, given the magnitude of the task. The other objectives especially mentioned are growth modernization, self-reliance and social justice. The objectives of Seventh Plan are not any different from those of Sixth. The document admits that the attainment of the goals require, among others, actions to sustain and enhance the momentum of economic expansion and technological development, adoption of effective promotional measures to increase the productivity and incomes of the poorer sections of the society, poorer regions and poorer states, expansion and quantitative improvements in health, and educational facilities and measures for bringing about a "sharp reduction" in the population growth rate. Sixth Plan document in its assessment of the development performance clearly states the two dimensions of social justice— "the first dimension is an improvement in the living standards of the poorest groups in society, and the second is a reduction in asset distribution." Also discussed there is the data showing gross inequalities with regard to share of the poorest in urban and rural consumer expenditure as well as in distribution of land and total assets in rural areas. However, in the Seventh Plan document the distributive justice or the equity dimension of social justice is conveniently forgotten. Ironically, even a mere mention of inequalities does not find a place in the discussion on social justice. The Eighth Plan was a plan for managing change, for managing the transition from centrally planned economy to market-led economy without tearing our socio-cultural fabric. From a highly centralized planning system, we are gradually moving towards indicative[57] planning.

At the same time, it was also recognized that one-third of our population lived in conditions of proverty, denied of basic minimum needs and that those very processes which stimulate growth sometimes tend to neglect the poor. The objectives of 'removing poverty and unemployment' are necessarily the objectives of every exercise in national planning irrespective of the growth model. Equity and social justice have been duly emphasized as main objectives of the development planning in the country. From the initial years of planning, it was realized by the government that necessary policy measures and institutional change had to be undertaken as part of the plan.

Over a period of time, goals of development have changed from mere economic growth to growth with justice and finally to growth for social justice. The orientation has shifted from welfare to development and from development to empowerment; the approach has shifted from promotion of welfare in all fragmented manner to holistic and integrated development of specific areas and target groups and the strategy has shifted from the provision of subsidies and loans by the government on its own creating a dependency syndrome[58] among the beneficiary groups to people themselves marching ahead through their own organizations and NGOs to undertake major responsibility of their development. *However, it is important to see that initiatives taken do not become stagnant or get concentrated under the influence of distributive justice.*

People-Centred Development

Development, as it most often is pursued, is intended to meet national goals and the interests of dominant and mainstream societies. Reducing poverty and improving the quality of life of people in general most often are the primary objectives of development. However, it is not always the cases that poverty reduction and improvement in the quality of life realized from development extend equally to all segments of society, or that improvement reaches each segment of society. Moreover, in mainstream-oriented economic development policies, poor and disadvantaged people may bear a disproportionate burden of the negative social, economic and environmental effects that such development projects may bring, without realizing commensurate benefits (ADB, 1999).

The further development proceeds, with the creation of great wealth, of high standards of living, and more sophisticated technology, the clearer it is that most societies are unable to accommodate all their citizens in terms of giving them a place within the increasing prosperity. Many countries are unable to provide an equal status in society for indigenous or other minority groups. India continues to present a large population living in poverty, which scarcely diminishes despite the country's overall development. It is a matter of leaving people behind and creating situations of relative poverty to a large degree. Being left behind in the development process seems to make many people highly vulnerable to other developments which can be more devastating than their initial poverty or underdevelopment like civil war,[59] ecological degradation, social unrest, etc.

Development process in India has been a distorted one. Distorted development is, to a large degree, a result of inequalities in the distribution of power in societies. Hence, it is often argued that the key to rectifying that situation is empowerment of those who are excluded from the development process and then build political, social and economic structures which are more participatory in nature. The development process must be people-centred, and highly participatory. That is, implementing an alternative development model such as People-Centred Development, which is consistent with the ecological resources, and social contexts within which we live.

The true meaning of convergence and synergy with diverse stakeholders, viz. corporate sector, NGO and government need to be spelt out more practically at the policy level which could facilitate the themes into reality.

People-centred development is defined by the UNDP as 'development of the people, by the people and for the people'. People should be involved in their own development and that they should be the chief beneficiaries of development. In effect, people-centred development can be said to rest on five foundations :

(1) Awareness-raising,
(2) Social mobilization,[60]
(3) Participation,
(4) Self-reliance, and
(5) Sustainability.

"Economics as if people mattered" is the crux of the issue. The British Economist E.F. Schumacher first coined this term over 25 years ago. He was among the earliest people to point out fundamental flaws in modern economics. 21st century economics must recognize that the basic questions about economics would be a system of rights and obligations, risks and rewards which (1) channels people's selfishness into the common good; (2) prevent people's selfishness from damaging other people's interests and especially the selfishness of the powerful from exploiting the weak; and (3) energizes the altruistic[61] desires and capacities of people to help one another as well as to contribute to creating a better society and better world (Kurian, 2001). The common risk should be to replace the *laissez faire*[62] model with some kind of new economics that takes care of everybody, the poor as well as the rich. Local people have to regain control of local resources and gear local economic systems in order to meet local resources needs rather than the needs of the international market. However, because the very poor also frequently face social exclusion, empowerment strategies will normally need to make use of community mobilizing and organizing techniques featuring group-based activities such as women's savings groups or community-based organizations. Empowerment can also be supported by introducing appropriate policies for equitable land distribution, tenurial reform, and security of property and user-group rights.

While individual projects and programmes can begin the process of empowering the poor, institutionalizing this process, and progressively building organizations in which the poor can participate as equals in all aspects of society can only assure sustainability. Once established, such organizations contribute to the strengthening of social capital. In this process civil society helps ensure more effective and equitable governance. Devolution[63] of government in the form of recently modified Panchayat Raj Legislation has ensured that the poor will not only participate in but will actually become leaders of local government institutions. This model thus offers the potential to break the stranglehold of traditional rural elite and provide a platform for the progressive empowerment of those who have been excluded in the past from participation in civil society, particularly rural poor women.

Social investment funds, while mainly used as a social protection strategy, are also being widely used to encourage asset-creating growth in areas of poverty. As part of broader targeted poverty reduction investments, government has sought to finance community-based infrastructure development in rural areas. In India's well-known Maharashtra Employment Guarantee Scheme, participants claimed excellent outcomes from infrastructure schemes undertaken in rural areas with strong community and NGO participation. Among the various components of the Integrated Rural Development Programme or the PRC's 7 Programmes, wage labour generation was likewise regarded as the most successful.

There is a transition required from 'charity-centred' approach to a more social-investment oriented one, the participation should not just be time-frame oriented but should be based on a more sutainable framework.[64]

A comprehensive framework for a people-centred development is likely to include the following components :

1. *Indirect Strategies :*

   (i) Removing obstacles to development,
   (ii) Improving governance,
   (iii) Reforming restrictive policies, and
   (iv) Developing capacities for sound public sector management.

2. *Direct Strategies :*

   (i) Enabling the poor to increase their human capital,
   (ii) Accelerating growth in priority poverty areas via targeted investments, and
   (iii) Providing social protection (for those awaiting the impact of the above strategies).

The importance of grassroots level initiation has to be understood, since it is here that more realistic assessment of the needs of the community can be obtained. Indian NGOs, for example, are questioning the implicit dependency they are creating in the thousands of self-help groups (SHGs) they have established among the poor, and are now experimenting with the promotion of direct linkages between SHGs and local government. Institutionalization of participation will, at the same time, strengthen the functioning of civil society and increase social capital. The importance of social capital in providing the institutions and values necessary for sustainable economic growth is now increasingly recognized. More positively, the private sector or the businesses can support appropriate local government programmes, social investment funds, capacity building of NGOs, community-based organizations, etc. Such social development areas inevitably require a much longer-term involvement and the private sector can play a major role in this process.

Making Face-Value by the Private (for profit) Organization

Corporate social responsibility (CSR) or corporate social development (CSD) may be a new term, but it is not new concept. In 1965, the then Prime Minister of India presided over a national meeting that issued the following declaration on the Social Responsibilities of Business :

> "......[Business has] responsibility to itself, to its customers, workers, shareholders and the community.... every enterprise, no matter how large or small, must, if it is to enjoy confidence and respect, seek actively to discharge its responsibilities in all directions...... and not to one or two groups, such as shareholders or workers, at the expense of community and consumer. Business must be just and humane, as well as efficient and dynamic."

Companies are taking an increasingly active role in the communities where they operate, forming partnership with non-profit organizations, governments agencies and other stakeholders to fulfil a wide variety of community needs. Companies are realizing the need to change their mindset from one of social obligation to one of social commitment. The rise of community partnerships also reflects a growing realization that individual entities—governments, non-profits, and businesses—which traditionally acted independent of one another, can create powerful synergies when working together. Benefits to companies include developing trust and goodwill in local communities, securing or expanding market position, enhancing brand image, attracting and retaining employees, and improving employee morale, productivity and due to this course of action they felt that they are also a 'stake-holder.'

Recent years have witnessed a growing shift in the corporate involvement in social development. Cases have been incorporated in the study which reveal creative and positive approaches taken by the corporate sector. But this massive and complex task of development requires a complementary effort on the part of all the three sectors. Partnerships between corporate bodies and non-profit organizations have already given rise to specific benefits in the following forms :

(i) *Expansion of markets and creation of new services*— Business houses like the Tatas, Birlas, Mahindras and the Murugappas have developed partnership with various forms of non-profit activities to help provide new services in the community as well as to expand existing markets.

(ii) *Enhancement of employee skills and training*—Evidence suggests that when employees participate in community partnership activities, they increase their skills and training.

(iii) *Lowering of employee turnover*—Research evidence suggests that companies participating in community partnership activities are more likely to increase employee retention. A company's community involvement activities directly influence employee's feelings about their jobs. Employees involved in their company's community activities are more likely to want to continue working for that company and help it succeed.

(iv) *Enhancement of brand image*—Companies participating in community partnerships can greatly enhance their brand awareness and positioning by linking marketing efforts to social causes.

(v) *Developing trust in the local community*—By engaging in community-focused partnerships, many companies are finding that they can gain the trust and goodwill of local community residents. The benefits of doing so can include opening new markets, reducing local regulatory obstacles, providing access to the local political process, generating positive media coverage, and increasing company or brand awareness.

Many factors have driven companies to realize their responsibility to society. Also, employees, consumer and shareholders prefer to be associated with such companies. Socially responsible companies frostier a sense of belonging and pride among its employees. Through globalization of the media, any urban India consumer is now aware of social issues. *The mindset has changed, people no longer associate business with just material aspects but the questions of social responsibility are seriously coming forward.* Consumers are prepared to pay a slightly higher price for products from companies doing good work. Similarly, shareholders prefer to invest in socially responsible companies. The investors expect such companies to adhere to 'best practices'[65] in the way they work and in their relations with the community.

Functioning of companies greatly affects local communities where they operate, both favourably and adversely. The adverse effects could be loss of a productive resource, pollution of the local area and income imbalances, to name a few. Therefore, companies should operate to directly benefit the community. Tax benefits have driven many companies towards social development and welfare programmes. Social imbalance also affects business to grow. Companies can help bridge this gap between the rich and the poor with the support of NGOs and the government.

A natural question that arises is what are the imperatives for private sector to be involved in development. First is "socio-econmic-moral", it appeals to the business of community, which is surely not unaware of the fact that the world's largest democracy and perhaps one of the largest markets is crippled by hopeless poverty and want in rural India. More than one-third of its population is classed as living below the poverty line. This equates to one-third of the world's poor. A business community, which is engaged in a society of this nature, cannot be oblivious to the magnitude of the problem, and do nothing about it. The second is the business imperative. The huge population of rural India is without effective purchasing power at all to enter the real economy of the country. If urban market is saturated, where will the business sector expand? On the other hand, if the most important asset in rural India, the huge workforce is trained and enabled, they could constitute the largest consumer market in the business sector. With little investment in human resource and infrastructure, business sector can secure good dividends. This can be done by building business civil society partnership in favour of the poor and disadvantaged. *The challenge is to overcome the cultural differences that exist between the traditional activities of the industry and the activities required in social development sector.*

Economic Determinism is Bringing in New Players

Economic prosperity has often been viewed as a market-driven management, that is expansion of economic activities. Market-driven economics is a process of increasing ecnomic integration and growing economic interdependence between economies around the world. It is associated not only with an increasing cross-border movement of goods, services, capital, technology, information and people, but also with an organization of economic activities. This process is driven by the lure of profit and the threat of competition in the market. In the context of social development, the most important economic priority of every nation has been towards creating more wealth. Unless more wealth is generated, there will be a slump in resource distribution for wealth and development. Structural changes which follow liberalization brought in new ways of representing, realizing and treating socio-economic and political problems. It marks the fundamental changes in all aspects of governance.

The emerging flexible production system, shaped by the nature of the technical progress, the changing output mix and the organizational characteristics, is forcing firms to constantly choose between trade and investment in their drive to expand activities across borders. The declining share of wages in production costs, the increasing importance of proximity between producers and consumers, and the growing externalization of services, are bound to influence the strategies and the behaviour of industries in the current period of globalization. A comparison of globalization in the late twentieth century with globalization in the late nineteenth century suggests that the game is similar, though not quite the same. But the players of the game are new. And the rules of the game are very different.

The process of globalization in the 19th century was dominated by imperial[66] nation states not only in the realm of politics but also in the sphere of economics. The process of globalization now has placed new players centrestage.

There are two main sets of players in this game : transnational corporations[67] that dominate investment, production and trade in the world economy, and international banks or financial intermediaries that control the world of finance. This has induced a strategic withdrawal on the part of the nation state in some important spheres. Thus, nation states are not the key players that they were in the late 19th century during the first incarnation of globalization. They remain the main political players but are no longer the main economic players. However, the benefits of integration with the world economy, through globalization, would accrue only to those countries which have laid the requisite foundations for industrialization and development. This means investing in the development of human resources and the creation of a physical infrastructure, i.e., raising productivity in the agricultural sector, acquisition of technological and managerial capabilities at micro-level, creation of institutions that would regulate, govern and facilitate the functioning of markets. In each of these pursuits, strategic forms of state intervention are essential. Evidence from several poor countries demonstrated that human development indicators[68] were not necessarily correlated with economic prosperity. Quality primary health care, maternal and child survival programmes, good sanitation and primary education can turn the tide (Ramachandran, 1996). Industry has made great strides and while generally there is much more prosperity in these 50 years, the income gap is rising, level of unemployment is also rising. So there is a need to analyse the costs/benefits of globalization and liberalization. To do that, there is a need for business, government and NGOs to work together for tackling issues of concerns both to business and community. The unprecedented scale towards upscalling the intervention has brought with it :

(1) High social/economic costs : unemployment, corruption, inequality and lack of social provisions for a majority of the population.
(2) The rise of myriad NGOs competing of ownership of projects, private sector resources and agency funds.

In the international debate on non-state players, NGOs are often referred to as representative or voice of civil society, but one must distinguish between the NGOs and civil society. The term civil society has been used to denote various bodies including NGOs, voluntary associations, non-profit sector, for-profit sector, charitable organizations and benevolent societies. In recent years, a number of NGOs, particularly the northern NGOs, have developed campaigns of 'responsible trade', 'green trade' and 'greening of trade.' Since NGO action is seen as representative of the civil society, the legitimacy of NGO action is substantial. Globalization has contributed to the increased activities of many NGOs and they have sought to play an increasingly political role in the international negotiations on trade as well. The developed countries' NGOs are very sophisticated players with abundant resources and power to influence both their respective governments and to some extent, international policies. The developing countries' NGOs, on the other hand, do not even have the mans to set up the basic infrastructure. *Corporations need to make a serious commitment to set aside at least some percentage of Profit After Tax (PAT) for social betterment. A part of it could be spent on local community safety nets, the balance be given to NGOs or individuals working at any level preferably in emerging and underfunded areas.* Economic policies in India have unergone much change over the last decade, and more changes are in the process of being implemented.

The central focus underlying these reforms has been the market mechanism which led to such public policies including deregulation and reduction of governmental controls, greater autonomy of private investment, less use of the public sector, more opening of the economy to international trade, and so on.

There have been controversial debates on these issues which concentrate on a particular class of means related to the use or non-use of markets (such as incentives for private investment, reliance on international trade, etc.). However, there are many other issues, especially those involving the 'social' aspect of economic operations and successes, which typically are conspicuously absent in these debates. *There is also lack of documentation*[69] *by which a more in-depth analysis can be carried out.*

Social Development and the Corporate Sector in the Light of LPG

Globalization is radically changing the face of human societies, shattering cultures and social systems. It has brought instant prosperity to a thin layer of society, but has consigned the rest to marginality. A vast majority number of the world's population has been excluded from the benefits of globalization. This includes workers laid off due to massive job cuts and the closure of factories, farmers dislocated by widespread land conversion schemes, indigenous peoples driven out of their ancestral lands, migrant workers forced to leave their jobs, and independent local entrepreneurs forced out of business. There are also certain possibilities and opportunities inherent in global economic dynamics. These include : spectacular breakthrough in science and technology, empowered voices of NGOs, people's movements, minority groups, marginalized people and small business, and exciting possibilities of knowledge-based growth (Jagadish Gandhi, 2001).

There is growing recognition among economists and lay people that human welfare are not profits. This feeling is rooted in the pain inflicted on millions of people by both the 'state' and the 'market' in the name of globalization and development. Globalization claims certain natural and inevitable 'price for progress' where human beings are conveniently forgotten. It has become impertinent for the business co-operations to involve themselves in programmes which bring benefits to the community. What is needed is perhaps a development that keeps people firmly in the picture. For this people must have control of what they want (Kurien, 2201). During the LPG period encouraging progress has also been made in the Indian economy in many dimensions. The percentage of population in poverty has continued to decline, even if not as much as was targeted. Population growth has decelerated below 2 per cent for the first time in four decades. Literacy has increased from 52 per cent in 1991 to 65 per cent in 2001 and the improvement is evident in all states. Sectors such as software services and IT-enabled services have emerged as new sources of strength creating confidence about India's potential to be competitive in the world economy. But now the economy is in a decelerating phase. Growth in the 1990s has generated less employment than was expected. The infant mortality rate has stagnated at 72 per 1000 for the last several years. As many as 60 per cent of rural households and about 20 per cent of urban households do not have a power connection. Only 60 per cent of urban households have taps within their houses and far fewer have latrines inside the house. Land and forest degradation in the rural areas, and over-exploitation of ground water are seriously threatening sustainability of food production. Pollution in the cities is on the increase. LPG has yet to have an impact on the people's lives in terms of speedy economic development and distributive justice to its stakeholders. Social harmony, efficacy of law, especially in finding a mean between the interests of the new businesses and its stakeholders such as the vast labourforce, are some of the principal issues to be tackled in the real earnest.

Globalization, Business Scenario and Social Development in India

The economic reforms, which began in 1991, still remain mired in controversy because in sensitive areas such as agriculture, labour, financial services and social sector development, the pace has been tardy, leaving the nation poor in terms of absorption of foreign direct investment, better managerial practices or technology. Liberalization has failed to address India's core economic problems. Poverty has grown, productivity has fallen and income inequality has widened. Liberalization was intended primarily to do two things. First and foremost, it was supposed to accelerate industrial growth.

Second to attract huge inflows of foreign investment to finance infrastructure development. Neither happened. Industrial growth in the decade 1981-91 was 7.7 per cent and since 1991-92, it has been 5.8 per cent. An analysis of the reforms between 1991-92 and 1999-2000 reveals that while after 1992-93, the growth rate picked up to around 6 per cent of GDP, on an average, the growth process did not reduce the percentage of population below the poverty line. The growth rate of employment in the organized sector decelerated to 0.6. per cent between 1990-91 and 1997-98, against 1.73 per cent between 1983 and 1990-91. Similarly, the employment growth rate in the unorganized sector fell to 1.1 per cent against the average growth rate of 2.4 per cent in the seven-year reform period. A basic flaw in the reform process is the neglect of agriculture. This is evidenced by decline in public investment in irrigation and the private sector's failure to fill the gap. This has resulted in sluggish growth in foodgrains output with serious implications for food security in the long run. The average annual price rise during the 1980s for food articles was: rice 5.6 per cent, wheat 5.7 per cent and pulses 11.2 per cent. During the following decade these changed to : rice 10.2 per cent, wheat 9.5 per cent and pulses 11.4 per cent. Surveys by the National Council for Applied Economic Research (NCAER) reveal that almost 59 per cent of all households accounting for 526 million people have an annual income of less than Rs. 12,500, i.e., a monthly household income of about Rs. 1,000 or about Rs. 200 per head. About 240 million people live below the poverty line. Though our economic programmes aim at the upliftment of the majority of people who are poor, in the last 10 years the economic debate was focused on the supposed industrial and infrastructure development of India. The budgetary allocations for most development programmes, in particularly in the social sectors, have been slashed. In the 15th Indian Economic Summit, jointly organized by the Confederation of Indian Industry (CII) and World Economic Forum on November 26, 2000, the then Prime Minister Atal Behari Vajpayee said the rapid changes brought about by technology and globalization had to be addressed with care and caution and the process of change had to be managed with sensitivity. In this regard, corporate sector must implement higher standards of corporate governance, which will enhance the people's confidence in the private sector. It would have to invest in human resource development, focus on research and development, innovation and technology building. There is a definite correlation between the direction of economic growth and poverty reduction. In the reform period, it is clear that the proportional plan budgetary allocation for the social sector spending on health, housing, nutrition, water supply, sanitation, education, roads and electrification has come down from 39.32 per cent in 1985-90 (pre-reforms) to 35.95 per cent in 1991-97 (post-reforms). Except for SC/ST welfare, the expenditure on all other sub-sectors under social services showed a declining trend. As a percentage of GDP, development expenditure by the Centre was 11.5 in 1985-90, but fell to 8.5 in 1991-97. Social sector expenditure was only around 2 per cent of GDP. According to the latest *Human Development Report*, the Human Poverty Index (based on a long healthy life, knowledge, economic provisioning and social inclusion) for India was as low as 34.5 per cent (Jagadish Gandhi, 2001). *The international funds are declining for the social sector and state governments are running out of money. Contrary to this, there is in-house up-tapped resources existing. It is here that the corporate sector has to step in so that these resources can be put to productive use.*

We may conclude that structural reform policies cannot succeed unless a degree of stabilization has been brought about. The reform programmes must be tailored to the socio-economic framework prevailing in the Indian economy and must take into account the political feasibility of the measures contained in them. Therefore, it is essential to promote shared growth in the sense of ensuring that the benefits of growth percolate to all sections rather than being the exclusive prerogative[70] of some pockets. In context with this, the corporate participation in social development is the only solution to achieve the real meaning of the sustainability to ensure the livelihood. India needs to follow the policy of sharing growth which provides a sustainable base for the long term. *What is required is the institutionalization of the process so that it will be easier to assess the potential and degree of responsibility borne by the business sector. The issue of transparency needs to be addressed so that better facilitation can take place by involving different channel partners.*

REFERENCES

1. State of transition to meet people's needs, capacities and values (Qizilbash, M., 2001; Sustainable development : Concept and rankings; *The Journal of Development Studies, Vol.* 37, No, 3, 134-164).
2. Involving different perspectives and skills to bear on a problem (Qizilbash, M., 2001; Sustainable development : Concept and rankings; *The Journal of Development Studies,* Vol. 37, No. 3, 134-161).
3. Continuous change from one state to another (Nayyar, D., 1996; Globalization : The past in our present; *Economic Growth and Social Change,* March, 11-16).
4. Characterized by or advocating or based upon the principles of democracy or social equality (Tandon, R. & Mohanty, R., 2000; *Civil society and governance : A research study in India;* New Delhi : Society for Participatory Research in Asia).
5. The purpose of social development is the ensure that people's needs, capacities and values are at the centre of development efforts (Bhattacharya, D., 1999; Political parties need to make commitments on social development; *Equinox,* Vol. I, issue 1, 3-5).
6. Representing or appealing to or adapted for the benefit of the people at large (Asian Development Bank, 1999; *Polity on indigenous people* Manila, Philippines : ADB Publications).
7. Sometimes called the voluntary agencies. Private independent, non-profit organisations of charitable, research or educational nature (Ball, C. & Dunn, L., 1995; *Non-government organizations : Guidelines for good policy and practice;* London : The Commonwealth Foundation).
8. Community Based Organisation (Ball, C. & Dunn, L., 1995; *Non-government organizations : Guidelines for good policy and practice;* London : The Commonwealth Foundation).
9. Inequality or difference in some respect (Suman Chandra K., 1998; Social justice and development; *Social Welfare,* March '98, 21-26).
10. Involving social as well as economic factors (Jalan, B., 1991; *India's Economic Crisis;* New Delhi : OUP).
11. The financial means whereby one lives (Beteille, A., 1999; *Economic and Political Weekly,* Vol. 34, Nos. 10&11, 589-597).
12. Susceptibility to injury or attack (ADITHI, 1996 : *Integration of Women in the Key Economic Sectors : A Report* (mineo.), Patna : ADITHI).
13. Collecective endeavours to form capital at the community level (Haq, M.U., 1996; *Reflections on human development.* New Delhi : Oxford University Press).
14. A manner of living that reflects the person's values and attitudes (Mitra, A., 2001; Civil society, globalization and sustainable development; *Seminar* 507, 47-52).
15. A manner of living that reflects the person's values and attitudes (Mitra, A., 2001; Civil society, globalization and sustainable development; *Seminar* 507, 47-52).
16. Well defined framework of society's attitude and values (Cherunilam,

F., 2001 : *Global Economy and Business Environment)* New Delhi : Himalaya Publishing House.

17. The biophysical aspects of distribution (Asian Development Bank, 1997; *Polity on indigenous people;* Manila, Philippines : ADB Publications).
18. Local self-governance (Government of India; 1996-97; *Statistical Outline of India,* 1996-97, p. 14).
19. Social insurance for the ill and injured, *Shaping policy;* Do NGOs matter? New Delhi : Society for Participatory Research in Asia, 1997).
20. Condition of social order legally recognized in ordinary affairs of life (Moen Mathiot, E., 1998; *NGOs and Grassroots Development Work in South India;* Lanham : University Press of America).
21. A process by which people take an active an influential hand in shaping decisions which affect their lives (Kurian, T., 2001; Rethinking on Globalization and development : A view. *Southern Economist, May* 1, p. 19).
22. Persons, groups or institutions with an interest in, or influence over, the success or failure of the project, issue and initiatives (Moen Mathiot, E., 1998; *NGOs and Grassroots Development Work in South India,* Lanham : University Press of America).
23. The organisation making a contribution towards the cost of a project. This contribution is usually in cash, but could also be in kind (Annual Report; 2000-2001; SDCA, Confederation of Indian Industry).
24. A group of people through the rational of activism create influence decisions of the Government (Asian Development Bank 1995; *Guidance note on how to do stakeholder analysis of aid projects as and programs;* Overseas Development, Social Development Division).
25. The recipient of funds or other benefits (World Bank, 1999; *Polity on indigenous people;* World Bank Publications).
26. Classified according to various criteria into successive levels or layers (Asian Development Bank, 1995; *Guidance note on how to do stakeholder analysis of aid projects and programs;* Overseas Development, Social Development Division).
27. The act of authorizing (Mitra, A., 2001; Civil society, globalization and sustainable development; *Seminar,* 507, 47-52).
28. The generally accepted perspective at any given time (Macchiwalla, T., 1997; Perspectives on sustainable development; *Search Bulletin,* Vol. 12, No. 2, 15-22).
29. The process of being highly sensitive to specific events or situations (Singh R.R, 1997; *Shaping policy; Delhi School of Social Work, University of Delhi,* New Delhi).
30. Relegated to a lower or outer edge, as of specific groups of people (Chowdhry, K., 1994; *Gandhi and agenda,* p. 21, New Delhi : Vikram Sarabhai Foundation).
31. Based on or prescribing a norm or standard (Chowdhry, K., 1994; *Gandhi and agenda,* p. 21, New Delhi : Vikram Sarabhai Foundation).
32. The members of a business venture created by contract (Aswathappa, K., 2001; *Essential of business environment,* New Delhi : Himalaya Publishing House).

33. The property intangible in nature, have the wisdom for change, being distributed (Mohanty, M. & Singh, A.K., 2001; *Voluntarism and Government; Policy, programme and assistance;* New Delhi : Voluntary Action Network India -VANI).
34. Inducing or aiding in a neural activity; (J. Bhagyalakshmi, 2001: New initiatives for poverty alleviation; *Yojana, November, 12-13).*
35. Applicable delegated authority in accordance with the legislation (Mukherjee, K.K., 1994; *Emerging Societal Challenges and Voluntary Organizations : Challenges and Responses;* Ghaziabad; Gram Niyojan Kendra).
36. Consisting of two or more associated entities (Narayan, J., 2001); Good governance is the key to prosperity; *Economic Times, August 18, 2001).*
37. A government that undertakes responsibility as a constitutional manage for the welfare of its citizens through programs (Planning Commission; Discussion Paper, 2001).
38. Not segregated; designated as available to all groups (Nayyar, D., 1996; Globalization : The past in our present; *Enonomic Growth and Social Change, March, 11-16).*
39. Lessen or to try tô lessen the seriousness or extent of (Sampradan, 2001; *Giving and Fund Raising in India,* New Delhi : Indian Centre for Philanthropy).
40. Accomplished by the act of working jointly (Overseas Development Institute, 1996; *The Impact of NGO Development Projects;* Briefing Paper 2/96).
41. Incorporating various sectors in the same scheme of things (Overseas Development Institute, 1997; *The Impact of NGO Development Projects;* Briefing Paper 2/96).
42. Not distribute equally in all directions, biased towards a particular direction (J. Bhagyalakshmi, 2001; New initiatives for poverty alleviation; *Yojana, November,* 12-13).
43. Measure of the economy; The total market value of goods and services produced by all citizens and capital during a given period (usually 1 yr.) (Holiday, C., 2001; Sustainable growth : The DuPont way; *Harvard Business Review, September,* 129-134).
44. An expected time to live as calculated on the basis of statistical probabilities (Government of India, 1996-97; *Statistical Outline of India,* 1996-97, p. 14).
45. Beauracratic monopoly; views of common people are not taken into account for policy decisions affecting them directly (Asian Development Bank, 1999; *Reducing poverty : Major findings and implications;* ADB Publications).
46. From the people to the decision makers (Asian Development Bank, 1995; *Guidance not on how to do stakeholder analysis of aid projects and programs;* Overseas Development, Social Development Division).
47. Different systems of traditional population; at community level (Mittal, L.N., 1997; Economic growth *vs.* social well-being; *Social Welfare, May,* 18-20).
48. Given the character of an institution or incorporated into a structured

and usually well-established system (Kabra, K.N., 1995; Social development : Elements of an alternative agenda; *Economic Growth and Social Change, March,* 91-92).

49. Having many aspects (Mittal, L.N., 1997; Economic growth *vs.* social well-being; *Social Welfare, May,* 18-20).
50. The restoration of someone to a useful place in society (Asian Development Bank, 1999; *Reducing poverty : Major findings and implications;* ADB Publications).
51. The State of being first in importance (Mittal, L.N., 1997; Economic growth vs. social well-being; *Social Welfare, May,* 18-20).
52. A complete extent or range (Chowdhy, K., 1994; *Gandhi and agenda;* p. 21, New Delhi : Vikram Sarabhai Foundation).
53. Defiling to the touch; Especially used in traditional Hindu belief of the lowest caste or castes (Chowdhry, K., 1994; *Gondhi and agenda;* p. 21, New Delhi : Vikram Sarabhai Foundation).
54. Spirit of Indianness (Chowdhry, K, 1994; *Gandhi and agenda,* p. 21, New Delhi ; Vikram Sarabhai Foundation).
55. The 73rd Constitutional Amendment (1993) provides for direct elections every five years to local bodies *(panchayats)* at three levels—village, taluka and district, and empowers them to assume development responsibilities for subjects which closely touch people's lives.
    The 74th Consitutional Amendment (1993) has similar provisions applicable to municipalities and metropolitan councils (J. Bhagyalakshmi, 2001; New initiative for poverty alleviation. *Yojana, November,* 12-13).
56. Guided by or in accordance with conscience or sense of right and wrong (Asian Development Bank, 1999; *Polity on indigenous people;* Manila, Philippines : ADB Publications).
57. Within a strategy or framework it is common practice to develop outline programmes. These give an indication of the type of projects that could brought forward, the likely resources and time scales, but they do not have to specify actual projects (Planning Commission, Government of India, 1993; Unpublished document).
58. A complex of concurrent things (Cherunilam, F., 2001; *Global economy and business environment;* New Delhi : Himalaya Publishing House).
59. A war between factions in the same country. (Cherunilam, F., 2001; *Global economy and business environment;* New Delhi : Himalaya Publishing House).
60. Act of marshalling and organizing and making ready for use or action human resources in the society (Goyder, G., 1951; *The future of private enterprise : A study in responsibility;* Oxford : Basil Blackwell).
61. Showing unselfish concern for the welfare of others (Garain, S., 2001; Corporate citizenship and corporate volunteering; *Yojana, December,* 12-14).
62. The doctrine that government should not interfere in commercial affairs (Guruswamy, M., 2001; How good is our liberalization? *Seminar, November,* 39-44).
63. The delegation of authority (especially from a central to a regional

government), (Cherunilam, F., 2001; *Global economy and business environment;* New Delhi : Himalaya Publishing House).

64. Continued economic and social development without detriment to the environment and the natural resources on which human activity and future development depend (Moen Mathiot, E., 1998; *NGOs and Grassroots Development Work in South India;* Lanham : University Press of America).
65. A customary way or socially most acceptable way of operation or behaviour (Confederation of Indian Industry, 1995; *A New India—The New Indian Industry;* New Delhi : CII).
66. Belonging to or befitting a supreme ruler (Narayan, J., 2001; Good governance is the key to prosperity; *Economic Times, August* 18, 2001).
67. Organisations who operate out of the physical boundaries of the state (Aswathappa, K., 2001; *Essential of business environment;* New Delhi : Himalaya Publishing House).
68. Data that provides a simple and reliable basis for measuring change or performance (Government of India, 1996-97; *Statistical Outline of India,* 1996-97, p. 4).
69. Confirmation that some fact or statement is true (Gandhi, P.J., 2001; Dynamics of global economy : Its diagnosis and prognosis; *Southern Economist, May,* 1, 11-14).
70. A right reserved exclusively by a particular person or group (Especially a hereditary or official right), (Asian Development Bank, 1999; *Polity on indigenous people;* Manila, Philippines : ADB Publications).

2 Historical and Contemporary Context of Corporate Social Development

Recently while receiving the Economic Times Award, Narayan Murthy, CEO, Infosys, said, "Unless we give back to society, some of what we are getting out of it, I foresee a very violent future for our country." Corporate charity or corporate philanthropy has graduated to corporate citizenship or corporate social responsibility. This is the justified initiative to forward-looking companies, which find contributions made to social causes will fetch rewards. Corporate participation in social development is considered good business, more rationally grounded than only doing business for profit. Bill Clinton, former President, U.S.A. during his visit to India in 1999, said, "The whole enterprise cannot be just about higher profits, there must also be a higher purpose." Here, higher purpose means humane understanding of human problems and pulling together all of our capabilities, mental and physical, towards the purpose of better quality of life. Corporate houses are in a better position to carry on this mission of higher purpose.

Business is a social organ, which cannot make its own world in a manner detrimental to the interests of the cross-sections of the society as also to the various constituents of business at large. Professionalization of corporate facilitates to reflect in the increasing acceptance of broader aspect of business ethics. The term business ethics refers to the set system of principles and rules of conduct applied to business. In practice, the term has been used to describe the do's and don'ts for business, the various things that business should or should not do, viz. not violating any law, avoiding unethical practices, making donations to charitable causes, taking up development projects in backward areas, paternalism towards employees, good public relations, etc. In the Indian perspective, business ethics has many dimensions, for example :

Table 2.1 : The Top 10 Most Respected Companies of India

Rank	*Believes in Transparency*	*Ethical Organization*	*Socially Responsive Conscious*	*Environ-mentally*	*Quality of Products*	*Good Returns to Share-holders*	*Ability Create Value for Stake-holders*
Infosys Technology	8.14	8.27	7.76	7.04	8.24	8.26	8.22
Hindustan Lever	7.84	7.59	7.25	7.21	7.92	7.59	7.63
Reliance Industries	6.95	6.81	7.48	7.32	7.95	8.10	8.09
Wipro	7.25	7.48	7.06	6.89	7.64	7.47	7.50
ICICI	7.28	7.44	7.01	6.56	7.69	7.01	7.14
ITC	7.00	7.21	6.87	6.67	7.64	6.49	6.68
L&T	6.71	6.78	6.70	7.78	7.34	7.10	7.01
Dr. Reddy's	6.86	7.20	7.05	7.14	7.56	7.21	7.30
Ranbaxy	6.92	7.11	6.93	7.35	7.53	7.01	7.06
Nestle	6.72	6.93	6.57	7.12	7.40	6.78	6.75

Source : Business World, 24 September, 2001.

Table 2.2 : Sector-wise Average of Top 6-10 Companies

Rank	*Believes in Transparency*	*Ethical Organization*	*Socially Responsive Consciousness*	*Environmentally*	*Quality of Products*	*Good Returns to Shareholders*	*Ability Create Value for Stakeholders*
Auto and Auto Ancillaries$_{10}$	7.15	7.46	7.07	7.46	7.49	6.77	6.80
Financial Services$_{10}$	6.90	7.08	6.98	6.93	7.20	6.60	6.58
FMCG$_{10}$	6.72	6.89	6.45	6.60	7.34	6.68	6.68
Infotech$_{10}$	7.04	7.31	6.91	7.06	7.38	7.14	7.21
Infrastructure$_{10}$	6.88	6.85	6.85	6.99	7.41	6.87	6.78
Media$_{10}$	6.81	6.77	6.99	7.07	7.17	6.73	6.77
Pharmaceuticals$_{10}$	6.57	6.80	6.80	6.35	6.72	6.94	6.50
Textiles & Garments$_{6}$	6.56	6.74	6.64	6.57	7.32	6.56	5.45
Services$_{10}$	6.80	6.90	6.78	6.70	7.21	6.00	6.06
Telecom$_{9}$	5.85	6.15	6.03	6.12	6.59	5.77	5.78

* The number subscripts indicate the total number of companies in each sector.

(i) Responsibility towards employees;
(ii) Responsibility towards consumers;
(iii) Responsibility towards government; and
(iv) Responsibility towards its own stakeholders.

Corporate participation in social development first wants a good conduct or character on the part of the corporate house. After extensive survey of secondary and primary sources, some of the parameters have been adopted to rank the Indian top 10 companies in corporate social development (CSD). Some of the statement criteria used to rate corporate respect are directly or indirectly related to corporate social development and business ethics. These statements are : (1) Ethical organizations , (2) Socially reponsive organization, (3) Environmentally conscious organization, (4) Quality of products/services provided, (5) Ability to create value for stakeholders, (6) Believes in transparency and (7) Good returns to shareholders. These are also the parameters which, if fulfilled will lead to a genuine pursuance of corporate participation in social development. Table 2.1 (on page 38) shows India's top 10 most respected companies and Table 2.2 (on page 39) shows the sector-wise average of top few companies in the seven selected statement parameters.

A recent survey on corporate involvement in social development in India conducted by Social and Rural Research Institute (1997) reveals some important information. Out of 354 companies surveyed the percentage of companies involved in particular sectors of social development are given in Table 2.3.

India's great business philanthropists foresaw the need to bring

Table 2.3 : Corporate Involvement Sector-wise

n=354

Social Sectors	*Corporate Involvement*	
	Number	*Percentage*
Health	81	23
Education	72	20.34
Environment	20	6
Infrastructure	74	21
Community	9	2.54
Art and Sports	47	13.28
Livelihood	4	1.13

technical, scientific, medical and management education and research into the country for the progress of India, and acted accordingly. It was private initiative which showed the way, whether in the field of art (JJ School of Art, Mumbai), social work (Tata Institute of Social Science, Mumbai), engineering (Birla Institute of Technology, Pilani) or commerce (Shri Ram College of Commerce, Delhi). Private initiative also pioneered many new fields of endeavour, such as cancer research, wildlife conservation, management education etc. The State later used the experience and expertise so gained to widen the field, and disseminated the gains more widely. The motive of philanthropy has not always been pure altruism, with no expectation of a *quid pro quo*. More generally, a mixture of motives has prevailed : religious belief; guilt; a need for spiritual fulfilment not met by material success; a feeling of obligation to society; patriotism; a desire for social prestige and status; need to memorialize a loved one or a noted personality; response to a personal tragedy or natural calamity; government pressure; the lure of tax benefits; and so on.

There have been two main approaches to altruistic giving typified by the 'Parsi' and 'Marwari' communities. Apart from being the two communities most noticed for their giving, each has followed a distinct style derived from a different socio-cultural background and religious belief. Parsi philanthropy, as typified by the Tatas, has followed a more Western approach, while the Birla approach, representative of Marwari philanthropy, is a more eclectic mixture of traditional merchant charity and modern ideas. Both approaches have proved equally valid, and each has made invaluable contributions to Indian society in their own way. Other business groups from other communities fall somewhere in between the two ends of this spectrum, with non-family owned or controlled business groups being nearer the Tata model, and the practices of 'Chettiar' and 'Gujarati' business houses being nearer the 'Birla' approach.

The Tatas have been quick to adopt and adapt progressive Western ideas, concepts and institutional forms such as philanthropy, social responsibility of business, corporate citizenship, grant-making foundations, professional social work and the like, ahead of others. Their business as well as philanthropic methods, from the earliest times, have been more Western than traditional. Mahindra is championing the cause of the girl child through "Nanni

Kali," the organization he set up for the purpose. Then there is Uday Khemka who, from a traditional Marwari business family, Harvard educated, is gathering together like-minded young business leaders and professionals to bring their skills, contacts and resources to organizations working for social development through his brainchild, "Youth Reach".

As companies now seek to integrate their business operations vertically as well as horizontally and to develop core competencies to meet the challenges of globalization, many are moving their philanthropic focus from the cities to village communities around their production units. It is expected to widen markets, help in sourcing inputs and reduce conflicts likely to arise from islands of prosperity in the midst of poverty and need. Dr. M.B. Athreya, a leading management expert, categorizes the four main types of challenges thrown up by globalization for industry as :

(1) Optimizing the positive economic impact and ensuring that they are more widely and equitably disseminated and shared;
(2) Minimizing the negative impacts and helping to cushion them as far as possible;
(3) Maximizing the positive social impacts by preparing the disadvantaged to participate and share in the growth process; and
(4) Minimizing the social impacts by providing mini private safety nets to supplement the macro ones provided by government agencies.

Far-sighted leaders realize that profits are a necessary, but not a sufficient condition of success and that, as Jamsetji, Jamnalal Bajaj and G.D. Birla before them have demonstrated, there is a difference between making money and making wealth.

Within companies, social development needs to move from a peripheral concern to becoming a core competence, with specialization to one particular area of development. This chapter is divided into three sections : Section I deals with the historical context of corporate social development, Section II deals with the contemporary context of corporate social development, and Section III gives an overall picture of government's role in social development in India.

SECTION I

Historical Context of Corporate Participation in India

The government always has adequate amount of resources at its command, the private sector, comprising both business as well as non-profit civil society organizations, has distinct advantages over the government in certain matters of development. While the government action is advantageous where huge resources and a large coverage is necessary, it is not so productive where experimentation with new ideas and directions is needed because of inflexibility, bureaucratic control, lack of political will, lack of genuine planning and red tapism. In recent years, many corporations are engaged in the development of communities and in finding solutions to national concerns, the business community's contributions for social development are made in three different ways : through trusts and foundations set up by wealthy industrial families or by corporations; donations by companies directly to philanthropic work being carried out by individuals and organizations; and operating corporate programmes for rural development, health care, education, promotion of art and culture and other community development activities. Indian business philanthropy dates back to century and a half and it can be divided into four phases is described in the following sections.

Historical Phases of Corporate Philanthropy in India

1. *The First Phase :* The first shift was from a more or less purely ameliorative charity for religious reasons and causes during the re-industrial era (pre-1850), towards the more Western form of philanthropy in the period 1850-1914. The period saw the beginnings of industrialization in India and like their counterparts in the West the newly rich business families began to set up trusts and endow a host of modern institutions such as schools, colleges, hospitals, etc. for the welfare of society. The 'Gujarati' and 'Parsi' business communities of Bombay in particular spearheaded the new trend.

2. *The Second Phase :* In the second phase (1914-1960), which was the golden period of both Indian capitalism and business philanthropy, there was a maturing of philanthropic practice. Apart from making political donations for the freedom struggle, business also contributed to many social and cultural causes associated with

movement such as revival of Indian art and culture, nationalist education, and so on. Many of India's leading businessmen—G.D. Birla, J. Bajaj, Lala Shri Ram, A. Sarabhai and others, came under the spell of Gandhi and his theory of trusteeship of wealth. They contributed liberally to his programmes for removal of untouchability, women's emancipation and rural construction, even as the earlier preoccupation with creating a physical and social institutional infrastructure continued.

3. *The Thrid Phase* : The nest shift came in the 1960s which ushered in an era of economic and political troubles and saw the business community operating under several constraints, i.e., political, financial, infrastructural and technological. Mistrust of business—consequent of sharp and unethical practices by some, coupled with high taxes to finance, state-led development, further contributed to disinclination to part with private wealth for public benefit. Ironically, the high tax regime aided by deterioration in business morality led to a large expansion in the establishment of charitable trusts for purpose of tax planning. Between 1951 and 1965, industrial production grew at almost 8 per cent per annum and the share of industry in GDP, at constant prices, increased from 11.8 per cent in 1950-51 to 15.8 per cent in 1960-61. By 1965, there were several new entrants into industry and into the top league.

Industrial entrepreneurship was becoming conditioned more by economic and industrial factors such as access to capital, possession of business experience, and opportunities to acquire technical and managerial training, than by social factors such as caste, community and social approval or disapproval. Till the 1950s, it was largely the first generation of industrialists who had dominated the business scene. By the 1960s, this picture had changed in many ways. The new generation of first time entrepreneurs, who had emerged, was also more educated and professionally qualified with a better awareness.

Government's Economic Policy and Philanthropy

Right from the beginning, the government's industrial policy incorporated certain social goals such as reduction of disparities in income and wealth; prevention of monopolies and concentration of economic power; reduction of regional disparities; and improving the living conditions of the workers. And the achieve these objectives, measures such as industrial licensing was introduced by the Industries (Development and Regulation) Act of 1952. Meant to be sparingly used, largely to direct and regulate the development of the private sector in conformity with plan priorities, the range and depth of regulation of business was continually expanded as a result of the economic and political troubles faced by then Prime Minister Indira Gandhi in the wake of the 1967 elections. It was also a fact that the concentration of economic power had been encouraged by the State through its industrial licensing system and the financial assistance provided by financial institutions. Some large industrial houses cornered both the licences and finances from financial institutions on whose boards many of the capitalists were directors. A protected market, inflationary budgetary policy and tax incentive, all aided the concentration of wealth in a few hands, while the sector at large was hamstrung for new growth as well as expansion of existing capacities.

Through the Monopolistic and Restrictive Trade Practices Act (MRTP) enacted in 1970, followed by the Foreign Exchange Regulation Act (FERA), tighter control was exercised on industrial expansion by big business houses, till industry was so comprehensively controlled. As against an annual rate of some 8 per cent during the 1950s and 1960s, the annual rate of growth of production was just about 4 per cent in the next decade and more. Along with controls and encroachment of private turf by the State, there was also heavy taxation to finance planned development and to bring about a more equitable distribution of income and wealth. Compulsory distribution of dividend till the measure was withdrawn, coupled with corporate taxation which took no account of the need for internally generated resources for expansion, made business divert available fund into working capital and development, rather than into charity.

The deceleration of industrial growth, controls on industry, a high tax regime and changes in the attitudes of the new business class had several adverse consequences for philanthropy :

(i) The industrial and fiscal policy sapped self-confidence and self-esteem, lowered business morale, and left little surplus for charity;

(ii) Paying heavy taxes for the sake of planned development

and anti-poverty programmes came to be perceived as an alternative to charity and having to contribute anything additionally to charity was considered double jeopardy;

(iii) High tax rates and the licence permit raj led to the growth of administrative and political corruption and huge black money economy. The Wanchoo Committee on Direct Taxes (1972) estimated the income on which tax evaded for 1968-69 to Rs. 1400 crore and the income tax evaded during the same period at Rs. 470 crores. One of the members of the Committee, D.K. Rangnekar, estimated the black money at an even higher figure of Rs. 2833 crore; and

(iv) The presence of black money, as well as the changed outlook of the new generation of businessmen, encouraged conspicuous consumption rather than investment in productive activity or charitable institutions, though donations of large cash amounts, dropped anonymously into temple hundis (donation boxes) became more common.

Government and Foreign Funding of Voluntary Action : A New Approach to Development

As the government became the biggest donor to social welfare organizations through the central and state welfare boards set up after independence, the private sector felt absolved of its responsibility, in contrast to the pre- and immediate post-independence period when charitable organizations relied greatly on private donors. Between 1953 and 1966, the Central Social Welfare Board (CSWB) santioned Rs. 61.6 million by way of grants to approximately 6000 institutions for the welfare of women, children and the handicapped, and more than half of the voluntary agencies established between 1951-1960 owed their existence to the large-scale grants-in-aid programme of the CSWB as part of the first two Plans (Paul Choudhury, 1971). In 1960-61, approximately 36 per cent of a voluntary agency's income came from Central, States and Local Governments. Social action thus came to be perceived as government's responsibility and the problem as too vast to be tackled by private charity.

Social Responsibility in the 70s

In the 1970s, which indicated that business attention was shifting from purely charitable behaviour measured in money terms to one where charity was only one aspect of socially responsible behaviour, and in which development of communities was considered as important as charitable giving through trusts and establishment of prestigious institutions. The credit for bringing social responsibility into the business community's consciousness goes principally to Kasturbhai Lalbhai, J.R.D Tata, Arvind Mafatlal and Ramakrishna Bajaj. All believed in the trusteeship ideals of Mahatma Gandhi and in sound business ethics, and were worried about the deterioration in the latter. The trusteeship theory therefore was seen as a safer way of bringing about social transformation without a violent social upheaval.

Industry and Social Development in the 80s

The 80s brought a new dimension to the concept of corporate social responsibility which had started in the 1970s. In the new paradigm, enlightened self-interest is more strongly stressed than before, and 'giving' and 'sharing' includes giving of all corporate resources—facilities, management know how, technological expertise, and employee time, and not just money resources. The goal is to establish a synergetic relationship between the community, business, and community development activities, such that each energizes the other. The decades of 80s and 90s witnessed a phenomenal growth in the corporate sector in terms of size, complexity and sophistication. The number of private companies increased from 61,000 in 1981 to 407,926 in 1996, while their assets increased from Rs. 49,141 million to Rs. 842,841 million during the same period. The share of industry in GDP at current prices went up from 25.9 per cent in 1980-81 to 29 per cent in 1995-96. The business community has been enlarged by the entry of several new business groups that have made it to the top in a short period. The country was experiencing changes in all aspects of life from traditional business practices to public attitude to business. Though whole of India saw mushrooming of industries, its concentration in south was dramatic. All over India, industrial space has been enlarged by numerous small and middle-level entrepreneurs from professional and non-traditional backgrounds. Proliferation of business groups also occurred through splits in several old industrial families. Younger generations of the business families have different visions and goals, and the politico-economic transformations both inside and outside of the country provided both challenges and opportunities to the new generations. Along with the division of assets division of the philanthropic assets and responsibilities has occurred also. Corporate attitude to social development has been changed during this period. Following the liberalization and globalization movement in the 80s and the 90s, a new wave of MNCs have set up their presence on their own or in collaboration with Indian companies. The business community during the late 90s comprised of five distinct categories :

(i) The old, established, family owned-controlled business like the Tatas, Birlas and Mahindras;
(ii) The old non-family owned and professionally managed groups like Hindustan Lever, ITC, and Larsen & Toubro;
(iii) New groups which have risen to the top of the league in the 80s and 90s such as Reliance, Escorts, Gujarat Ambuja and Ranbaxy, as well as medium-sized groups like Excel and TVS Suzuki;
(iv) Upcoming companies like Sona Steering, Microland, and Malladi; and
(v) Finally, multinationals like Pepsi, Coca-Cola, Daewoo, Samsung, HP, Bridgestone, and Motorola.

The Government's Contribution to Boost Corporate Participation in Social Development

In 1978, Section 35 CC had been introduced into the Income Tax Act to provide for 100 per cent deductions to a company in respect of expenses incurred on approved programmes of rural development, as well as for contributions made to approved organizations undertaking such work. From 1983, such deductions were allowed only for contributions made to the Prime Minister's Rural Development Fund. But as environmental issues came to the fore, Sec. 35 CC (b) was introduced to allow 100 per cent deduction for conservation of natural resources; and Section 35 AC was inserted to give 100 per cent exemption to donors who contributed to associations or institutions carrying out projects approved by the specially constituted 14-member 'National Committee for Promotion of Social and Economic Welfare.' The eligible projects covered, under both the sechemes, a wide range of social development subjects including provision of drinking water, construction of housing for the economically weaker sections, promotion of sports, and so on.

In 1995, Prime Minister P.V. Narasimha Rao reminded that the government had tried to meet the industry's aspirations for liberalization and reforms on the economic front and he urged the industry to share the benefitss with the common people of India. He warned the idustry that if the poor perceived that the disparities had widened in the wake of liberalization or that unemployment in some regions and units was increasing due to free imports and increased competition from foreign investment, then the reforms process would be jeopardized.

The various arms of the government—Union, State, Municipal/ Panchayat—are the biggest agents of development in the country. Their combined resources run into crores of rupees which are spent on many different schemes and plans. The Union Government has many departments and ministries that are directly involved in social development. These include :

1. Ministry of Rural Development
   (i) Department of Land Resources;
   (ii) Department of Drinking water; and
   (iii) Council for Advancement of People's Action and Rural Technology (CAPART).
2. Ministry of Health and Family Welfare
   (i) Department of Health; and
   (ii) Department of Family Welfare.
3. Ministry of Human Resource Development
   (i) Department of Education and
   (ii) Department of Women and Child Development.
4. Ministry of Environment and Forest
5. Ministry of Social Justice and Empowerment;
6. Ministry of Tribal Affairs;
7. Ministry of Urban Development and Ministry of Urban Employment Poverty Allevaition
   (i) Ministry of Urban Development;
   (ii) Ministry of Urban Employment and Poverty Alleviation; and
   (iii) Ministry of Youth Affairs and Sports.
8. Ministry of Food and Civil Supplies; and
9. Ministry of Labour.

In states and districts too, there are different government departments involved in social development. In the districts, the District Rural Development Agency (DRDA) is a coordinating body for all such work. Apart from providing basic social infrastructure for education and health, the government has a large number of development schemes. Many are aimed at economically and socially disadvantaged sections. These schemes address income, credit, water and sanitation, housing and other such needs, typically at an individual or household level.

SECTION II

Contemporary Overview of Corporate Participation in Social Developmental (1995 Onwards)

In its values and management style the Indian corporates are more akin to global, rather than traditional Indian business culture. Amongst the inheritors of dynastic philanthropic traditions such as Rahul Bajaj, Ratan Tata, C.K. Birla, A.C. Muthiah, Siddharth Shriram, Venu Srinivasan, B.K. Modi and a host of others, only a few are personally committed to social development to the extent that their elders had been. The new leadership has come from three other categories—the progressive CEOs of the older, professionally managed corporations like Larsen & Toubro; the entrepreneurs who had started from scratch and made it to the top, and now want to repay their debt to society; and CEOs of international companies in India, who are either seeking to extend the parent company's policy to India or view philanthropy as an auxiliary activity necessary for winning friends and influencing people.

One of the most important reasons for a grater willingness on the part of business to participate in, and contribute more to social development is the improvement in the economic environment of business. The rate of growth of industrial products went up from 4 per cent in 1969-1980 to 7.7 per cent between 1981-1989 (Statistical Outline, 1996-97), and stood at 8.5 per cent in 1997. By the end of 1996, the country had made an almost coplete turnaround from Nehruvian socialism to a Western style market economy, and foreign private investment was once again being welcomed. Private industry was again being given a more critical role in development, and was encouraged to become a global player. Though globalization and economic reforms are far from complete, they imparted a new dynamism to the economy which was reflected in profitability. A 1995 survey of 979 private sector companies by the Confederation of Indian Industry (CII, 1995) found that profitability had shown a dramatic increase from 7 per cent in 1992 to 94 per cent in 1995; turnover growth had gone up from 13 per cent in 1992 to 25 per cent in 1995. Eight Indian companies—Reliance, Hindustan Lever, Telco, Tata Steel, L&T, ITC, Bajaj Auto, Grasim (Birlas)—were among the 200 fastest growing companies in the world, and a number of Indian companies including Dabur, Grasim, Hero and Ranbaxy had become international. Phenomenal growth has occurred in the information technology and pharmaceutical sectors. Companies in these sectors, i.e Wipro, Infosys, Satyam, NIIT, HCL, PCL, Microland, etc. in the first category and Dr. Reddy's, Ranbaxy, Sun Pharma, Cipla, Lupin, Morepen, Torrent, Cadila, etc. in the second category have managed to go global with much confidence.

The Need

There had been great progress on many fronts, for some of which at least the private sector could legitimately claim some credit:

(i) The institutional infrastructure of cities had increased enormously so that each city was endowed not only with several colleges and hospitals but also parks, auditoria, public libraries and art galleries.
(ii) India had a vast reservoir of technically skilled manpower.
(iii) Life expectancy had gone up from 32.1 in 1951 to 60.8 in 1992.
(iv) Participation of women in the workforce had gone up from 14.22 per cent in 1971 to 19.67 per cent in 1981 and to 22.27 per cent in 1991.
(v) The 73rd and 74th Constitutional Amendments had made possible the democratic participation of people in local government. But the bad news was that there were, and still are, great areas of need.
(vi) As late as 1995, 17 million people (equal to the total population of Australia) were being added to an already enormous population of 930 million.
(vii) In spite of nine Five Year Plans, India continued to rank low in the Human Development Index, the Gender Development Index and the Gender Empowerment

Index—below other developing countries like Sri Lanka, Indonesia, Pakistan and Thailand.

(viii) There was only a marginal reduction in rural and urban educated unemployment.

(ix) Though there was an apparent decline in the percentage of people living below the poverty line from about 50 per cent in 1972-73 to about 37.4 per cent in 1983-84, the absolute number of the poor in mid-1980s remained over 270 million. In 1977, there were still 329 million or 36 per cent of the total population living below the poverty line (UNDP Report, 1997).

(x) Only 50 per cent of the adult population was literate as against 69 per cent in China, and women's literacy rate at 35 per cent was half that of the males'.

(xi) Since the poorest among the rural population did not have access to basic health services, the maternal mortality rate at 550 per 100,000 live births was one of the highest in the world, while the infant mortality rate at 89 per 1000 births was also one of the highest, even among developing countries.

(xii) Nearly 36 per cent of school children were dropping out before completing primary school and the girl child, in particular, suffered from discrimination of every sort.

(xiii) Many villages had no potable drinking water facilities.

(xiv) New social problems had been added to the old: AIDS, drug addiction, environmental pollution, shrinking forest cover, child labour, and human rights abuse.

Overall fiscal deficit in 1998-99 was as high as 10.26 per cent compared to below 6 per cent during 1999-2000. The axe has fallen mainly on capital expenditure and social sector spending. The central plan outlay on the social sector was almost unchanged at 1.12 per cent of GDP in 1999-2000 (Budget Estimate) compared to 1.09 per cent in 1993-94.

The Development Sector

By the 1980s, the development sector had become a significant third force, having in size, acquired considerable sophistication in approach, and become more dynamic in implementation. 'Empowerment' was the central piece of the new strategy for decentralized development, formalized by the 73rd and 74th Constitutional Amendments of 1992 introducing Panchayati Raj in rural areas and municipal elections for local self-governance in urban areas.

To traditional charities providing welfare services (hospitals, orphanages, homes for the disabled) were now added community and people's organizations; activist groups working to 'conscientise' people about their rights and offering legal aid and legal literacy programmes; groups working on environment, consumer rights, heritage conservation, women's rights; and think tanks, research centres, training organizations, resource centres, advocacy groups, and networks of NGOs to lobby with government and to offer back up support to the sector as a whole. The NGOs have distinguished themselves by their dedication, flexible and innovative approaches to solving problems of poverty, targeted delivery to the poorest, and ability to mobilize quickly in times of distress. In recognition, the government and foreign donors have channellized an increasing amount of funds through them for development activities.

By 1994, the external resources channelled to the NGO sector through government were nearly Rs. 32 billion, or 7 per cent of the total external aid to India. In addition, funds were contributed by private foreign donors governed by the Foreign Contribution Act (FCRA) such as Ford Foundation, Plan International, and so on. These funds increased from Rs. 100 crore in 1979 to Rs. 253 crore in 1984, and to Rs. 1865 crore in 1994, with the major donor countries being Germany, the USA, the UK, the Netherlands and Italy. Approximately 10,963 NGOs from all over India received the money. Almost 200 foreign donors have set up establishments in India (GOI, 1994).

Compared to foreign funding of NCOs, the average corporate contributions have become insignificant. For instance, ADITHI, an NGO working on income generation and empowerment of women in Bihar, received in 1994-95, 40.25 per cent of its funds from foreign funders; 48.8 per cent from the Central Government, and less than 1 per cent from private sources. In 1995-96, the contribution from foreign agencies had gone up to 67 per cent while that from private agencies increased marginally 1.3 per cent (ADITHI, 1996).

The Specialist Organizations which Negotiate Corporate Partnerships for Social Development

There are, at present, two organizations in India which specialize in building corporate partnerships. The advantage companies have in dealing with these specialized organizations is that they will be able to devote resources and effort to the process, thereby being more responsive and focused:

(1) *Partners in Change (PiC):* Established in 1995, Partners in Change is a not-for-profit organization, registered under the Societies' Registration Act and promoted by the international NGO Action Aid. Its mission is to build sustainable partnerships between the corporate sector and social development initiatives in India aimed at the eradication of poverty. Therefore, it works with all 'good' NGOs and companies and does not restrict itself only to its membership or to certain NGOs. The main client of PiC is the company with whom it plays its basic role of building partnerships with development initiatives. It also plays an advisory role, especially to help develop corporate policies on development and identify developmentally sound activities that companies can take up or support. The main strength of the organization is its understanding of social development issues and its links with NGOs through its relationship with Action Aid India and many development NGOs that it is closely networking with.

(2) *The Business and Community Foundation (BCF):* BCF is the Indian associate of the Prince of Wales Business Leaders' Forum. The latter is an UK-based not-for-profit organization, initiated by Prince Charles, to promote corporate citizenship around the world. Like its international associate, BCF is a membership organization whose members are companies, both Indian and multinational. Its members include, among the Indian companies, Tata Steel and Bajaj, and among international companies, Cadbury's, SmithKline Beecham, to name a few. Thus, it is essentially a corporate driven initiative. BCF plays a facilitating role, i.e., promotional, partnership building and advisory, which, along with its international pedigree, are its biggest strengths. Its work is mainly restricted to its members (existing and potential) who pay an annual fees.

The Business—Society Interface

The presence of a large NGO sector has had a threefold effect on corporate or community interface:

(1) It had to motivate the business community and to catalyze corporate action by creating awareness of different social problems and issues and ways of working with communities;
(2) It has acted as a watchdog towards the corporate sector, especially in the area of environment pollution where many corporations were culpable; and
(3) It has offered companies a viable alternative to operating their own sustainable community programmes.

Corporations could either donate to NGOs or build partnerships with them for working in particular communities and on particular issues. In the 1990s, the NGO sector began to look increasingly to the corporate world for financial support due to the following reasons:

International political developments had demonstrated that foreign assistance could be fickle, even in the humanitarian field. Geopolitical considerations and fashions in funding governed foreign aid. The dismantling of the communist block in eastern Europe and of apartheid in South Africa, the opening up of China, and the need for rehabilitation of Vietnam in the aftermath of war had led to a reordering of priorities by Northern donors, away from the developing countries of the South. For another reason, priorities for causes towards funded tended to change unexpectedly, and periodically. Government efforts to curb the flow of subversive foreign funds had led to cumbersome restrictions under the Foreign Contributions Regulation Act which hamstring many genuine organizations.

NGOs began to make a greater effort to mobilize local private resources. A number of new support organizations such as the Indian Centre for Philanthropy, Partners in Change, South Asian Fund Raising Group, and the India Business and Community Partnership Trust in Delhi, and the Centre for Advancement of Philanthropy in Mumbai, emerged to motivate and to link the corporate sector with non-profit groups, and to facilitate fund raising techniques.

The more sensitive business houses realized that unless they did something to change the state of affairs, the increasing reflection on social tension and conflict would surely drag individuals and businesses into its vortex. By education, training or capacity building they favoured more direct action at community level to solve social problems, rather than old style charity or institutional philanthropy, and they believed that business was uniquely placed to make a difference. It could not only offer money resources but also organization and management skills, vision, leadership and an ability to take risks on new ideas.

Corporate Associations: Mobilizing Industry towards Social Development

Of the several initiatives that facilitate corporate partnerships, the most significant are the industry associations — at the apex and regional and industry sector levels. All the apex associations, i.e., CII, FICCI and ASSOCHAM, actively promote corporate social responsibility among its members. These organizé workshops and seminars on the subject or set up committees to sensitize and advise on what initiatives can be adopted. FICCI has also set up a Foundation that implements its own programmes. It is supported by members who help leverage funds from various donors. In its Annual Report for 1987, FICCI explicitly stated that the business community is part and parcel of the society in which it functions and could not remain aloof from it, and the speeches at various mouthpices of FICCI reflects for over the years the need for participation of industrial houses in social development was in their own self-interest towards long-terms sustainability.

In 1990, a FICCI Report titled Business in the Service of Rural India, based on a survey done by it, noted that nine affiliated chambers and 36 industrial houses had undertaken several programmes of development. These included promotion of cottage industries, development on infrastructure like construction of roads, digging wells, providing for irrigation, drinking water and electrification; development of dairies and piggeries; improving farm technologies and farm management; and promoting health and family welfare.

The Confederation of Indian Industry, the primier national chamber, too initiated similar measures to involve its 4000 members, representing small, medium and large industries. To the committees for assisting rural development (through adoption of villages for promotion of rural employment through small industries, vocational training and prototype development) it added committees on occupational health, environmental planning and preservation, and pollution control. A scheme of awards was instituted in 1988 to recognize outstanding achievement by member companies in these fields. Development of skills and infrastructure, promotion of non-conventional energy use, preservation of the environment, AIDS prevention, promotion of literacy at the workplace and in the community, community health, sports, consumer affairs, and industrial training were all placed before its members as concerns which deserved their attention. At the regional level too, there is considerable promotional activity. The regional offices of CII have set up corporate citizenship committees that organize many events locally.

ASSOCHAM, the third major apex body, began its education and action programmes later than the other two chambers, though many of its members like Mafatlals, Lupin Laboratories, Armour Chemicals and others had been engaged in rural development, family planning and educational activities of their own since long. Its one major initiative has been the launch in 1994 of drinking water initiatives as part of its Platinum Jubilee celebration.

In the regions, Bombay and Calcutta chambers took the lead. In Bombay too, the leading chambers—the Bombay Chamber of Commerce (BCC), and the Indian Merchants Chamber (IMC)— took civic facilities of the city as their first priority. The BCC has concentrated on the population problem and on civic issues of Bombay city. Through its Population Cell (established in 1991), it launched an active advertising campaign to promote small families, and organized activities around issues such as infant mortality, nutrition and literacy. Some industry sectors too actively promote corporate social responsibility. The Organization of Pharmaceutical Producers of India (OPPI), for instance, had a separate session on the subject in its last international symposium. The Joint Plant Committee of the steel industry did likewise in one of its seminars on growing markets.

Initiatives of the industry associations are characterized in the following way :

(i) A strong promotional role but a limited advisory and partnership building role;

(ii) Focusing on what member companies are doing, though NGOs are increasingly being seen as important partners; and

(iii) There are some not-for-profit and for-profit consulting organizations who have started to provide advisory services on corporate partnerships.

Corporate Participation in Social Development: Current Perspective

At present, corporate contributions for public welfare take six different forms:

(i) Establishment of trusts and channelling of funds through these;

(ii) Establishment of mega institutions for public causes;

(iii) Operation of community programmes directly by companies;

(iv) Giving donations on request to individuals or organizations;

(v) Forming partnerships with government or NGOs for particular projects; and

(vi) Sponsorship for social development programmes.

Of these various ways of meeting social need, direct company involvement seems to be the most prevalent new trend along with the trend to form partnerships with NGOs.

Only a few partial attempts have been made to systematically survey the field, and that too without quantifying the contributions in monetary terms, so that it is difficult to say how much of the total given by business to social concerns goes to each of the above categories.

In 1984, the Delhi office of the Ford Foundation sponsored a sample survey of 39 companies and four philanthropic organizations in Bombay. The survey found that several companies were spending substantial amounts on social development activities, but the largest amount went to a company's own programme (47 per cent), followed by aid to outside organizations (39 per cent), and only 14 per cent went to company trusts. In responding to requests, companies usually considered integrity of the person or organization making the request and the need to maintain good relations with them; the standing of the person making the appeal; appeal of the cause to the company; whether employees were involved with the charity; whether the company itself was involved with the organization in some way (e.g. the hospital seeking a donation is one which usually treats company employees); and whether the cause or organization was related to company business in some way.

Two surveys, commissioned by Action Aid in 1992 and 1996 (SRI, 1992), updated the information on corporate attitudes and practice. The 1992 survey identified only 44 companies as being receptive to the idea of partnership with NGOs, though to varying degrees. The survey also found that more of the older companies (85 per cent), established 40 years ago or more, were engaged in philanthropic activities and had firm policies compared to younger companies; and that a larger proportion of MNCs had a stated policy than did Indian companies which worked according to unstated policies. Middle-sized companies (turnover of Rs. 100-500 crore) were mostly engaged in running schools and hospitals and providing donations to the poor. By contrast, companies with less than a Rs. 100 crore turnover had adopted surrounding villages for development while others provided medical services to the poor and contributed to relief funds for natural calamities. The older and larger companies had established large institutions, helped out the poor and also undertook community development. What's more, they made long-term, rather than *ad hoc* commitments.

In the 1996 survey of Action Aid (SRI, 1997), 647 large modern corporations in India, including both public and private sector enterprises, were covered. It revealed the following :

(i) Nearly 36 per cent had some sort of policy on their support to social service and 7 per cent had a clearly stated written policy.

(ii) It also revealed that out of 295 companies involved in social work, about 16 per cent worked through civil society organizations other than their own foundations and trusts. Most of these CSOs interested in relief type of organizations such as Lions, Rotary Clubs, Jaycees and YMCAs. Although, the trend is gradually changing. Now many corporates are coming forward for partnerships with grassroots and activist types of orgnisations as well.

(iii) A majority of those with policy had a person or department responsible for its implementation, and typically, they supported long-term interventions.

(iv) About 46 per cent were involved in development activities. The reasons ranged from a purely philanthropic impulse to getting goodwill and good image, saving, on tax, and boosting employee morale.

(v) Companies involved in development tended to be larger and older companies.

(vi) Cash donations were the most preferred form of support. Non-cash forms of support included management assistance, sharing of skills, allowing use of company facilities, preferential purchase of products from the disadvantaged communities, creating employment opportunities through ancilarization, donation/discounts on company products and facilities, and least used, staff secondment.

(vii) The most popular causes remained health, education, creation of physical infrastructure and sports and arts. Natural resource management, community support and livelihood were less favoured red, while more radical causes like consumer rights, promotion of legal aid and literacy, human rights, helping the aged, and rehabilitation of bonded labour, had very few takers.

(viii) In deciding where and what to support, the surveys found that those projects were selected which were in or around the locations where the company had its offices and units; financial aspects, both in terms of investment required and potential returns were of less importance.

(ix) Decisions were mostly made at the senior-most levels of chairman, or managing director or senior management. The budgets ranged from as low as Rs. 25,000 to Rs. 50 million, with a nodal range being between Rs. 100,000 and Rs. 1 million.

The companies did not find it easy to engage in community level philanthropy. There responses cited problems of cooperation from villagers and beneficiaries; of having to deal with government agencies and statutory bodies; financial and manpower constraints; illiteracy and lack of awareness amongst target groups; and of maintenance of the infrastructure so created. Due to these reasons, at least half the companies surveyed preferred to donate to or work with NGOs rather than do the work themselves, though a majority believed that they had an obligations to and could make a contribution to development, and that it was good for their reputation and image.

Action Aid's 2000 survey (SRI, 2000) has promising implications for business social responsibility. Some of the findings are outlined below:

(i) More than 85 per cent of the companies out of 600 agreed to have a role to play in social development.

(ii) 71 per cent of the companies mentioned that community (either near the workplace or anywhere) should be the beneficiaries of social development activities of the companies.

(iii) Nearly 20 per cent has a policy on involvement in social development. Public sector undertakings were more likely to have a policy. A higher percentage of MNCs have a policy compared to Indian private companies, but the difference between them was not significant.

(iv) Nearly 70 per cent, i.e. 414 companies were undertaking social developmental activities. In the similar kind of survey conducted in 1996, at least 62 per cent of the companies were undertaking social developmental activities. The 2000 survey indicated a marked improvement in corporate involvement in social developmental activities.

(v) 17 per cent of the total number of companies involved in social development (414 companies) had worked in partnerships with NGOs or development agency and local government.

(vi) Monetary donations were made by 78 per cent (324 out of 414) of the companies and were the most commonly adopted method of supporting developmental activities.

(vii) Having a policy whether written/unwritten has a definite impact on undertaking of social development activities.

(viii) The percentage of companies involved in donation on subsidization of the products/services has not shown any significant differences since the 1996 survey (in which the corresponding figure was 16 per cent, out of 647).

(ix) 20 per cent of the companies out of the 600 were involved in preferential purchasing and 16 per cent were found to be involved in enabling employment.

(x) It was found that there is a significant increase in per cent of companies undertaking ongoing projects from 81 per cent in 1996 to 88 per cent in 1999.

(xi) It seems that companies who undertake social development activities have belief in efficacy of long term projects.

Entry of Indian MNCs

ITC, apart from setting up the Sangeet Research Academy as a modern gurukul for training young musicians, has also established a corporate contributions programme covering a variety of fields—education, health, environment, arts, employment training, welfare of disabled and wildlife. It operates at all levels—region, city, national and project. Currently, its contribution is said to total around Rs. 100 million. Larsen and Toubro fulfils its social commitment mission by offering medical assistance to the community for family planning, mother and child health, TB and leprosy control through its L&T Welfare Centre at Andheri in Mumbai; through its Lifeline Express train which takes treatment on wheels to remote areas of tribal Maharashtra; and through its AIDS awareness campaign. In its non-metropolitan locations, it is engaged in rural development programmes of health, education, employment generation and afforestation. It has also contributed to older style philanthropy by setting up the L&T Institute of Technology and endowing lectures and chairs in academic institutions. Equally important, as a corporate citizen, it is promoting fair and ethical business practices and exemplary standards for employee welfare and customer satisfaction.

Today almost all the companies in the top 100 bracket, barring a few, have some kind of philanthropic programme. The shift in style is most noticeable in the South where corporate philanthropy was perhaps on a lower scale and more religion-oriented than elsewhere.

Corporate-NGO Partnership

Among those who have set up an NGO are Tatas, Godrej, Escorts,

Lupin, IPCL, Usha Martin, Excel and Arvind Mills. Many of these organizations were established in response to the government's call to help with rural development, and to take advantage of the tax deductions offered under Section 35 CC of the Income Tax Act.

In recent years, there has been the trend towards forming partnerships with NGOs and public agencies for particular projects. Many companies in Kolkata are contributing regularly to the Ramakrishna Mission's work in rural development, while the Mafatlal group has for long been involved with the Bharatiya Agro Industries Foundations. Ranbaxy, a leading Delhi-based Indian multinational pharmaceutical company, works with Navjyoti Development Society on integrated community development with a special focus on women and children to provide healthcare services in the industrial slum where Navjyoti works. Bata is supporting the All Bengal Women's Union to help destitute women become self-reliant by giving production and marketing support.

In Bangalore, two corporations, AEG NGLF and Madura Coats, have a long association with the Cheshire Homes to teach employment skills and provide income to the inmates. LML Vespa is now seeking to associate itself with two NGOs, Shramik Bharti and Sakhi Kendra in Kanpur to support vocational training to underprivileged youth in two wheeler repair; subcontracting the tailoring of worker uniforms to NGOs, and carrying out a tree planting programme near their plant in Kanpur. The Chennai-based Rane group, manufacturing automobile ancillary equipment, is developing a partnership with Tribal Health Initiatives, an NGO of Dharmapuri in Tamil Nadu. The Mumbai based NGO, Pratham, addresses the deficiencies in primary schools of the municipal corporations with corporate support from Gujurat Ambuja and others. The Taj group of hotels is partnering Katha Khazana, an NGO working for empowerment of women and children in one of the largest slums of Delhi.

Public-Private Partnerships and Corporate Sponsorships

The common perception is that the role of industry is to create wealth through the production of goods and services. This production is to be carried out within a legal framework. The industry is expected to obey labour laws, pay taxes to the government and to respect the environment. Industries working within this framework are fulfilling their 'social responsibility.' Most of the companies do not want to go beyond this. Certain corporates have, since their inception, made special efforts to go beyond their normal idea of business. Traditionally, the driving force behind such efforts has been philanthropy. But philanthropy has not been able to do justice to social development. Mere donation of funds does not provide any long-term solution to any problem, rather it does have some sporadic success.

The Indian corporate sector possesses a unique strength *vis-a-vis* NGOs, especially the ones dependent on foreign funding. This is the ability to set its own agenda and work in a professional manner. It has the ability to take risks and test out new ideas. Self-funding and local accountability gives Indian corporates tremendous flexibility in day-to-day functioning, solid credibility and sound monitoring. Whether they admit it or not, NGOs are bound to work in sectors for which foreign funding is forthcoming. Very often, the Indian NGOs' development agenda is influenced by funding agencies on the other side of the globe.

According to Singh and Sah (2001), the ethical aspects of business also include a healthy cooperative inter-business relationship between different businesses and avoidance of such unfair practices as price rigging undercutting, patronage and so on. The social and ethical responsibilities of business towards the state demand that the businessman should (a) respect law of the land, (b) pay his taxes and dues to the state honestly, (c) not corrupt public servants and the democratic processes for his selfish interest, (d) not buy undue political support or patronage by money, and (e) pursue a fair trade policy and avoid activities leading to restraint of trade.

The very purpose of an alliance is to ensure a greater chance of success through co-operative activity than from going it alone. The unique strength of NGOs is their ability to communicate effectively with the poor. Their role could be basically to work with the community to facilitate the physical upgrading work, as well as manage the community-based components. The unique strength of the corporate sector is its managerial capability and its competence in mapping out competitive business strategies. Therefore, the corporate sector could shouldering play the role of project manager and co-financier. It can also focus on the skill upgrading and income generation component of the project.

Private-public partnerships have emerged as one of the options to direct the growth of private sector towards public goals. In general, the focus of various private-public collaborations has been on:

(i) Developing strategies to utilize untapped resources and strengths of the private sector; and
(ii) Improving efficiency through evolving new management structures.

Some companies are partnering government departments for accomplishing some of the social goals like population management. In Mumbai, Bangalore and Delhi, municipal corporations have invited corporate houses to participate in the upkeep of the cities' infrastructure of parks, municipal schools, garbage collection centres, traffic, islands and so on.

Corporate sponsorships, though not philanthropy in the true meaning of the word because of the expectation of some benefit in return, has become a popular way of contributing to social causes and getting immediate returns for the company in the form of publicity and goodwill. Sports and cultural performances are the causes most, favoured for sponsorship and companies like MRF and JK are known for the support given to sports in this way.

Primary health care (PHC) forms the backbone of the health delivery system in each state. Surveys have shown that PHCs do not have adequate facilities to provide health services effectively and utilization of these facilities is very low. A number of surveys have highlighted that many PHCs are without doctors and where there are doctors, they do not attend the facilities regularly. Under this scenario, harnessing local level support and private initiatives is emerging as an important option to improve the performance of the PHCs in various states. Public-private partnerships in the health sector can solve government's resource problem to a large extent and also take care that the vulnerable groups— the poor and majority of rural population—have access to health facilities. State governments of Punjab, Rajasthan and Delhi have devised important policy initiatives towards developing partnerships with industry in the health sector. Many other states are also exploring this new system of sharing development responsibilities with the industry. The cases of Tamil Nadu and Gujarat highlight the nature of these initiatives.

Tamil Nadu : In Tamil Nadu the state government has involved industry in improving the performance of PHCs. The primary role of industry was envisioned to adopt a local PHC, health sub-centre or district hospital. They have the responsibility of building, maintaining and equipping the facility. Under this collaborative arrangement, the state government continues to provide staff and medicine. Most of the industry houses choose the PHCs around their plants. Of the total budget of Rs. 10,450 million, Rs. 250 million are allocated to maintenance of PHCs. Industry has committed to spend up to Rs. 13 million. The collaboration also provides opportunity to the state government to get feedback from industry on various management issues of the PHCs.

Gujarat : In Gujarat, SEWA-Rural was given the entire primary health care services in one district by the state government. Under the agreement, the government agreed to finance the entire PHC services in SEWA-Rural's project area. These services were planned to be run on the same pattern as that in the government, but managed wholly by SEWA-Rural.

The Partnership between Civil Society Organizations (CSOs) and Business

Historically, civil society organizations (CSOs) have taken one of the three stances to the business sector : financial resource mobilization, protest and advocacy, or non-engagement. This paradigm governing most intersectoral relationships was either that of donor-recipient or adversary. With the emergence of neo-liberal policy agendas at global and national levels, some observers are claiming that new terms of engagement between the sectors are not only possible, but also being applied around the world. "Strategic partnership" is the new paradigm for civil society—business relationships with advance the core strategies of both sectors. The most common motivation for civil society cooperation was resource mobilization, and businesses were primarily interested in responding to societal pressures to be more socially responsible.

Benefits to CSOs : In general, the CSOs mobilized increased resources that contributed three types of benefits : increased development reach and impact, strengthened organizational capacity, and enhanced relationships with business and donor communities. In a case study of Southern American countries, it was found that joint activities fell in the areas of education and employment opportunities for the poor and marginalized communities.

Social stratification, organizational sphere, stereotypical attitudes and lack of mutual knowledge separate many CSOs and businesses. Since business tend to contribute resources like funds and technical assistance, traditions of donor-recipient relationship get reproduced with the result that CSOs become dissatisfied with joint projects and participants fail to realize intended benefits. Cooperation with business often requires CSOs to develop new competencies and change organizational policies, practices and structures.

Contemporary Context of Corporate Participation

The issue of interaction between the business community and the civil society actors is not new in India. Historically, Mahatma Gandhi during the freedom movement called upon the industrialists to help him and his initiatives, both in the area of constructive social work as well as in the struggle for freedom. Since then, the share of private sector in Indian development has been rather weak and only recently that space for private economic development has been provided in the Indian development policy framework. Yet, there are many examples of collaboration between the business sector and civil society organizations, particularly around disaster relief or in respect of service provision in areas of health, education, safe drinking water, etc. By and large, the Indian business community prefers to do things on its own, primarily looking at its immediate self interest in communities where its business activities are being carried out. Business organizations setting up social foundations for general support is a rather exceptional phenomenon in the Indian context today. However, with increasing discourse on corporate citizenship and socially responsible corporate actions gaining importance in the current context, with the presence of multinational companies with a growing recognition that the private business sector has a legitimate role in the country's development, there is now an increasing responsibility of building partnerships between CBOs and the Indian business sector, particularly the more progressive and professional segments of the same.

The corporate sector involvement has been in philanthropic activities and the concept of corporate partnership or corporate social responsibility, as it is often called, is comparatively new. Traditionally, most businesses, small or big, professional or traditional, have helped a social cause, but such support was mostly *ad hoc* for religious causes like building temples or rest houses for pilgrims, or for humanitarian relief or for social welfare. Such support has largely been individualized barring a few who have set up special trusts for the purpose. However, it is seen that most businesses have very little or superficial knowledge about the issues on social development in India. Activities like bringing awareness among the poor, mobilizing and organizing them or capacity building for the poor to give them greater control over their destinies, etc. are largely absent from the corporate agenda of social work.

Currently, the government is giving more and more concessions to industry by reducting taxes and tariffs. It is for this reason that it has been often agrued that as a result of liberalization, the corporate sectior is becoming a major force in the Indian economy and thereby affects the lives of the poor. A point to be noted in the context of liberalization is that the culture of business is becoming pervasive. Values of self-financing, self-sufficiency and market approaches are spreading to all sectors. Anybody seeking to support social developement is being asked as to how soon it will pay for itself. Outlook on the part of the corporate as they are adopting a more professional stand towards business and therefore, towards social development (Ashman, 1999). Besides the tradition of corporate philanthropy, tax benefits is an important consideration for some companies and in most cases the corporate sector would prefer to give to an activity which would give them tax benefits under Section 80G and Section 35A.

Rationale of Partnership and Role of Business Association

Two lines of agruments are put forward for corporate involvement in social work. The first line of agrument takes and ideological stand and argues that corporates take so much from the society creating several social and environmental problems, therefore, it is their duty to give some amount back to the society on which they survive. The second line of agrument takes a more pragmatic and conciliatory approach by saying that it is in the company's own interest, direct or indirect, short-term or long-term, that it gets involved in social development.

It is often seen that business organizations that are interested in social development prefer to do it themselves threough a Trust established for the purpose, rather than therough NGOs. Mutual suspicions and prejudices are quite wide spread. Since corporate culture is politically conservative, it tends to view NGOs, particularly the activist types, as socialists and leftists. NGOs, too, are generally afraid that if they collaborate with the market enterprises they may be seen as having been coopted by vested interests and would lose their credibility. Also, some NGOs working at the grassroots, directly or indirectly, confornt the industry. NGO's opposition to such projects as ENRON in Maharashtra, Narmada Dam in Gujurat, indiscriminate mining in Sourthern Rajasthan are seen by the corporates as NGO's anti-industry stance.

In the 4th 'Social Summit' 2001, organized by the Confederation of Indian Industry (CII), certain resolutions were passed by the participating representatives of the corporate sector in combating problems in the areas of health, education, population control, employment generation, etc. They called for starting with the workers, and then followed by their families and finally, the communities. Experience shows that most often these partnerships are not accountable to each other. Initial interventions or one-time interventions have veen the modus operandi. This calls for active networking amongst NGOs and the corporate sector, arriving at a common platform of social understanding and social responsibility.

The Partnership : India has witnessed considerable shift from socialism to liberalism and nationalization to privatization. There has been emphasis not only on industrialization but also privatization. While the private sector is being encouraged to establish more businesses, the government has begun to reduce its stake in business enterprises run by it till now. Today the government is giving more and more concessions to industry. State governments are inviting industries to come to their states offering all kinds of facilities and concessions.

There has been a noticeable shift on the part of the business towards the social concerns. Business organizations are beginning to view their business in the context of the existing socio-political environment, broadening their perspectives of development beyond GNP and per capita income. Recent years have also witnessed a marked shift from charity and relief to a more totalistic approach to social development. More and more companies are increasingly recognizing their social responsibility and getting involved in social development, either through their own foundations and trusts or in partnership with civil society organizations.

Industry associations like CII, ASSOCHAM, FICCI and intermediate organizations like Partners in Change, India Business and Community Partnership Trust, Indian Centre for Philanthropy and others are playing an important role in broadening the scope of the business-civil society partnerships. Partnerships are beginning to come out of the shells of only funding relations to assistance by corporations in providing technical and management skills to the NGOs.

CSOs efficiency, performance and outcomes are now more systematically planned, organized and managed in a more professional way with more and more technical and management professionals being recruited. Many NGOs have started adopting company form of organization. Non-profit company form seems to be more in vogue today as compared to the charitable trust and society form that NGOs had most commonly preferred so far.

As yet, the partnerships are confined to a certain type of corporates and a certain type of CBOs and for certain type of developmental activities. Generally, the corporates that have entered into partnerships are fairly large, modern and professionally oriented organizations. Small and medium corporations, involvement in social development has so far not been in vogue through now and then they contribute to some social cause. There exists tremendous potential in small non-professional industries, large trading and other commercial establishments that needs to be tapped. The case of the collaborating NGO partners is similar. There are a large number of small and medium sized NGOs that are doing very crucial work in awareness generation, mobilization and organization of the rural poor, increasing the access of the poor to various government schemes and programmes, and working on the related issues of citizen empowerment although they do not have professional characteristics.

Civil society and business are slowly coming together and as a joint formidable alliance on large issues of development on a formal and sustained basis. They are forming task forces and working groups on critical issues, study the situation, and influence the concerned institutions and establishments and influence policy of the government, bilateral and international development agencies.

SECTION III

The Government's Involvment in Social Development in India

Jawaharlal Nehru, the first Prime Minister of India, was so fascinated by the Western models of development that even Mahatma Gandhi, who had constructed and experimented with indigenous models of development, was sidelined and ignored. Nehru was hightly influenced by the Russian model of planning for development and use of gigantic machines making use of high energy technology for raising the production of different types of goods and services especially railways, moter vehicles, shipping, electricty, and so on, for consumption of Indian masses. Undoubtedly, after independence, a plethora of steps were taken by the Government of India to protect and promote the interests of the working class through the enactment of progressive legislation like Industrial Disputes Act, 1947; the Factories Act, 1948; the Employees State Insurance Act, 1948; the Minimum Wages Act, 1948; and so on.

In the Nehru era, beginning from the late forties to the early sixties, there was development of large-scale industries, emergence of new industrial townships, continuous expansion and enlargement of cities, concentration of wealth in a few families, monopolization of trade and industry, greater empowerment of bureaucracy which started treating itself as masters of people instead of considering themselves as public servants, and emergence of a big gulf between rulers and the ruled. Undoubtedly, it was realized that the government alone could not undertake the entire responsibility of social welfare; the cooperation of non-government organizations were essential and as a consequence, the Central Social Welfare Board (CSWB) was established in 1953 to aid and assist the non-government organizations in the country.

The era of planned development started in the 1950s when the First Five Year Plan (1951-56) commenced. With special emphasis on agricultural development to attain self-sufficiency in foodgrains, the first Plan tried to double the per capita income within a period of 25 years. A massive programme of community development was launched for the development of rural communities in India. The Panchayati Raj System was introduced in order to provide power to the people at the grassroots level to enable them to take decisions for themselves. A number of non-government organizations started working in the area of nation-building and social reform.

The Second Five Year Plan, which started in 1956, laid emphasis on the industrial development of the country in order to ensure supply of goods and services required for the minimum desirable standard of living to all. It also stressed on raising the gross national product and on the expansion of employment opportunities. Thus, the decade of 1950-1960 was mainly concerned with economic growth and it was the government which took major initiative. Of course, the non-government organizations also played a significant role in promoting welfare of women, children, scheduled castes and the scheduled tribes. The uneven distribution of the benefits of development— social and economic —over the years has led to fairly widespread inequality.

In the Third Five Year Plan (1961-66), the programme of intensive agricultural development leading to the green revolution was organized. Non-government organizations, with trained manpower, started organizing innovative programmes in the field of education, health, etc. It was also realized that the fruits of development could not reach the general masses and, therefore, it was clearly stated that the objective was to establish progressively greater equality of opportunity and to bring about reduction in disparities in income and wealth and a more even distribution of economic power.

The Fourth Five Year Plan commenced in 1969 in which one of the principal tasks was to provide substantial additional facilities in the social service sector, especially for the rural areas. Due to the active role played by the government in promoting the process of development, dependence of people on the government considerably increased. There was emergence of an elite class, particularly of professionals who monopolized knowledge leading to their control over the centres of power. Establishment of new industries and provision of varied kinds of services in and around big cities and towns speeded up the process of urbanization and led to the emergence of big slums and degradation in the quality of environment.

In the decade of 1970-80, there was a major shift in the approach towards development. 'The general approach was substituted by target group and area approach. *Garibi Hatao* (eradicate poverty) was the slogan of the ruling party. Indira Gandhi, very rightly thought for the poor. The Twenty Point Programme was launched in 1975 in order to eradicate poverty and promote multi-dimensional development, especially of weaker and vulnerable sections. Varied kinds of programmes like Cash Scheme for Rural Employment, Marginal Farmers and Agricultural Labourer's Development Agency (MEAL), Small Farmers Development Agency (SFDA), Integrated Rural Development Programme (IRDP), Training of Rural Unemployed Youth for Self-Employment (TRYSEM), Development of Women and Children in Rural Areas (DWCRA), etc. were stated during this decade. Indira Gandhi made special efforts in the area of environmental conservation and development, women's development, particularly in the area of reproductive health of women, special protection and development programmes for minorities, etc.

The Janata Party with Morarji Desai as the Prime Minister of India stressed the eradication of illiteracy, elimination of poverty and improvement of health, particularly through the programmes of National Adult Education Programmes (NAEP), Antyodaya and Village Health Workers.

The Fifth Five Year Plan (1974-79) was launched which clearly stated that 'the objectives in view are removal of poverty and achievement of self-reliance... The strategies relate to growth in the three leading sectors, namely, agriculture, energy and critical intermediaries and the creation of additional employment opportunities' (India, 1976:5). It was in this plan that a comprehensive sub-plan approach to tribal development was introduced. There was considerable growth in the development sector also which concentrated on the development of the poor and the downtrodden. Special concern was shown towards people below the poverty line. Varied kinds of efforts were made to organize and mobilize the poor.

The Sixth Five Year Plan, launched in 1980, *inter alia*, aimed at 'a progressive reduction in the incidence of poverty and unemployment...improving the quality of life of the people in general with special reference to the economically and socially handicapped population....strengthening the redistributive bias of public policies and services in favour of the poor....a progressive reduction in regional inequalities....promoting the active involvement of all sections of the people in the process of development through appropriate education, communications and institutional strategies' (India, 1980:34). During this decade, the government as well as NGOs organized a number of programmes relating to women's development and environmental protection. The social forestry programme was organized on a massive scale to improve the quality of the environment. There was a special concern for women's participation and sustainable development. As a consequence, participation of people in the development process considerably increased.

The Seventh Five Year Plan, launched in 1985, unequivocally stated, 'Removal of poverty, the building of a modern society making maximum possible use of science and technology and attainment of self reliance are the objective of planning in India...the aim is to create by the year 2000 the condition necessary for self sustaining growth and to provide the basic material requisites of well-being of all our people' (India, 1985:viii). This Plan sought to emphasize those policies and programmes which could be instrumental in accelerating the growth in foodgrain production, expansion of employment opportunities and increase in the level of productivity. The central development strategy was geared towards the generation of productive employment. There was development not only of the rural infrastructure but also creation of opportunities for employment of the rural poor.

It was during the Rajiv Gandhi's government (from 1984 to 1989), that a separate Ministry of Human Resource Development, consisting of Departments of Education, Women and Child Development and Youth Affairs and Sports was created; the New Education Policy was formulated which stressed on the vocationalization and professionalism and linking of degrees from job. The National Literacy Mission was started; the revised 20-Point Programme was launched; the Tribal Sub-Plan was started; the JRY commenced, especially with a view to winning over the Gram Pradhans (the political heads at the lowest level of village); a beginning in the area of entrusting power to the people, particularly through the participation of weaker sections, was made, and the National Youth Policy was formulated. Another spectular contribution of Rajiv Gandhi was introducting 'computer and IT'; revitalising the PRI and make 33 per cent reservation for woman in PRI.

V.P. Singh took over as the Prime Minister of India in 1989, and his main contribution to the field of human development was the implementation of the Mandal Commission which had recommended 27 per cent reservation for the OBCs on the principle of social justice. The Chandra Shekhar government's main contribution was the introduction of reservation for economically poor sections of society, irrespective of their religion and caste. In fact, he was forced to do so by the then circumstances in which upper caste people were highly agitated over the issue of reservation for the OBCs and the exclusion of the poor upper castes from the ambit of reservation.

During the Prime Ministership of P.V. Narasimha Rao, the New Economic Policy providing for liberalization, privatization and globalization was adopted and the Dunkal proposals incorporating TRIPS and TRIMS were accepted due to the pressure of IMF and the World Bank and a very bad situation of balance of payments running into billions. A number of programmes relating to poverty removal such as Urban Basic Services for Poor, provision of employment under the Special Employment Programme, shelter for the poor through the Indira Avas Yojana, among others, were started.

The Eighth Five Year Plan (1992-97) clearly stated that, 'The Plan will have to work out the ways and means of involving people in the developmental task and social evolution. It will have to strengthen the people's participatory institution (India,1992:1): The 73rd and 74th Constitutional Amendments were made in 1992 to ensure wider participation of people, especially SCs, STs, Other Backward Castes (OBCs) and women in local self-governments.'

Nabhi's Approach Paper to the Ninth Five Year Plan (1997-2002) has observed that 'the principal task of planning in the federal system is to evolve a shared vision of a shared commitment to the national objectives' (India,1997:69). It emphasized human development—food and nutritional security for all, particularly the vulnerable sections of society; provision of basic minimum services of safe drinking water; primary health centre facilities; universal primary education; shelter and connectivity to all; curb on the rate of population growth; environment friendly and sustainable development; empowerment of women and socially disadvantaged groups; and development of institutions of people's participation such as the Panchayati Raj, cooperatives and self-help groups. Since the Sixth Five Year Plan, the scope and coverage of these anti-poverty programmes have greatly expanded. However, the success of these programmes will depend on the ability of the fiscal system to mobilize enough surpluses of finance for both productive investments and socially oriented programmes (Suman Chandra, 1998).

Initially it was the government, which took initiatives by formulating policies and plans and launching programmes, providing extension services, financial help, and infrastructural support which resulted in the promotion of economic development. The NGOs were mainly concerned with promoting welfare of people and bringing about reforms in society. Today, it is primarily the people's own organizations that are striving hard for promoting integrated development, especially of the marginalized sections of society. Development today is conceived in its totality and the policies, plans and programmes of development are being formulated by prospective beneficiaries themselves and their representatives by giving special consideration to the promotion of social justice and environmental implications of development projects in order to ensure that the overall quality of life of people gets improved and enough resources are left for future generations also (Singh, 1999). In favour of the above, some examples are given below:

It is being realised that the duty and responsibility of any vigilant civil society to have introspection about the essence of the core structure of the Constitution. Here the context is, by principle, India has the basic character of a welfare state. Therefore, business as a major stakeholder of the civil society has to play a very proactive role in social development, especially at this juncture. The Directive Principles of State Policy in the Constitution suggest the launching of an intensive programme of bringing about desired changes in the rural society by enacting legislations. Since 1950, a large number of such legislations have been enacted and claims made in reforming and restructuring aspects of rural society through constitutional provisions, e.g., Article 45: "The State shall endeavour to provide, within a period of ten years from the commencement of this Constitution, for free and compulsory education for all children until they complete the age of fourteen years." The essence of Directive Principles lies in Article 38: "The Constitution was to foster the achievement of many goals, transcendent among them was that of social revolution. Through this revolution would be filled the basic needs of the common man, and it was hoped, this revolution would bring about fundamental changes in the structure of Indian society—a society with a long, a glorious cultural tradition.

The Private (not for profit) Sector: Its Limitations in Social Development

The remarkable proliferation of private (not-for-profit) organizations in India marks a paradigm shift in the view of the development process, and the emergence of new actors in the development arena, long dominated by the state and the market. Popularly known as NGOs, these have emerged as an alternative to the conventional liberal solutions for development involving the state and market, and have become important catalysts of social and economic change. Because NGOs offer a different approach to development than the state or market, they have been collectively referred to as the Third Sector of development. However, NGOs face formidable internal and external obstacles as they seek to develop effective programmes in the face of social inertia, political opposition, and an unpredictable funding environment.

By the early 1990's, NGOs in India had become heavily dependent on foreign disbursements for their operating and programming budgets. NGOs in India received approximately $520 million from all sources in 1992 (Moen Mathiot, 1998), making up approximately 30 per cent of the total ODA disbursed to India in that year. The U.S., Canada, Norway and Sweden constituted the main donors to NGOs in India in the early 1990s. One estimate suggests that 90 per cent of NGO income came from foreign sources in 1992—about Rs. 9 billion out of Rs. 10 billion in NGO income (Moen Mathiot, 1998). The difficulties involved in seeking funds from donors include refusal to fund overheads, and delays in decision making and remitting funds in general. Donors prefer to provide seed-money for ground-breaking, innovative programmes with a clear rationale and limited time horizon (typically for two to three years). Further, donors projects for particular groups or particular types of activities, i.e. education of rural girls and women, or working children, or bonded labourers.

NGO personnel in India, felt that targeted funding of specific components made it difficult for smaller NGOs to fund entire projects. Furthermore, short-term funding makes it difficult to plan ahead, and to create long-term budgets for ongoing programmes. Consequently, there is a tendency to move towards programmes that are likely to receive funding at the expense of programmes that may be worthwhile, but that are more difficult to "sell." A recent assessment of Indian NGOs by a member of the NGO Gram Niyojan Kendra suggests that reliance on outside funding encourages specific type of proposal writing and discourages experimentation and innovation due to the fear that novel approaches will not be understood (Mukherjee, 1994).

Patterns of expenditure, programme content and organizational issues are likely to come under increasing scrutiny in the future. Many donors have already begun to demand that NGOs conduct evaluation studies, and provide evidence that donor funds are being used effectively (Overseas Development Institute, 1996). Multilateral donors such as the World Bank are also in the process of finalizing their evaluation systems. The trend towards more evaluation of NGO programmes is a logical outcome of trends in funding. Because the NGOs are receiving a larger share of development assistance, there will be more demands for accountability, and for evidence that NGO programmes perform more effectively than comparable official development programmes.

India is a vast country with a huge population with problems in almost all areas and at all levels of life. Though the government of India has been working towards overall socio-economic-political development since its inception, it has failed to achieve big success. CSOs joined in the efforts of the government to attain overall social development. Their combined strength has worked productively. But the level of social development attained so far is nowhere near the ideal target. NGOs are working with a lot of limitations. The government does not generate enough money to sustain its overall basic commitments in infrastructure building and service sectors and in other public sector undertakings (PSUs). The government funding to NGO activities is not adequate and also on many occasions the government funding comes with bureaucratic hassles and political impingement, which is inimical to a smooth functioning of developmental activities of the NGOs. Many NGOs also lack professionalism, good management practice, noble purpose, and independent decision-making capacity. They, on many occasions, fail to mobilize grassroots participation of people.

They find it difficult to generate money on their own. In pretext of historical context. It has been seen that there is a tremendous potentiality for a third party, which is large and all-pervasive in the country, and has the financial capacity and administrative maturity to provide and carry out substantial structural support to the growing need towards making a sustainable febric for the civil society. And also it has been seen that for the long-term sustenance for both, doing business in a longer perspectives, the strategic involvement of the corporate and social development is leading towards the direct intervention as 'Corporate Social Development' in very near future.

The decade of 1990s has been marked by radical changes in the policies and approach of the government towards development. In 1991, the government took a drastic step by adopting liberalization, privatization and globalization. The unnecessary restrictions, that were imposed on industries and businesses which thwarted their development, most of them were removed.

3 Contemporary Views and Concept

In recent years, industry has been increasingly recognized as partners to government and civil society in the process of social development. Corporates and business associations are making serious efforts to address social concerns, in addition to pursuing their business goals. Along with traditional philanthropy, there is a lively debate in developing countries on how corporates can adopt a proactive approach and involvement in development. There is clearly a marked trend, especially in India, towards corporate social responsibility (CSR) or corporate social development (CSD) being business rather than individual driven. CSR is generally seen as an activity that companies add, with varying degrees of integration, towards their mainstream activities.

As part of the broad UN initiative to develop closer links with the corporate sector, UNDP is promoting the concept of meeting point for business and other stakeholders to develop partnerships to strengthening human development. To take this agenda forward, UNDP and CII jointly launched the 'India Partnership Forum' in February 2001. The forum's objectives are (CII, 2001):

(i) Provide a platform to facilitate dialogue, including policy and action on the role and responsibilities of business in development;
(ii) Exchange views and experience on issues related to CSR;
(iii) Build bridges across different social groups: business, civil society organizations and government;
(iv) Build a 'shared social vision' and create an environment for interactive discussions with new partners;
(v) Build 'societal capital' to foster linkage for the creation and implementation of bussiness—civil society partnership initiatives with least advantaged groups; and
(vi) Institutionalize interaction with the private sector.

The need to build social capital across traditional notions of private sector, public sector, NGOs and other multisectoral actors is now more apparent than ever. The private sector has a unique role in building social capital in the developmental context. Given this new reality, businesses are increasingly being asked to play an active role in development efforts. What is interesting is that the field of corporate responsibility is also changing from philanthropy to social investment. Today some of the major companies are developing innovative and sustainable funding mechanisms, mobilizing core competencies, developing partnerships and undertaking community capacity building efforts.

The focus of this study is to address Corporate Social Development (CSD) issues in the Indian context and understand the transitional way which has been marked as the paradigm shift in CSD trend that is being witnessed in the last couple of years in India. In and extensive manner, very few studies have been made in this area and related issues. And throughly these have been reviewed for the purpose of this study. Here studies related to NGOs, VOs, Civil Societies and CSD are discussed in consonance with the present study.

Views and Concept

Traditionally, the role of the business sector in community development has been that of philanthropist. But businesses benefit substantially from reforms and programme that foster stable, healthy communities, and can do more than create wealth. They can also widen economic opportunity, invest in human capital, promote environmental sustainability, and enhance social cohesion. Increasingly, they are becoming equal partners and contributors in efforts to create sustainable economies.

Shrivastava and Venkateswaran (2000) in their book *The Business of Social Responsibility* have argued that there is a need for companies to develop an Indian attitude to social responsibility which should address problems that India, and perhaps the rest of the developing world, face. It goes on to say that companies would do well to adapt the western experience to problems that exist here and it also illustrates the need for companies to develop a social responsibility. The book has dealt with how companies can partner communities and NGOs to pursue their social responsibility programmes.

Singhania (1980) has classified the nature of the social responsibility of business into two categories :

(i) The manner in which a business carries out its own business activity. This involves the acceptance of the fact that business is not merely a profit-making occupation but a social function which involves certain duties, and requires that appropriate ethics are followed; and
(ii) The welfare activity that it takes upon itself as an additional function. In addition to its commercial activity, business also plays a role in promoting social welfare activity, even directly.

George Goyder (1951), in his famous book, *The Future of Private Enterprise: A Study in Responsibility*, mentions the following as the principal objectives of a responsible company:

(i) The extension, development and improvement of the company's business and the building up of its financial independence;
(ii) The payment of fair and regular dividends to the shareholders;
(iii) The payment of fair wages under the best possible conditions to the workers; and
(iv) The reduction in the prices to be charged to consumers.

Another aspact of the book says that the primary objectives of a socially responsible business should be to strengthen itself with due regard to the interests of the shareholders, employees and consumers.

The important among them are:

(i) To enhance labour welfare;
(ii) To enhance customer service and goodwill;
(iii) To assist in developing and promoting the amenities in the locality;
(iv) To assist in developing the industry in which the firm is a member; and
(v) To contribute to national goals.

Table 3.1: Ackerman's Three Stages of Social Responsibility

Organizational Level	*Phases of Organizational Involvement*		
	Phase I	*Phase II*	*Phase III*
Chief Executive	*Issue:* Corporate Obligation *Action:* Write and Communicate policy *Outcome:* Enriched purpose, increased awareness	Obtain knowledge Add staff specialists	Obtain organizational commitment. Change performance expectations
Staff Specialists		*Issue:* Technical problem *Action:* Design data system and inerpret environment *Outcome:* Technical and informational groundwork	Provoke response from operating units. Apply data system to performance measurement
Division Management			*Issue:* Management problem *Action:* Commit resources and modify procedures *Outcome:* Increased responsiveness

Therefore, the business needs to pay due attention to the long-term welfare of society.

Corporate Social Responsibility: A Theoretical Backdrop

There are two basic approaches to the concept of corporate social responsibility. Some theorists, focusing on the 'micro' level of analysis, try to show individual companies how they can be more socially responsive. Other researchers concern themselves with the 'macro' level of analysis, assuming that the government, viz. other civil society stockholders, not individual companies, should establish a country's social goals. It is the micro level of analysis which is significant.

Micro-level theorist Robert Ackerman described three phases through which companies commonly tend to pass in developing a response to social issues (Table 3.1) (Aswathappa, 2001):

(i) *In Phase I,* a corporation's top managers learn of an existing social problem. At this stage, no one asks the company to deal with it. The chief executive officer merely acknowledges the problem by making a written or oral statement of the company's policy towards it.
(ii) *In phase II,* the company hires staff specialists or engages external consultants to study the problem and to suggest ways of dealing with it.
(iii) *In phase III,* it is implementation. The company now integrates the policy into its ongoing operations. Unfortunately, implementation often comes slowly and often not until the government or public opinion forces the company to act.

Carroll's Four-Part Model discusses the nature of social responsibility (Figure 3.1) (Aswathappa, 2001). Discretionary responsibilities are purely voluntary obligations that an organization assumes. Examples are philanthropic contributions, training the hard-core unemployed, and providing day-care centres.

Economic Responsibilities	*Legal Responsibilities*	*Ethical Responsibilities*	*Dicretionary Responsibilities*

Fig. 3.1. Total Social Responsibilities of Carroll's models

The difference between ethical and discretionary responsibilities is that few people expect organizations to fulfil discretionary responsibilities, but all expect a firm to satisfy its ethical obligations.

The four responsibilities are listed in order of priority. A business unit must earn profit first in order to satisfy its economic responsibilities. In order to continue to exist it must follow law thus fulfilling legal responsibilities. After these basic responsibilities have been satisfied, the firm should seek to fulfil its social responsibilities. It can then fulfil its ethical responsibilities by doing those things that society tends to value but have not been brought under legal frame. After satisfying its ethical responsibilities, the company can focus on discretionary responsibilities, the purely voluntary actions that society has not yet considered as important.

Business responses to social responsibility tend to fall within four categories: (i) social opposition, (ii) social obligation, (iii) social response, and (iv) social contribution. As illustrated in Fig. 3.2.,

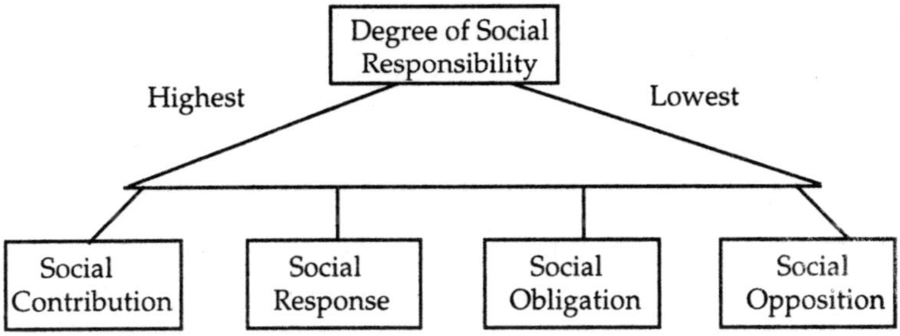

Fig. 3.2 : Approaches to Social Responsibility

these positions fall along a continuum, ranging from low to high levels of socially responsible behaviour (Aswathappa, 2001).

Social opposition: This view is taken by the businesses which feel that they have no obligation to society in which they operate.

Social obligation: This view is held by the companies which believe that they have an obligation to obey the law. That is, the only socially responsible behaviour that is appropriate and is the one prescribed by the law.

Social response: Social response is the position taken by companies that meet their social responsibilities as dictated by the law, and will, on selective basis, go beyond the legal requirements.

These units may volunteer to participate in limited socially responsible efforts, but not until they are convinced that the benefits outweigh the costs.

Social contribution: It is the position taken by the companies which believe that they have a deep obligation to serve the society. Such companies consider themselves to be responsible citizens in society and are eager to contribute whatever they can for the improvement of the society.

The Concept of Corporate Social Performance

The influential contribution of Wartick and Cochran (1985) describes corporate social performance as the integration of principles of social responsibility, the processes of social responsiveness, and those company policies developed to adequately address social issues. Wood's (1991) forward-thinking treatise reformulates and expands upon Wartick and Cochran's framework by offering a definition of CSP that comprise a business organization's configuration of principles of social responsibility (e.g. the consequences of business activities, with the implicit involvement of economic activity in social development), processes of social responsiveness (e.g. the action phase of management responding in the social sphere), and policies, programmes, and observable outcomes of corporate behaviour as they relate to an organization's internal and external constituencies and societal relationships.

The 'charity, principle,' the idea that wealthier members of society should be charitable towards those less fortunate. The'stewardship principle,' whereby corporate management has an obligation to see that everyone, particularly those in need, benefit from a company's actions, and the profit-seeking enterprise deploys its resources in ways that are good not just for stockholders alone but for society generally. CSP tends to distinguish between two major aspects of performance: (a) internal social performance, which is centred around the response to social considerations within an organization, such as worker occupational health and safety, personal development and equal employment opportunity practices, waste reduction, and resource conservations, and (b) external social performance, which focuses upon a company's relations with the outside environment, such as efforts to help strengthen local community services and foster economic revitalization, pollution control initiatives, customer care and protection, and ethical sourcing. Furthermore, two fundamental components of the firm's social performance have been identified, namely "corporate social responsibility" (CSR1) and "corporate social responsiveness" (CSR2) (Wood & Jones, 1996; Swanson, 1999).

The American-based Committee for Economic Development (CED) in its 1971 report, Social Responsibilities of Business Corporations, articulated a three concentric circles model of CSRl. The CED conceptual framework depicts an inner circle (including clear-cut basic responsibilities for efficient execution of the firm's economic function—products, jobs, and maximizing shareholder wealth), an intermediate circle (encompassing responsibility to exercise the firm's economic function with a sensitive awareness of changing social values and priorities), and an outer circle (identifying newly emerging and still amorphous responsibilities that a business enterprise would prepare to take on board for the betterment of society. According to Davis (1973) and Epstein (1987), corporate social responsibility generally refers to an organization's consideration of, and outcomes associated with, issues transcending the narrow economic, technical and legal requirements of the firm.

Corporate social responsiveness moves away from principled reflection and philosophical precepts and provides an action, counterpoint, or "managerial phase," in responding to developments in the corporate social environment (i.e. a micro emphasis). CSR2 entails the management of an organization's processes and activities through which public expectations are anticipated and identified, placed within the context of other corporate concerns and, in some fashion, woven into the ways of doing business. That is, CSR2 tends to be anticipatory and preventive in nature with a systems orientation.

Work of Sethi (1987) suggests that contemporary approaches to analyzing corporate social performance can be grouped under two broad categories: (a) a "window-in" approach, which assumes that it is primarily the external environment which is dominant in affecting changes in corporate behaviour and responses; (b) a "window-out" approach, which is internally focused and emphasizes the effects of structural design, leadership style, and organizational culture on corporate performance in response to externally defined constraints on corporate behaviour. Such variables as the quality of personnel involved, the firm's ability to secure employee input and support for policy changes, and the company's capacity to follow through on implementing CSP initiatives and activities can greatly impact the social performance achievements of an organization.

A growing number of firms, mostly in developed countries like Europe, Canada, Japan, USA, are stepping up efforts at measuring their social and environmental performance. Important developments that seem to be responsible for stimulating such activity include: (a) intensified pressure on senior-level management to deal with social responsibility issues; (b) corporate managers adopting new attitudes about the kinds of activities their companies should undertake; and (c) many of the arguments against some form of corporate social involvement have, for the most part, been dispelled or refuted by persuasive counter-arguments. According to Wartick and Wood (1998), the salience of social issues affecting particular business policies and practices may vary over time, across industries, nations and cultures. Anshen (1980) and Clarkson (1995) offer several important arguments favouring a firm's interest in CSP, such as: enhanced public image and credibility within the community, and being viewed as a "neighbour of choice"; increased employee loyalty, commitment, and morale; the avoidance of burdensome government regulations; and strengthening the competitive position and continued viability of the organization.

Corporate Social Responsibility: Global Developments

Philanthropy and related activities have long been a crucial part of American life, though there are signs that it is becoming increasingly important in other countries too. However, most philanthropy is tax-motivated. Giving favourable tax treatment to charitable donations is on the political agenda in many countries. Charity is one way of supplementing the services provided by the state, which are becoming ever harder to finance out of taxation. In Europe, the state's leading role in areas such as higher education, health care and civic amenities like museums may have discouraged private philanthropy. Tax concessions on private giving may help to change that. Philanthropy may not be able to achieve the scale of some state-financed activities, but this could engage the creativity of a country's most successful people, rather than causing their resentment by confiscating some of their wealth in tax. Perhaps the most interesting change in approach to philanthropy is taking place in Latin America. There is a mindset change regarding poverty as a permanent aspect of civilization. From almost nothing, philanthropy is increasing rapidly in Brazil, led by big business. Multinationals operating in Brazil have put a lot of effort into improving education and childcare, shaming domestic firms into following suit, mainly by trying to stop children working. This is an area in which the government has failed to deliver (The Economist, 2001). In the US, charitable giving of all sorts totalled $203 billion in 2000, around 2 per cent 'of Gross Domestic Product (GDP) (up sharply from 1995, when the ratio was 1 per cent of GDP). Americans seem to start giving chunks of their money away once they are worth around $20 million, where as in other countries the threshold is more like $100 million. In case of USA, the philanthropic activities have taken the nature of motivated giving—a genuine act of giving backed by goodwill to meet the need of others. Charities can complement and influence government policy. Philanthropy is increasing rapidly in many countries. In the past two years, the concept of Corporate Social Responsibility has become so popular that it has acquired its own abbreviation: CSR. In India also, it is resurfacing as corporate social development (CSD) with a new structure. Some advocates of corporate "social responsibility" take a somewhat different track. They argue that what's good for the company's shareholders for the short term is also good for its other stakeholders over the long term. That is, all interests converge; all stakeholders are ultimately the same. Many American corporations continue to be exemplars of "responsibility" to their employees and communities (Reich, 1998).

The key factor in the growth and increasingly organized nature of social development activities in the UK has been the efforts of business in the community. And it is a sign of how far corporate social responsibility has moved into the mainstream that the government has appointed a minister for CSR whose job is to encourage companies to step up their activities in their areas. A recent Company Law Review considered placing a requirement on companies to pay greater attention to interest groups other than the shareholders in UK. This is a sharp break with the past, when governments tended to believe that firms should confine themselves to maximizing profits for shareholders (Trapp, 2001).

What started for many in the 1980s as a focus on environmental issues has evolved to take in such wide-ranging concerns as business ethics, employee volunteering programmes, a company's role in society at large and the extent to which the interests of employees, customers and other "stakeholders," as well as shareholders, are met. More recently, it has become focused on the issue of child labour and other aspects of the growing trend for Western consumer goods to be made in Third-World countries. One catch-all definition has been "sustainable development." But lately that has given way to "CSR" and, more recently, "corporate citizenship." John Elkington, chairman of the sustain ability consultancy and one of the best-known advocates of this balanced approach to corporate performance, says the late 1990s saw "extraordinary corporate transformations being driven both by emerging societal values and by 'triple bottom line' performance (meeting various social, ethical and environmental objectives as well as financial aims) and targets demanded by customers and markets" (Trapp, 2001).

Historical analysis of the nonprofit sector of Thailand shows the significant shift away from traditional religious-based organizations providing social services to members of society, towards groups organized to support marginal people in their everyday lives. Another shift has involved non-profit organizations assuming a more developmental role, bringing about local-level changes with "participation" and "self-reliance." Through local-level development, a democratization process has evolved. The degree to which these nonprofit organizations can function for the benefit of the people depends in part on the government. The government can neither ignore the existence of the nonprofit sector nor reject requests and/or demands from influential members of the sector. The government will have to learn to work with the nonprofit sector for the benefit of the poor people who have been left out of the development process. The nonprofit sector will continue the role of the people's advocate, particularly by raising the awareness of government officials and monitoring government activities (Pongsapich and Kataleeradabhan, 1997).

South Asia Partnership (SAP) in Sri Lanka was a development-oriented NGO operating in the South Asian Region. The mission statement of South Asia Partnership was to revitalize and enhance the capacities of the powerless members of civil society through a process of participation and partnership to achieve peace and prosperity. SAP believed that development came from within, it could not be done to people or for people, but must come from people. The goals of SAP, Sri Lanka, were promoting peace through ethnic and religious amity and cultural harmony, raising the standard of living of people by addressing issues of poverty, deprivation, unemployment and social exclusion; facilitating an educative process to empower individuals, initiating creative alliances with civil society organization, the state and the corporate sector through mutually beneficial partnerships. That was why social responsibility was important. Corporate citizenship was a win-win partnership that helped to create wealth and stimulate development. Socially responsible investment was the acceptance of responsibility by the business community for the impacts of financial decisions not just for themselves but on others, for future generation, not only looking at short-term benefits. But social responsibility could not be considered in isolation; it had to be an integral part of corporate culture and should be included in each company's strategic plan. SAP started having educational sessions with the corporate sectors, especially with the Rotary Club and the Lions, where the corporate sector people were the members. Their CSR programmes started in 1996, as a partnership programme with a commercial bank—HNB, the idea being to be partners in supporting the disadvantaged communities in the places of work. The understanding was to give credit by HNB to all partners, without collateral, based only on recommendation by SAPSRI. In that process, a beneficial partnership was built between the branch managers and the people. The second initiative was with Citibank, in 2000. The idea was to initiate a bakery and help women to become bakers. Everybody benefited, but there was a weakness, because the bank people could not commit much time, and it was far away from the central area. All these development works had been taken with foreign funds, now, in the future, all these initiatives would be connected with some corporate sector company (CII, 2001).

Community development meant direct involvement. In Philippines, 180 companies had come together to form a group called the Philippines Business for Social Progress, which gave in funds for various projects. Other ways of directly involving companies in community development would be by way of the programme where one company developed one village, through training, capacity building etc. In the Philippines, groups put together assistance at the times of calamity, for example, at the time of cyclones and so on. But the problem was that most coalitions came together only in response to some crisis. Another example of two banks, the first was the largest development bank for farmers in the Philippines, which indulged in special lending directly to the farmers. The idea was that they work with farmers, who are not yet bankable, but given access to credit, could be potentially bankable. The second one was a commercial bank in the country, which chose not to mix its lending programme (through micro-credit) with its profit business.

The business sector in Bangladesh is small, but it is vibrant. The area of corporate social responsibility is not very organized or formalized, it is emerging. Yet, in Bangladesh, there was already a tradition of charity and philanthropy, people did it in private, individual capacities. A very large amount of CSR was taking place in the fields of health, education and environment. In the last 5 years, 16 private universities had come up, accredited to the universities in the United States, solely by grants and donations, from the corporates; there had been no government loans or subsidy. Recently, there has also been a move to get the private sector involvement even in the field of health.

The Prince of Wales International Business Leaders Forum (PWIBLF) over the last decade has focused on encouraging business to take collective action on issues where business and the community share common concerns, such as:

(i) Support for new enterprise and the social impacts of industrial restructuring;
(ii) Opportunities for the disadvantaged and minorities;
(iii) Strengthening of links between school and work;
(iv) Raising of management standards, particularly with regard to the environment; and
(v) Corporate social governance and social exclusion.

To promote this mission, the Forum (2000), as a pioneer in the Central and Eastern European region in promoting corporate social responsibility, has devised a strategy dubbed as the 'A-B-C-D' approach. This stands for:

(a) Advocacy of the need for business to adopt socially responsible business practices that benefit business and society.

(b) Brokerage of partnerships between business, government agencies and not-for-profits as a means for tackling issues of concern both to business and the community.

(c) Capacity building of individuals within business, government, public sector institutions and the non-profit sectors to enable them to work in partnerships for sustainable development.

(d) Dissemination of information and experience on the subject of corporate social responsibility.

Collective action by companies in the Central and Eastern European countries like Poland, Bulgaria, Slovakia, Hungary, Czech Republic is gaining ground among certain sectors of business. Professional services firms, for example, are giving time and expertise to NGOs and authorities in the areas of legal and technical issues, the carrying out of feasibility studies, the transfer of management techniques such as marketing and training. Local companies too are developing reputations of their own in being socially responsible. However, whilst the trend towards companies exhibiting a sense of social responsibility is growing, it is still a long way off from being the norm. The way in which a company meets the expectations of all its societal stakeholders, from shareholders to employees, suppliers to customers, national governments and local authorities, to the communities in which it operates, both large and small, local and international. It demands a strategy that maximizes the company's positive impact and minimizes the negative on its social and physical environment, all the while providing a competitive return to its financial stakeholders (IBLF, 2000).

The globalization of trade and the expanding interconnectedness of markets and citizens in the last decade have drawn attention to the power of business in terms of its social, environmental and economic impact. Micro-entrepreneurs to multinationals are paying—or are being forced to pay— greater attention to the ways they operate, to the direct and indirect impact they are having on communities, to the size of ecological imprint they are leaving behind. CSR is beginning to appear on the formal and informal agendas of the Canadian Federal Government. The Canadian government is currently assuming more of a facilitative role when it comes to CSR issues, leaving leadership to industry (Kerby, 2001).

Corporate social responsibility is a well-established concept in the United Kingdom. A long history of corporate philanthropy has set the stage for current CSR practices; for example, business have developed productive relationships with government and NGOs; they have acknowledged their broader role in society; and they are willing to put in place the processes, resources and leadership with which to make a meaningful, sustainable and visible contribution. In Denmark, the main focus of corporate social responsibility follows two major themes: social inclusion (ensuring marginalized groups have the opportunity to be contributing citizens) and employment integration (maximizing the number of gainfully employed citizens in the labour market). Denmark uses CSR as a framework to address a company's role in relation to general social problems, primarily focusing on employment as an important and integral part of life for the majority of the population. The Netherlands has a tradition of a strong welfare state that has taken the lead in addressing social issues. Recently, government's role has shifted from acting as a strong welfare state, taking responsibility for social issues, to a facilitative role, sharing the increasing costs of addressing social issues with private and public partners. The result is that companies are increasing their involvement in addressing social issues through government-initiated social and environmental projects emphasizing community involvement (Kerby, 2001).

Intermediary Institutions and Civil Society: Instruments for Social Development

It has been widely recognized that modern economic growth, industrialization, associated technical change, urbanization and changes in social norms, behaviour and organization are associated with endemic and sizeable open unemployment, insecurity, inequities, eco-disaster crime and disenchantment in the West and intractable structural unemployment, mass poverty, inhuman inequities and dehumanizing levels and styles of living in the Third World (Kabra,1995).

Towards the beginning of 1960s, it became increasingly clear that the Government of India had not been able to fulfil majority of people's need in the field of education, health, livelihood and shelter, etc. Civil society initiatives in India got momentum to express in many ways in the post-independence period:

(i) Emergence of a large number of self- initiated organizations to create alternate channels for delivery of basic services like health and education,
(ii) Students and industrial workers movements in different parts of the country, and
(iii) Political movements.

NGOs-organized activities promoting development had a cooperative attitude towards the government as large number of these organizations being Gandhian. Two pioneering institutions—Khadi and Village Industries Corporation (KVIC) and the Central Social Welfare Board (CSWB)— were set up by the government in the 1950s to further support the NGOs (Tandon and Mohanty, 2000).

The 1970s saw a new kind of social movement. Civil liberty, ecology, women and dalit movements captured the civil society space to make demands on the state in an unprecedented way. 1n contemporary Indian context, a number of social movements have emerged as major manifestations of civil society. The primary function of social movements has been reform of society, institutions and governance through membership associations in India. A variety of business associations and traders' associations have also been building membership to advance the interests of trading and business community like CII, FICCI, which are also civil society associations. In recent years, many development programmes of the government and NGOs have also enabled the formation of community based organizations. Several intermediary civil society organizations have been set up to provide support to other community based organizations or other intermediary organizations in India today. Such support functions are focused on themes like income generation (Udyogini), environment (Centre for Science and Environment), health (Centre for Health Education, Training and Nutrition Awareness—CHETNA), housing (Society for Promotion of Area Resource Centres—SPARC) etc. Some support organizations are more generic in nature like the Organization for Development Education (Unnati), the Society for Participatory Research in Asia (PRIA), the National Centre for Advocacy Studies (NCAS), the Center for Educational Development (CED), etc. Some intermediary civil society organizations provide resources to other civil society organizations in the country. Child Relief and You (CRY), the National Foundation of India (NFI), the Rajiv Gandhi Foundation (RGF) are some examples of the same.

Several corporate houses have philanthropy programmes like the Tata Trusts. New approaches for mobilizing resources like the Charities Aid Foundation (CAF) are also emerging in the Indian context. Some intermediary civil society organizations are associations of other intermediaries and act as networks to extend their collective voice and strength. Some networks are focused on a theme like Voluntary Health Association of India (VHAI), Association of Voluntary Agencies in Rural Development (AVARD), etc. Some are generic and cover a specific geographical area such as the Uttar Pradesh Voluntary Action Network (UPVAN) or the country as a whole like Voluntary Action Network India (VANI). As a category of civil society organizations, such intermediaries have a growing influence on the policies and practices of the government in India.

In the contemporary era, NGOs play the role of promoters of development, catalysts of social and emotional changes, are a mechanism for popular participation in influencing public policy and public opinion, act as motivators, play a role in the enforcement of law and social legislation and are a vital link between the people and the government.

During the Eighth Five Year Plan (1992-97), a high level NGO-Government Meeting, organized by the Planning Commission in 1994, identified a number of areas for NGOs participation. These include: watershed management, sanitation and drinking water, integrated rural development, family welfare, education, health, development of women and children, social welfare, labour, science and technology, non-conventional energy source, urban development dealing with the problems of urban slum dwellers, street children and environment and forests. Many NGOs have taken up ecological issues in their agenda for action towards a sustainable development (Planning Commission, 1995).

Corporate Participation in Social Development

Successful companies not only make profit in their business, but also develop niche for themselves in the competitive market through quality product or service. Inner strength of a company lies in its human resources that are competent, professional, innovative and visionary. With privatization, liberalization and globalization, realignment of interrelationships among the various stakeholders is taking place. Corporates are increasing their involvement in the social sector and thereby enhancing the sphere of influence. Corporates have the resources, both financial and managerial, for enhancing the efficiency of service delivery and effectiveness of the NGOs. Corporates can share their business-like approach to managing its affairs to the NGOs. The involvement of corporate sector in providing financial and infrastructural support to projects carried out by the NGOs has greatly enhanced the effectiveness of these efforts. It also provides an opportunity for the corporate sector to carry out its agenda in contributing to social development. In the changing situations, the corporates seek to strengthen their unique relationship, wherein corporate organizations provide support for projects undertaken by the NGOs in the social sector. It provides the business the opportunity to network with the local community, meet challenging situations and endeavours to provide solutions that are beneficial to the NGO concerned as well as the underprivileged sector.

The process of developing corporate volunteering programme in the NGO involves the following steps for the corporates (Garain, 2001):

(1) Defining the vision;
(2) Determining the interventions;
(3) Planning the interventions; and
(4) Monitoring, evaluation and social audit.

The benefits of corporate volunteering are reached out to the community in two forms. Firstly, the corporate volunteers get engaged in their own company initiated community initiatives although their engagement is voluntary and contribution is planned and managed systematically, often synchronizing with their official expertise. Secondly, the corporate volunteers on their own individual initiatives get involved with various NGOs and community groups. Corporates are encountering an incredible opportunity for showing its concern for the community and to its other stakeholders.

Corporate social responsibility is towards (i) employees, (ii) consumers, and (iii) civil society at large. Responsibility towards employees is in the form of just selection, training, promotion, fair wages, levelling out variations in employment, comfortable working conditions, safety and health, social measures, scope for initiation and advancement, participative management, workers' education and the like. Responsibility towards consumers include such aspects as producing and supplying quality goods at reasonable prices, avoiding creation of artificial scarcities, revealing truth in advertising and labels, preventing formation of monopolies with the intention of exploiting customers and guaranteeing the buyers about the lifetime performances of the products. Business responsibility towards the civil society covers such areas of complying with holistic sustainable development which upholds cross-sectoral strategic requirements, issues of livelihood, honestly, executing jointly and implementing projects and acting as a willing partner with the government in pursuit of sustainable development.

There is a growing recognition that the business could pay due attention to the long-term development of society. In other words, the primary objectives of a socially responsible business would be to strengthen itself with due regard to the interests of the shareholders, employees, consumers and civil society at large and to strengthen itself with due regard to the interests of the shareholders, employees and consumers.

In the 1990s, more and more companies realized that they could no more function or be judged solely on the basis of their thick bottom lines. According to Aswathappa (2001), all companies with social orientation exhibit 14 characteristics as shown below :

(1) Initially founded by far-sighted people who visibly set the firm's moral tone;
(2) Stuck to the basic and produced only high quality goods and services for specific market niches;
(3) Developed a public image that emphasized their commitment to quality and often used non-traditional means to promote it;
(4) Firmly practiced the dual principles of self-management and decentralization;
(5) Brought in outside people to provide needed talent and additional perspectives;
(6) Encouraged all employees to become part of the shared mission through full worker participation in decisions;
(7) Paid fairly and usually offered benefit packages exceeding the competition;
(8) Emphasized a democratic people orientation and did without executive perks;

(9) Constantly solicited feedback from customers on all subjects from product direction to corporate donations;
(10) Top managers possessed an extensive knowledge of current events and took a wide-ranging interest in affairs outside their business;
(11) Offered donations in cash or services to people in need of help;
(12) Took an active role in the operation of their local communities;
(13) Deal with like-minded businesses and encourage their employees to do the same; and
(14) Constantly look to the future but always pay attention to the past.

In the concluding note, it can be mentioned that the corporate participation in social development literature reviwed has shown that a possesses certainly get strengths with the government and NGO sector. One of the major constrains is that very few literature is available in Indian context. From the above literature review, corporate social responsibility, viz. corporate social development is understood as the trend, viz. obligation of decision-makers to take actions which protect and improve the welfare of society as a whole along with their own interests. Every decision the corporate sector takes and every action it contemplates have social implications. Corporate social development in business is a new thrust to our country. The contemporary history of India has experienced a magnificent shift in business towards social development in real life with commitment.

4 Methodology of the Study

Statement of the Problem

The effects of globalization have given ample scope to various actors to participate in social development, that is private (for profit), private (not for profit), bilateral and multilateral agencies. This phase in the process of evolution can be translated as transitional convergence. In view of these recent developments in the field of social development, no comprehensive study has been conducted which looks into the nature and scope of participation of these emerging actors.

The new players that are entering into social developmental activities have a different background. In fact, the old players themselves have changed over time. On the one hand are today's NGOs, a far cry from the voluntary social worker or agency *vis-a-vis* the entire dynamics of raising funds to implementation of action plans in light of liberalization, privatization and globalization. On the other, there is the corporate sector, which is supposedly driven by the profit motive alone, which have started advocating ethical business practices and social audit for their sustainable economic gain.

Change is an integral part of history, and this transitional phase is also part of the ongoing history, which cannot be projected for negative or pessimistic change because within this a better effort is coming out. Better effort would be to find out a path that could be marked as one of the future strategic examples for sustainable replication. Therefore, the process of change, has to be recognized. But in the process of change, there are no in-built mechanism for checks and balances and, therefore, it is equally important to see that this change is a solution rather than the compounding of the problem. This change is a unique phase in the history of social development and its impact cannot be predicted.

There is a need to engage business, the public sector and NGOs in a partnership approach to socio-economic developmental problems inherent in this transition economy through engagement in practical and financially viable projects with definable outcomes. There is also the need for the direct involvement of the businesses to help tackle socio-economic problems. Businesses can a make a huge difference by not only giving time and effort but also through money. This study plans to look into the paradigm shift in corporate sector's participation for funding in social development in India and to identify its merits and demerits, so that necessary recommendations can be made.

The problem is that of overall development of the society. In developing countries like India, development is in its true sense has not taken place. Government has not been able to bring development to its desired level. It has been felt that government can take the whole responsibility of social development. Government cannot reach each and every household to initiate and monitor developmental programmes there. Business is a powerful structure in the society. It affects the society but cannot reach to everybody. It has the financial and professional resources to pursue social developmental works.

There are many reasons and arguments in support of socially responsive actions.

Some important of them are given below :

(i) *Changed Public Expectations of Business* : One of the most potent arguments for social responsibility is that public expectations from business have changed. Society gave business its charter to exist, and the charter can be amended or revoked at any time that the business fails to live up to society's expectations.

(ii) *Better Environment for Business:* Social responsibility creates better environment for business. The firm, which is more responsive to the improvement of community's quality of life, will as a result have a better community in which to conduct its business.

(iii) *Public Image:* Social responsibility improves public image. A firm which seeks better public image needs to support social goals.

(iv) *Balance of Responsibility with Power:* Business responsibility needs to be more related to its power. It is reasoned that businessmen have vast amounts of social power. They do affect the economy, minorities and other social problems. If each institution is to perform its social role in an orderly relationship with other institutions, then responsibilities must be accepted whenever there is power.

(v) *Business has the Resources:* Another argument for social responsibility is that business has a vast pool of resources in terms of men, talent, functional expertise and money. With these resources at its command, business is in a better position to work for social goals.

(vi) *Moral Responsibility:* Modern industrial society faces many serious social problems brought on, to a large extent, by large corporations. The corporations, therefore, have a moral responsibility to help solve or ameliorate these problems.

(vii) *Citizenship Argument:* Corporations are institutional members of society. Corporations are citizens, and citizens have civic duties and responsibilities.

Objectives of the Study

After analyzing the developmental strategies and roles played by the Government, the amount of development achieved so far, the current socio-economic conditions, the basic problems in the society, on the basis of these a set of observations and objectives are made. A comprehensive review of literature has been made to know the state of affairs in the realm of social development in India and other countries in the world. After consulting information from all these sources a set of hypotheses has been devised. Following are the objectives of the study:

(1) To identify past and present players in social development;

(2) To study the changing pattern of funding for social development;

(3) To study the changing social development projects/ programmes *vis-á-vis* beneficiaries; and

(4) To suggest possible alternative strategies for funding social development projects/programmes in the future.

Hypotheses of the study:

(1) The government plays a dominant role in social development;
(2) The role of private (not for profit) sector in social development is limited;
(3) Funds for social development by private (not for profit), multilateral and bilateral agencies are declining;
(4) Funding by private (for profit) multinationals and national corporations for social development is rising;
(5) Sustainability towards social development to be a major criteria to achieve long-term human development;
(6) Participatory approach to be an integral part of social development project/programmes; and
(7) The private (for profit) multinational and national corporate sector is emerging as a major source of funding for social development.

Methods of the Study

The study attempts to analyze the role of corporate sector funding in social development on the basis of empirical data collected from various sources which includes the corporate sector, NGOs, multilateral and bilateral agencies and the beneficiaries. The information collected for the study is for the periods 1998, 1999 and 2000. These three years period is chosen to justify the paradigm shift of corporate sector's participation in funding for social development. Also, the choice of the time period is based on data availability for all the relevant variables in the analysis. This paradigm shift is considered to be a post-liberalization phenomenon in India and hence it is relevant to study the trend during the period 1998-2000 with reference to the period 1994-95 wherever necessary. This is a national level (data is collected from all the five zones—north, south, east, west and central), empirical, analytical and in-depth study on the corporate sector's role in funding for social development. The methodology consists of the following steps:

1. Carry out a primary survey of periodicals and existing literature on the topic to identify the important issues and develop questionnaires for various, sectors that play an important role in social development, viz.. corporates,

government, multilateral and bilateral agencies, NGOs, and beneficiaries. An in-depth survey of available literature on the government's role in social development was carried out because social development issues have been the constitutional responsibility of the government (Central and States).

2. Conduct a sector-level interview-based survey on the basis of issue-based questionnaire. The study covered the following purposively selected sectors that are involved in social development in India. They are:

   (i) The Government of India;
   (ii) Private (for profit) multinational companies;
   (iii) Private (for profit) national companies;
   (iv) Private (not for profit) multilateral and bilateral agencies;
   (v) Private (not for profit) Non-Governmental Organizations (NGOs);
   (vi) Private (not for profit) Community Based Organizations (CBO); and
   (v) Beneficiaries of social development projects and programmes implemented by corporate and NGOs.

3. Analysis and Interpretation of Data. Results are based on the case study of all the sectors as mentioned above. Methodology to arrive at conclusion ranges from using simple tabular analysis based on percentages to graphical representation.

The main challenge before the present study is to explore the role of corporate sector as a major funding agency for various social developmental activities in India. For the study, it is difficult to formulate a structured objective questionnaire, as the questions in that case would be limited by the existing knowledge of the researcher about the sectors. On the contrary, the objective was to capture the ongoing changes, both in terms of direction as well as magnitudes. For this purpose, issue-based questionnaires were developed in discussion mode rather than a purely objective type questionnaire for the different sectors under study. During the survey, the questionnaire was presented before the concerned person/contact person for discussion. This methodology gives the respondent a greater amount of flexibility, which often helps bring out the underlying factors driving a particular strategy from an insider's perspective. The study also explores and reviews various parameters of social development as perceived by the corporate sector and NGO sector. The current pattern of corporate sector participation is analyzed with the help of both qualitatively and quantitatively.

The Sample

The sample for the study covers corporates and NGOs in all the four regions of India, i.e., East, West, South and North. The key players in social development in the country have been selected for this study. They are randomly selected according to the area of operation so that social development in different parts of the country would be assessed. The sample frame from which the samples were drawn in the case of the corporate sector comprised the top 500 companies in India ranked on the basis of sales turnover published in successive editions of Business India. The sample selected for the study comprised of 16 companies actively participating in social developmental activities, 16 non-government organizations, 7 bilateral organizations, 7 multilateral organizations and 320 beneficiaries. As a part of this work, 400 companies were also contacted through e-mail to know about how they perceive their role in social development. The top ranking officials of the companies were contacted. A set of 7 questions was sent to each of the companies for the purpose. A request was made to them to provide detailed information about their social developmental activities and the manner/mechanisms of their activities. Out of the 400 companies contacted, 300 companies responded and provided information as per the requirement of the questions.

Samples for the bilateral and multilateral organizations were selected from available government data and the sample for NGOs was selected from the NGO directory of Development Alternative. A participatory approach to the study has also been adopted by studying the beneficiaries' local perception, attitudes, and knowledge as part of the development activities undertaken by the corporate sector/government/ NGOs for their well-being. Data was collected from the people in concerned localities where the NGOs and corporates, which have been taken as sample in this study, are pursuing developmental works. Field study method was adopted to collect data from the people about their participation and benefits from the developmental works. This is a more comprehensive feedback for the analysis of the study. The purpose of qualitative inquiry is to produce findings.

Due to the small size of the sample in the case of companies, NGOs, multilateral and bilateral agencies, statistical operation could not be carried out. Therefore, a qualitative analysis of the sample regarding sustainability and social development, as operationalized below, was carried out. The qualitative analysis was done after having in-depth discussion with the concerned person of each of the 16 companies and NGOs.

Operationalization of the Study

The core developmental issues and concepts used to substantiate the focus of the study, i.e., corporate social development can be shown as follows:

1. Sustainability

(i) Socio-cultural factors
(ii) Institutional factors
(iii) Financial factors
(iv) Economic factors
(v) Demographical factors
(vi) Policies

2. Poverty Reduction

3. (Unequal) Social Relations

(i) Social groups and classes
(ii) Important stakeholders

4. Human Development

(i) Education
(ii) Income generation
(iii) Life expectancy

5. Participation

(i) People-centred development

(ii) Empowerment
(iii) Mobilization
(iv) Participatory planning and evaluation

6. Institutional Development

(i) At local, district, state and national levels
(ii) Good governance
(iii) Capacity and capability
(iv) Formal and non-formal groups and organizations

7. Structural Adjustment

(i) Market *vs.* state
(ii) Liberalization, privatization and globalization

A few indicators of social development have been identified as the focal concerns of each sector selected. These are the areas for which case studies is carried out :

(i) Health
(ii) Education
(iii) Community development
(iv) Rural development
(v) Environment
(vi) Infrastructure

Plan of Analysis

The analysis of the study is carried out with the help of descriptive statistical tools like percentages and charts. Cross-tabulation is done wherever required. The analysis is done both quantitatively and qualitatively. For the quantitative analysis, data is collected from the corporate sector, NGOs, multilateral and bilateral agencies and beneficiaries. Simple tools are used to find out the performance of various sectors. The purpose of the study was to glean out an integrational or holistic view of social development in India and, particularly, how the corporate has been participating in this joint venture in recent years. A parallel study of the corporate sector was done by collection of information through e-mail. For the qualitative study, case studies of corporates and NGOs are analyzed on the basis of issues related to social, cultural, ethical, empowerment, governance, etc.

The analysis of the study was carried out in the following manner :

(a) A sector-based analysis method was adopted. The five sectors actively involved in social development selected for the study include the government sector, the corporate sector, NGO sector, multilateral and bilateral agencies and the beneficiaries. Various agents have supported the entire social development works in India. On many instances they work also in tandem with each other. Relevant secondary and primary data has been collected from these five sectors under study. Descriptive statistics have been used to explain the data collected through questionnaire method, observation and interviews. Data collected from secondary sources have been used to provide a broader background to the study also to see how the primary data are related to secondary data.

(b) After a comprehensive review of the entire set of secondary and primary data of the five sectors, tabulation was carried out as follows:

(i) *The Corporate Sector:* Indian corporates are gradually formalizing their responsibilities in social development in the country. Some case studies have been made to get a clear view of the hypotheses. Primary information was collected from 16 corporates through discussion mode based on the questionnaire developed for this sector. Secondary information was also collected from various sources like CMIE, companies' annual reports, etc. to complement our findings. Innformation about the sales turnover and profit after tax of the companies for the period 1998-99 and 1999-2000, are gathered to look at the potential of this sector in terms of financial stronghold and logistic support to sustain social development in the country and also support to the large scale social development work of the Government of India.

Also, 300 corporate houses were contacted through e-mail to provide information regarding their participation in social development. The responses collected have been provided in tabular and graphical form and analyses are provided to bring out the emerging pattern or system of corporate social development.

(ii) *The NGO Sector:* The role of NGOs in social development is very crucial in the country. However, their role has been very limited in comparison to the government's massive scale operation in this area. To analyze the prospects and shortcomings of NGOs, case studies of 16 region-specific NGOs have been done. These NGOs represent the various regions of the country, viz., north, south, east, west and the central. Information was again collected through discussion mode based on issue-based questionnaire which was developed and supported by information from secondary sources like the NGOs' annual reports. NGO participation in various social developmental activities was calculated as percentage after analyzing the responses given by the 16 NGOs. In support of our objectives, information was also collected regarding the sources of funding of these NGOs. This was to find out the financial support provided to NGOs by various sources like the government, multilateral and bilateral agencies and the corporate sector.

(iii) *The Government Sector:* Extensive review of literature was carried out to study the role of the government in the social sectors. Government reports, books, journals/periodicals were extensively studied to gather information about government's annual spending in social sectors. The government has provided substantial additional facilities in the social service sector in succeeding years, especially for the rural areas. The government has also been providing financial assistance to the NGOs. Tabular representation of government spending in various social service sectors have been provided to facilitate comparative analysis between the government and the other players in social development.

(iv) *The Multilateral and Bilateral Agencies:* The major role of Official Development Assistance (ODA) provided by various multilateral and bilateral agencies has been of financing public expenditure and investment in various sectors of the economy including the social sectors in the developing countries. This has been very important for most low-income countries. ODA has often been considered for financing the so-called global public goods, whose services benefit mankind in general, rather than any particular country, and are non-excludable and non-rival between different countries. However, in recent years funding by the multilateral and bilateral agencies has revealed a declining trend. To substantiate our hypothesis, extensive study has been made from both secondary and primary sources. Our dataset for empirical analysis contained information about the funding pattern of 7 multilateral and 7 bilateral agencies selected on the basis of the magnitude of assistance to India. The information has been given in tabular form to provide a vivid picture of the declining trend in funding pattern of these prominent multilateral and bilateral agencies in India.

(v) *The Beneficiaries:* To assess people's participation in development projects undertaken by the NGOs and corporates in their respective areas of operation, a structured questionnaire was developed with a set of 12 questions considering relevant issues. The scores are ranked on a scale of four (0 to 3). The four alternative rankings for each indicator provides judgements on the level of participation existing within the project. Each question adds up to a score of 480 in the cases of 160 NGO beneficiaries and 160 corporate sector beneficiaries. Total scores and the mean scores was calculated for each of the 12 questions based on the responses given by the beneficiaries. A comparative analysis of the scores was done for NGO beneficiaries and the corporate sector beneficiaries.

(c) The final stage of analysis includes application/ administration of descriptive statistical tools to arrive at the conclusions.

(i) *The Corporate Sector:* The broad social development activities in which the corporate sector has been actively participating in recent years are health, education, natural resource management, infrastructure, community support, livelihood, to name a few. From the primary sources, percentage and its graphical representation (pie chart) was calculated to find out the major or significant social development activities which has attracted the corporate sector to participate. Similar descriptive statistical tools were administered on the primary data collected through e-mail from 300 companies. Percentages of participation in various categories of social sectors have been calculated and represented in the form of bar chart.

An attempt has also been made to see the relation between the 16 companies' PAT and social developmental activities like health, education, environment, infrastructure, community development, art and sports, and livelihood for the period 1998-99 and 1999-2000. Tabulation is done according to the responses of the companies:

(ii) *The NGO Sector:* The 16 NGOs in our sample provide a broad picture of how they perform in various developmental activities. The responses and information regarding the broad activities provided by the NGOs are computed in percentages terms and represented in the form of a pie chart. For our purpose, the broad areas of activities of NGOs have been categorized as health, education, environment, awareness generation, gender equity and sustainability. A comparative analysis of the scores on the basis of performance of the corporate and NGO sectors has been done with the help of percentages and bar chart.

(iii) *The Government Sector:* The shares of government expenditure for the social sectors like education, housing and urban development, social security and welfare and other social services have been studied extensively. Attempt has also been made to evaluate the changes in the composition of total social sector expenditure of the government, combined expenditure of the Centre and States as a per cent of total public expenditure, per capita expenditure in total social services of the government to explore interrelations among various indicators and also to support our hypothesis that a higher proportion of government expenditure has been allocated to the social sector. This extensive survey has been represented in the form of tables and cross tables.

(iv) *The Multilateral and Bilateral Agencies:* Promoting economic and social growth in developing countries has been the main motivation for ODA. Policy reforms and flow of external assistance are complementary to each other and not substitutes. But policy reforms also cannot be successfully implemented if they are not supported by adequate flows of external assistance. Our analysis suggests that over the years official bilateral and multilateral assistance has declined or more or less remained stagnant. To capture this declining trend, bar charts and percentages have been administered on our primary dataset. Various aspects of external assistance like authorization and utilization of external assistance, loans and grants etc. from secondary survey has also been evaluated. An attempt has been made to bring out a comparative picture of sector-wise distribution of external aid in tabular form.

(v) *The Beneficiaries:* Governments, international agencies and foundations have a constant need for estimating various aspects of the development process to inform resource allocation decisions and formulate appropriate development programmes. The task for development research has been to develop theories and methods to illuminate our understanding of social phenomena. However, we need to identify a variety of quantifiable aspects of the phenomenon called 'social development.' Therefore, in our study data were collected from the beneficiaries of social development to capture the success or disparities in the levels of achievement of social developmental activities being carried out by the corporate and the NGO sectors. Statistical tools like averages and percentages have been administered to calculate the scores obtained from the responses of 320 beneficiaries. For the comparative assessment of NGO and corporate beneficiaries, bar chart has been used using mean scores of the responses provided by the beneficiaries.

The aim of the study has been to explain the dynamics of social development in India. The dynamics of social development is built upon the involvement and participation of forces, viz., the government, the NGO, and the corporate sector. One of the main objectives of this study is to outline the nature and kinds of the developmental works done by various players in the field, thereby outlining the pattern and system of social developmental work in the past, present and its orientation towards the future. For this purpose, existing data have been collected and put in right statistical description in order to obtain an organized and condensed pattern. An attempt has been made to single out the new developments/dynamics in the field of social development.

The socio-economic and political background of the country has changed drastically in the last two decades. All through the movement has been towards growth and development. The roles and responsibilities of all those involved in development of the country have taken on new dimensions. Descriptive statistics has been used in order to bring all the past and present developments into a single platform in a lucid manner where various problems, drawbacks, loopholes and also positive aspects could be explained and understood in a better manner. This way, more realistic and strategic actions/decisions undertaken by various agents of development could be represented comprehensively.

5 Trends of Funding for Social Development

In the Human Development Report 2001 of UNDP, India ranks 115 in a list of 162 countries. It is an improvement over last year when India's position was 128. Taking into account the overall development in the areas like health, technology, gender development (equal development of men and women), the UNDP prepares its development index. India moving up a few notches in developmental index indicating better quality of life does not mean everything has been achieved. The then Prime Minister the Atal Behari Bajpayee said in his Independence Day speech on 15 August 2001. "In spite of the population trebled in the past five decades, we have been able to reduce the percentage of people living below poverty line from 36 to 26. I do not claim that we have been able to eradicate poverty as rapidly as we should or could have. But I am confident that abject poverty is on its way out in India." There is still, however, high incidence of poverty, illiteracy and backwardness in India, especially in the rural areas. The Government of India is committed in bringing about rapid and sustainable development in the country. The thrust of the government's development programmes is an all-round economic and social transformation of the Indian economy through a multi-pronged strategy aiming at reaching out to the most disadvantaged sections of society.

In the contemporary economic situation, disparities between the rich and the poor have widened. It has also forced people to look at the wider consequences of economic development. Politicians, business people and nonprofit organizations understand that building an equitable economy requires solid political, economic and social foundations and that these three areas, once thought to be separate, are indeed tied at the core. These three sectors, viz. the government, nonprofit organizations and the private sector can play a major role in funding social development programmes. To have a better insight into the funding aspect of social and economic development programmes, there is a need to study the contemporary funding pattern of various sources towards the social sector. In this chapter, we have focused on the funding status of the government, bilateral agencies, multilateral agencies, NGOs and finally, the pattern of funding by the corporate sector. It is important to recognize that the corporate sector does business for profit, therefore, the role of the corporate sector is distinct in the process of social development. Non-governmental organizations and community groups which understand local needs have a major contribution in lending their special expertise in programme implementation and service delivery at the grassroots level.

Foreign Aid : A Backdrop

The flow of external assistance or aid, directly or indirectly, has aimed at alleviation of poverty by contributing to growth and development and improving people's empowerment through basic services like education, health and livelihood, etc. and bringing forth social change. The flow of concessional assistance to developing countries has emerged in different forms such as financial, technical and aid for sessions asistance.

External assistance or 'aid' simply refers to resources on concessional terms, that are transferred or channelled to the developing countries, either directly or through the intermediaries or a multilateral institution or private voluntary organizations, for social and economic development. The 'developmental aid' excludes resources provided for relief, emergency and humanitarian purposes. The Official Development Assistance (ODA) is the public transfer of economic resources on concessional terms for development purposes. The Organizations for Economic Cooperation and Development (OECD), comprising of the industrialized countries of the world, is the largest group of aid donors. The transfer of ODA takes place from the donor government to the recipient country either directly or through multilateral and private organizations. The aid is transferred from North to South in four different forms :

(i) Official Development Assistance (ODA), as bilateral aid or contribution to multilateral agencies;
(ii) Other Official Flows (OOF), comprising both bilateral and multilateral institutions;
(iii) Private aid flows through direct investment, bilateral and multilateral portfolio investment and private export credits; and
(iv) Grants by NGOs and Private Voluntary Organizations.

The aid of the Development Assistance Committee's (DAC) countries qualifies as ODA on the basis of three basic criteria :

(i) It has to be undertaken by official agencies;
(ii) It has to be administered with promotion of economic development and welfare of the developing countries as its basic objectives; and
(iii) It should be concessional, in character, containing a grant element of at least 25 per cent.

The ODA, the common form of economic aid, involves both bilateral and multilateral transfer of resources for promoting development in the developing world. The coordinated efforts in the flow of concessional aid emerged in response to the widely perceived economic disparities between North and South. The volume of aid through bilateral channel has increased manifold and it still dominates the world's aid regime. While the bilateral transfer accounted for more than two-third of the DAC aid, the aid through multilateral channel, accounted for less than one-third in the late 1980s (Mohanty and Singh, 1996).

Foreign Aid and NGOs in India

The aid transfer from North to South through NGO channel had increased rapidly after the late 1970s, due to growing recognition of NGOs by the official aid agencies. NGO activities have become a significant element in the development cooperation, providing an alternative to the development strategy of bilateral and multilateral donors. The NGOs began their involvement in the development process by providing welfare and relief services, and then they moved towards implementing developmental projects. This process of shift from welfare to developmental approach was a gradual one. They are now acting as 'facilitators' or 'catalysts' of local developmental efforts.

India maintains bilateral cooperation with almost all DAC countries and receives aid from all the multilateral donors. They provide funding to Indian VOs through various channels by the approval of Government of India. By and large, the major part of funding to the voluntary sector in India comes from the international NGOs, and specially from NGOs of Europe and North America. The volume of aid channelled to India by the bilateral agencies account for nearly one-third of the total foreign aid (i.e., 425 billion rupees by 1994), while the multilateral aid accounts for more than half of the total volume of aid. The external resources channelled to the NGO sector through the government was nearly 32 billion rupees by 1994, i.e., over seven per cent of the total external aid to India (Table 5.1).

Table 5.1 : External Aid to India and NGO Funding (up to March 1994)

Aid Donors	*Volume of Aid (in billion rupees)*	*Proportion of Total Aid (%)*
OECD (DAC)	126.0	30.0
CMEA	32.0	7.5
Arab and OPEC	13.3	3.1
Multilateral	222.5	52.0
Non-governmental Acct.	31.6	7.4
Total Aid*	425.0	100.0

* Excluding grants of 66 billion rupees.

Source : Government of India : The Ministry of Finance, Department of Economic Affairs, External Assistance, 1993-94.

The total foreign aid received by NGOs in India amounted to approximately 50,000 million rupees in four years during 1990-91 to 1993-94 (Table 5.2).

Table 5.2 : NGOs in India receiving Foreign Aid during 1990-91 to 1993-94

Year	*Number of NGOs*	*Total Foreign Aid (million rupees)*
1990-91	9,316	945.7
1991-92	9,012	10,201
1992-93	10,963	14,121.3
1993-94	15,843.0	18,657.0

Source : *The Week*, September 15, 1996, Kerala, India.

According to Foreign Contribution Regulation Act (FCRA), there were about 16,000 voluntary agencies in India, which received foreign aid during 1992-93. The total foreign aid received by the NGOs of the country amounted to 15,842 million rupees. USA and Germany contributed half of the total aid.

Resource Mobilization in the Voluntary Sector

The VOs mobilize resources from two broad sources, i.e., internal and external. Historically, voluntary organizations acquired funding from diverse sources, i.e., non-institutional and institutional sources. In the pre-independence era, the communities pooled their resources to help those affected in contingencies. Philanthropists came forward to contribute much to voluntary action. In the post-independence era, non-institutional funding in the form of donations from the community has decreased dramatically. The advent of state welfarism and electoral politics in the post-independence era has changed the sensibility of the community and people gradually withdrew as the government support came in to take initiatives to build and sustain their own institutions. In addition, an unprecedented rural de-population through city-ward migration has also reduced the mobilized community resources by the grassroots level VOs and they have gradually lost their popular support base and have become increasingly dependent on the political and government supports.

Over the last two decades, the nature of funding has changed significantly. There has not only been an increase in volume of funds for development but also a diversification in the origin of their sources. Besides the bilateral and multilateral aid, channelled to the developing countries, the NGO funding through the Northern NGOs has emerged as one of the major sources of funding to the South. There is an increasing role played by international NGOs in raising private funds for development and channelling them to the NGOs in South. Over 4000 NGOs mobilize financial and human resources in DAC member countries for projects they operate directly or in partnership with developing countries. There are two major sources of funding of Northern NGOs (Mohanty and Singh, 1996) :

(i) Funds raised by NGOs from their own channels—for

example, contribution by individuals, foundations, corporate sector and philanthropic organizations, etc.

(ii) Official contributions to NGOs by various governments.

The flow of government funds through the introduction of grants-in-aid since the early 1950s and the flow of foreign funds to the voluntary sector since late 1960s, made the VOs over-dependent on external sources rather than relying on the resource mobilization internally. The two most dominant sources of funding to VOs in India today have been international sources (foreign contribution) and the national level funding. These include funding both from private and government sources and also include institutional as well as non-institutional sources. It is difficult to cover all donors providing support, however, for simplicity they may be classified into six broad types of funding as described below.

International Funding

The international funding or contribution is one of the major sources of funding to voluntary efforts in India and has multiplied in manifold dimensions. A foreign contribution in India is defined as "the donation, delivery or transfer made by any foreign source of any article, currency or foreign security." An overall external assistance to India is given in the following table:

Table 5.3 : Utilization and Authorization of External Assistance

(in US $ million)

External Assistance	*1990-91*	*1994-95*	*1998-99*	*1999-2000*
Authorization	291.0	343.8	49.9	604.4
Utilization	297.8	292.7	213.0	248.2

Source: Economic Survey, 2000-2001, Government of India.

The foreign sources of funding are divided into the following categories:

(a) *International Private Non-institutional Funding:* The private non-institutional funding to NGOs at the international level include resources mobilized from philanthropists and individual donors.

(b) *International Private Institutional Funding:* This category of funding includes funding from international NGOs such as Lions Club, International Red Cross Society, Amnesty Internationals, etc. This category also includes grants from the NGOs of industrialized countries like Oxfam-America, CARE, Action Aid, U.IG. etc. Another source of international funding is from solidarity groups, international trade unions etc. of the developed nations. This type of funding is mainly confined to the issues relating to human rights, women and child development and the environment etc. Most of the private institutional funding of NGOs come from the international corporate bodies.

Overseas NGOs, foundations and trusts also raise financial resources for development funding. However, they are more into providing manpower from the developed world interested in third world countries as also supporting NGO functionaries from third world nations for higher learning and exposure in the developed countries. They usually have a greater flexibility with regard to funding institutional infrastructure development of NGOs in third world countries.

Apart from development programme/project funding, overseas agencies are known to fund the setting up of buildings, creating corpus funds etc. for NGOs. They are also involved in advocacy efforts, i.e. raising their voice when actions of private business or governments result in environmental problems, specially radioactive contamination and such issues as global warming, ozone layer depletion, urban pollution or infringement of human rights. From the perspective of developing countries, the greatest importance of NGOs from the North lies in meeting the co-financing requirements for projects with agencies like the European Commission.

(c) *International Institutional/ Government Funding*: Institutional funding of NGOs at the international level comes from two major sources, i.e., from bilateral and multilateral donor agencies.

Bilateral Institutional Funding

Bilateral aid is one of the three channels of aid to the developing countries, representing the government to government cooperation. There are four major groups of bilateral aid donors: The

Organization for Economic Cooperation and Development (DECD), the Council for Mutual Economic Assistance (CMEA), Arab and OPEC Bilateral Donors and other developing country donors. Bilateral funding also includes aid from agencies, departments and ministries of the developed countries such as U.S.A., U.K., Japan, Sweden, Denmark, Norway, Canada and Australia. However, the substantial portion of this aid is made available to the government sponsored programmes, while a very small proportion is made available to VOs under the approval of the government for a specific programme and it is largely regulated by the Government of India through FCRA. The DECD is by far the largest bilateral aid donor. Among the bilateral aid donors to India, USA is the leading country followed by Germany, Italy, Denmark and the United Kingdom. A major trend in the current global aid regime is the emergence of Japan as the major ODA donor, surpassing USA aid regime.

The diversity of bilateral aid programmes was reflected in the multiple purposes and terms under which resources were transferred. The most common forms of bilateral aid transfer are grant aid, food aid, technical cooperation and concessional loans. Nearly one-quarter of bilateral aid is for the agricultural, social and political infrastructure sector. The organizational characteristics and roles played by bilateral donor and funding organizations include providing finances to NGOs for carrying out developmental activities and funding Government Departments and Ministries responsible for developmental initiatives in the Third World. The roles also include identifying strategic priorities and thematic areas for providing financial support; assessing feasibility of proposals or developmental plans; selecting promising developmental proposals for funding support; organizing assessments and conducting impact assessment studies.

Multilateral Institutional Funding

Multilateral funding includes funds from various agencies of the United Nations like WHO, UNESCO, UNICEF, FAO, UNFPA, UNDP, ILO, UNEP, etc. Some of these are sectoral while other focus on specific target groups. The other multilateral institutions, such as the World Bank and International Monetary Fund (IMF), also provide funding to the NGOs in India under the overall supervision and regulation of the government. The other sources of multilateral assistance to VOs include the Regional Development Banks such as Asian Development Bank (ADB), African Development Bank, Islamic Development Bank, the Commonwealth Development Corporation (CDC) and the Arab and OPEC multilateral agencies. The multilateral funding is very limited and is confined largely to the major voluntary organizations in India.

By and large, the major source of international funding to the voluntary efforts in India comes from the international non-government sector. This funding is restricted to specialized institutions or available by the approval of the government of India. For receiving any kind of assistance from the international donors, the NGOs required to register under the Foreign Contribution and Regulation Act (FCRA), 1976, under the Ministry of Home Affairs, Government of India. An amendment has been made in the Act in January 1985, under which the Government of India has imposed certain restrictions and regulations on the foreign contribution under FCRA. The thrust areas of the major international funding have been in the sectors like environment, health and family welfare, social welfare, women and children, education, rural development and science and technology. Though international funding brings new initiatives, new ideas and approaches in a wide range of areas, however, the international funding has certain limitations, i.e. being temporary in nature and for short duration action oriented projects. Over dependence on foreign funding becomes counter-productive as a considerable degree of uncertainty exists in regard to the flow of funds on a sustained basis. Besides, it affects, to a large extent, the autonomy, independence and transparency of the organizations.

The multilateral organizations are distinctly different from the bilateral ones as they usually provide soft loans to developing country Governments/State Governments with larger project budgets unlike the bilateral organizations who give outright grants. Otherwise, both the bilateral and multilateral organizations play a similar role in selecting promising financial developmental proposals for funding support, organizing assessments and evaluations and conducting impact assessment studies. Curiously enough, in the recent decades, even the multilateral organizations are increasingly demanding that the concerned governments involve NGOs in specific aspects of project implementation.

The trends in utilization of external assistance (both bilateral and multilateral) to India is given in Table 5.4.

Table 5.4 : Trend in Utilization of External Assistance to India

(US $ millions)

Source	*1980-81*	*1990-91*	*1997-98*
Bilateral Organizations	1100.3	1466.7	1056.0
Multilateral Organizations	1633.4	2269.8	2106.6
World Bank	835.6	1991.4	1415.7
European Economic Community	104.6	28.5	63.6
Asian Development Bank	-	212.4	601.1
IMF Trust Fund	679.7	-	0.2
Others	4.3	37.5	26.4
Grand Total	2733.7	3736.5	3164.7

Source : Economic Survey (1998-99), Government of India.

General trends in external assistance has been derived from the Economic Survey (1998-99) of the Government of India which captures loans and grants from bilateral and multilateral sources that are directly channelled through the Government's budget. Table 5.4 shows that the utilization of external assistance stood at $ 2.7 billion in 1980-81, peaked at $ 3.8 billion in 1990-91 and since have shown a declining trend. Funding from bilateral sources accounted for 33.5 per cent and multilateral sources accounted for 66.5 per cent of the total external assistance received by India in 1997-98. Of the total external assistance utilized in 1997-98, loans accounted for 92.2 per cent and grants for 7.8 per cent. These figures underestimate the grant component, as technical assistance which is directly administered by the Development Partner Organizations is not reflected. This is also the reason for the lack of data on UN assistance in this table. The latest data on ODA that also includes technical assistance is shown in Table 5.5.

The largest source for UN Development Assistance to India is the International Development Association (IDA) of the World Bank Group, accounting for a range of 84 to 95 per cent of total UN assistance between 1991 and 1998. From a total of $1.5 billion in 1991, total UN development assistance reached $ 3.5 billion in 1993 and subsequently declined to $ 0. 9 billion in 1998. The same trend has also been observed for UN development assistance excluding IDA.

Table 5.5 : Total Development Assistance in 1995 (latest year available)

Source of Aid	*US Dollars (Millions)*	*Percentage*
Multilateral Organizations	–	–
UN System (excluding the IFIs)	144.6	6.0
World Bank	757.2	31.1
Other IFIs	N/A	-
Non-United Nations System	31.7	1.3
Bilateral Organizations	1483.6	61.1
Sub-Total ODA	2417.1	99.5
NGOs	12.0	0.5
Total Development Assistance	2429.1	100

Source : UNDP, India.

Internal and National Funding

The internal or national level funding to NGOs is derived from diverse sources which include both private and government, and non-institutional and institutional sources:

(a) *National Private Non-Institutional Funding:* This category includes funding from the organization's own sources including philanthropist's and individual donations, contributions from the community, funds generated from membership, sponsorship fees, sales and interests, endowment funds, etc.

(b) *National Private Institutional Funding:* This includes funding from socio-cultural and religious bodies, trusts, trade unions and corporate bodies or business houses. This type of funding also includes resources generated from the national level funding NGOs such as Ashoka Foundation, Gandhi Peace Foundation, Family Planning Foundation, Aga Khan Foundation etc.

(c) *National Level Government Funding*: In pursuance of its policy to support and encourage development efforts, the Government of India through various departments and ministries has initiated centrally-sponsored programmes providing financial assistance to development organizations through grants-in-aid. Limited funding is also available with the state governments and at the local institutional levels. Besides, many governmental and semi or quasi-governmental agencies like National Children's

Fund, Central Social Welfare Board, CAPART, etc. provide funding for development efforts. However, they are for specific purposes and in a limited scale. At the local level, funds are provided largely through the District Rural Development Agencies, Zilla Parishads, Panchayati Raj Institutions, etc.

At present, the Government of India has several programmes and schemes to reduce urban as well as rural poverty, to provide shelter and to develop infrastructure, which lead to overall development. Since the majority of population lives in rural India, poverty alleviation programmes have acquired renewed importance in rural areas and for these schemes alone the government spends about Rs. 9000 crore annually.

Some of the important schemes aimed at poverty alleviation are : Pradhan Mantri Gram Sadak Yojana (PMGSY), Rural Housing, Rural Water Supply Programme, Rural Sanitation Programme, Jawahar Gram Samridhi Yojana, National Social Assistance Programme, Annapurna, Swarnajayanti Gram Swarozgar Yojana, Inegrated Wasteland Development Programme and Drought Prone Areas Programme and Desert Development Programme. The Ministry of Rural Development launched the PMGSY aimed at construction of rural roads. Though the rural roads are growing in length, according to an estimate, more than 2.5 lakh villages are still unconnected. The cost of the implementation of the programme is totally met by the Government of India (Bhagyalakshmi, 2001). So far the Centre has made Rs. 5000 crore available for the project. The project would need Rs. 60,000 crore for completion. The National Highways Development Project of Rs. 55,000 crore is one of the ambitious projects of independent India. These two major road connectivity programmes would create lakhs of new employment opportunities.

Empowerment of women has been another major concern of the government. Self-help groups started by women began a silent socio-economic revolution. There are many success stories in India, and also in the South Asia region where self-help groups using micro credit from banks made a significant dent in rural and urban poverty. Therefore, the government has decided to facilitate the setting up of at least one self-help group in each of the 14 lakh habitations in the country by the end of 2004. Over the next three years, all public sector banks will lend five per cent of the net bank credit to women entrepreneurs. This will make Rs. 17,000 crore of bank credit available for women specified business. Almost all the programmes launched by the Government have component for women. The 73rd Amendment Act of the Constitution, 1992 provides for reservation of women at all three tiers of Panchayati Raj Institutions. Thus at Gram Panchayat, Pachayat Samiti and Zilla Parishad one-third of members and chairpersons are women.

The Swarnajayanti Gram Swarozgar Yojana, launched in 1999, covers all aspects of self-employment including organization of self-help groups, training, credit, technology, infrastructure and marketing. It is envisaged that 50 per cent of the groups formed in each block should be exclusively for women who will account for at least 40 per cent of the self-employed persons. The Jawahar Gram Samridhi Yojana (JGSY) launched in 1999 has two objectives—creation of infrastructure and generation of supplementary employment for unemployed poor in rural areas. Here again, 30 per cent of the employment opportunities are reserved for women.

According to the new policy announcement of the Prime Minister, the Central Government will launch a new scheme of Rs. 10,000 crore to provide additional and guaranteed employment in rural areas. This scheme will be known as "Sampoorna Grameen Rozgar Yojana." All the existing employment schemes of the government will be merged into this scheme. It is expected to generate one hundred crore man-days of employment. Under this scheme "those who take employment from panchayats to build durable rural assets will be paid wages in cash and in foodgrains. For 50 lakh tonnes of foodgrains worth Rs. 5000 crore will be provided to state governments every year" (Bhagyalakshmi, 2001).

Housing shortage is another major problem in India. 137.20 lakh houses which need to be constructed or upgraded to achieve the target of providing shelter to all in the rural areas by 2002. In 1998, the Government of India announced a National Housing and Habitat Polity to provide "housing for all" and to facilitate building of twenty lakh houses annually (13 lakh in rural areas and 7 lakh in urban areas). Under Indira Awas Yojana, which is already being implemented, a total of 56,93,645 houses had been built up till December 1999 at a cost of Rs. 9173.24 crore. A comprehensive housing scheme called Samagra Awas Yojana was also launched to ensure integrated provision of shelter, sanitation and drinking water. Twenty-five districts of 24 states and one union territory had been identified for implementing the participatory approach under the Accelerated Rural Water Supply Programme. The Prime Minister in his Independence Day (2001) speech said that the government has decided to launch 'Ambedkar-Valmiki Malin Bastic Awas Yojana' to benefit especially those belonging to the scheduled castes, scheduled tribes, backward classes, and other weaker sections. The Ministry of Urban Development will give a yearly grant of Rs. 1000 crore to this project. HUDCO, which will implement this scheme, will make available another Rs. 2000 crore as loan amount.

Social Sector Spending by the Government

Education, health, family welfare, nutrition, sanitation, water supply, roads and social security—these constitute the basic social needs. The role of the government is vital for meeting these basic needs. Plan and Non-plan expenditure of the Central Government on various social sector services increased from a level of Rs. 9608 crore in 1992-93 to Rs. 36,270 crore in 2000-2001, an increase of about four times in eight years. In spite of the budgetary pressures faced by the Central Government, it has attempted to enhance outlays for the social sectors. Expenditures on social services increased from 1.28 per cent of GDP in 1992-93 to 1.66 per cent in 2000-2001. Significant increases in central plan outlay is observed in education, especially elementary education, health, women and child development, and family welfare programmes. The central plan outlay's budgeted estimate (BE) in 2000-2001 as compared to the previous year's revised estimate (RE) increased by 24.3 per cent for education and 26.5 per cent for elementary education programmes; by 29.8 per cent for health sector programmes; by 16.8 per cent for women and child development; and by 12.8 per cent for family welfare schemes (Economic Survey, 2000-2001). The planned expenditure of the government on major schemes of social sectors is given in Table 5.6.

The increasing diversification of the economy together with acceleration in economic growth has caused structural changes in the nature of the job market. The annual growth of employment in the organized sector, both public and private, has steadily declined during the last five years. The major contribution in the overall growth of organized employment is made by the private sector in

Table 5.6 : Central Government Expenditure (Plan and Non-Plan) on Social Services (Rs. crores)

Item	*1992-93*	*1996-97*	*1997-98*	*1998-99*	*1999-00 (RE)*	*2000-01. (BE)*
1. Social Services:	6397	13659	15894	19729	23727	25873
(a) Education, sports & youth affairs	1878	3988	5012	6550	7115	8416
(b) Health and family welfare	1722	2751	3174	3615	5110	5860
(c) Water supply, sanitation, housing and urban development	788	2957	3304	4190	4619	5087
(d) Information and abroad casting	371	593	898	1074	1230	1368
(e) Welfare of SC/ST and OBC	488	833	725	946	1083	1267
(f) Labour, employment and labour welfare	347	587	562	758	868	941
(g) Social welfare and nutrition	803	1950	2219	2295	3702	2935
2 Rural Development	3211	5081	5583	5403	5185	5397
3. Basic Minimum Services—BMS *including slum devp.	–	2466	2873	3684	4048	–
4. Pradhan Mantri Gramodaya Yojana (PMGY)	–	–	–	–	–	5000
5. Social Services, Rural Dev. BMS and PMGY(1+2+3+4)	9608	21206	24350	28816	32960	36270
Total Central Government Expenditure as percentages of GDP at current market prices**	15.8	13.9	14.2	14.6	15.5	15.5
Social Services, Rural Dev. BMS & PMGY as a percentage of Total Expenditure**	8.12	11.14	11.26	11.24	10.85	10.72
Social Services, Rural Dev. BMS & PMGY as a percentage of GDP at market prices $	1.28	1.55	1.59	1.60	1.68	1.66

Note : Figures for the years 1992-93 to 1998-99 are actuals.
* : Came into operation from 1996-97.
@: Launched in 2000-01(BE) as a new initiative for basic rural needs.
**: The total Central Govt. expenditure excludes the transfer of State's/UT's share of small saving collections.
$: Ratios to GDP are at current market prices (Base: 1992-93) released by CSO. GDP for 2000-01 is based on CSO's Advance Estimates.

Source : Economic Survey, 2000-2001.

the post-reform period, whereas there was hardly any growth of employment in the public sector.

Education is the key to all processes of development. Universalization of Elementary Education (UEE) has been accepted as a national goal of educational policy and programming. The government continues to provide financial assistance to voluntary organizations and NGOs under its various educational development programmes. National Child Labour Projects (NCLPs) have been set up in different areas to rehabilitate child labour. Major activities undertaken under the NCPL is the establishment of special schools to provide non-formal, vocational training, supplementary nutrition, etc. to children withdrawn from employment. So far 94 child labour projects under the NCLP covering 1.8 lakh children have been sanctioned in states where the child labour use is relatively high. However, children's care and the problem of child labour remains an area of concern. According to 1991 census, the number of working children in the country was of the order of 11.28 million.

Though, in absolute terms, the number of women workers during the last four decades has more than doubled from 40 million in 1951 to 90 million in 1991, the percentage of women labour to total work force may have declined marginally. A Central Advisory Committee has been set up under the Act to advise the government on providing increasing employment opportunities for women and generally reviewing the steps taken for effective implementation of the Act. The state government and UTIs have also set up similar committees. There are various other enactments applicable to women labour governing their working conditions. Despite marginal declines for the years 1994-95 and 1998-99, the all-India average real wages for the unskilled agricultural workers have risen continuously and at an average rate of about 3 per cent per annum during the 8 year span of 1992-2000.

Alleviation of poverty remains a major challenge before the nation. While there has been a steady decline in poverty over the last two decades, the total number of poor people has perhaps, remained constant because of growth in population. The specifically designed anti-poverty programmes for generation of both self-employment and wage employment have been redesigned and restructured in 1999-2000 in order to make these programmes more effective. For the year 2000-01, an outlay of Rs. 9760 crore (budget estimate) was provided as compared to Rs. 9351 crore (revised estimate) for 1999-2000. The major poverty alleviation programmes in operation in rural and urban areas are: (1) Jawahar Gram Samridhi Yojana (JGSY), (2) Swarna Jayanti Gram Swarozgar Yojana (SGSY), (3) National Social Assistance Programme (NSAP), (4) Employment Assurance Scheme (EAS), (5) Pradhan Mantri Gramodya Yojana (PMGY), and (6) Swarna Jayanti Shahari Rozgar Yojana (SJSRY). Several schemes were launched by the government to meet the needs of not only the educationally disadvantaged but also for the overall strengthening of the social infrastructure for education. The total Central Plan allocation on education has been raised from Rs. 4385 crore in 1999-2000 to Rs. 54,419 crore in 2000-01.

Women and children, who represent 67.7 per cent of the country's total population, constitute the most important target groups in the present day context of developmental planning. To empower the women, efforts are being made: (a) to finalize the draft National Policy for Empowerment of Women, (b) to legislate reservation of not less than 1/3 seats for women in the Lok Sabha and in the State Legislative Assemblies so as to ensure adequate representation of women in decision making, (c) to adopt an integrated approach towards empowering women through effective convergence of existing services, financial and human resources, and infrastructure in both women specific and women-related sectors, (d) to adopt a special strategy of Women's Component Plan (WCP) to ensure funds flow to women from other relevant sectors, and (e) to organize women into self-help groups. A task force on women and children has been constituted to review the existing legislation and the government schemes for improving the asset base of women to improve their social status, i.e., WCP, The Indira Mahila Yojana, The Rural Women's Development and Empowerment Project, Rashtriya Mahila Kosh.

The Ninth Plan (1997-2002) specifically stipulated identifying 'Women Component Plans' for which at least 30 per cent of funds flow to women development schemes. There are women-specific welfare schemes/programmes that receive funds under the annual budgetary allocations, 29 identifiable women-specific schemes that received Rs. 856.64 crores in 2000-01 as against Rs. 605.46 crores in 1999-2000. In India, the life expectancy at birth for females has increased from 44.7 years in 1971 to 60.9 years in 1994. The increase has been faster than that of men. The life expectancy at birth for women was, however, lower than that for men until 1981 but it surpassed that of men in 1991. The infant mortality rate (IMR) and child mortality rate (CMR) declined during 1980s and 1990s, but are still very high in comparison to many other developing countries.

Socially disadvantaged groups such as Scheduled Castes (SCs), Scheduled Tribes (STs), Other Backward Classes (OBCs) and minorities have received special focus over the years. Various programmes for welfare and development of SCs, OBCs and minorities are implemented by the Ministry of Social Justice and Empowerment. For STs the Ministry of Tribal Affairs was set up in October 1999 exclusively to attend to the needs of tribal population keeping in view their special needs and problems. The Persons with Disability (Equal Opportunities, Protection of Rights and Full Participation) Act, 1995 has become the anchor for rendering help to the disabled to become, as far as possible, self-reliant and productive. A National Programme for Rehabilitation of the Persons with Disabilities (NPRPD) has been launched for 'Reaching the Unreached,' which envisages rehabilitation services right from the village level.

Dimension of Funding by the Government : The Present Status

Recognizing the productive role of NGOs in the socio-economic activities, the Government of India earmarked nearly Rs. 1,500 million for the NGO sector during the Seventh Five Year Plan period. The Estimates Committee of Parliament reported that, for the year 1989, government sources alone provided funds to the voluntary sector to the tune of Rs. 2,500 million. The funding by the Central Government to the voluntary sector is now estimated to cross about 10 billion rupees. The Ministry of Social Justice and Empowerment with the largest number of welfare and developmental programmes have supported with funding to more than 2,100 voluntary organizations in the country upto December 1999. This ministry alone has released funds upto the tune of nearly 1,800 million rupees to the voluntary sector during 1999-2000 as against 1,110 million rupees in the year 1998-99 (Mohanty and Singh, 2001).

On the other hand, funds from inbemational donors reached a figure of Rs. 7 billion in 1988, providing assistance to 8,782 agencies in India. This has crossed over rupees 39 billion today. Over 21000 societies registered under FCRA have been eligible for foreign funding upto the end of 1999 since its inception. In addition, approximately 6,000 societies were granted prior permission by the Central Government for obtaining foreign grants during this period.

A classification of funding to NGOs is outlined in Table 5.7 :

Grants-In-Aid

The Government of India has been providing financial assistance to the voluntary organizations through an instrument called grants-in-aid. Grants-in-aid may be defined as an instrument of transfer of funds from a higher level federal authority to lower level authority under certain guidelines governing procedure, conditions and obligations. The basis objectives of grant-in-aid are:

(i) Promotion of voluntary action and people's participation,
(ii) Promotion of innovation and experimentation of programmes,
(iii) Provide service delivery with speed and flexibility,
(iv) Bring about decentralization,
(v) Cover the uncovered areas, sectors and groups, and
(vi) Sharing tax funds for welfare and development etc.

The main purpose of grants-in-aid is to encourage innovation and promotion of voluntary effort in areas where it is non-existent. It is also meant to help NGO agencies develop a professional approach through the induction of trained manpower and build their administrative and organizational competence. The Government of India, apart from giving financial assistance, provides technical, material and training assistance and guidelines to NGO organizations in different forms. The central funding to NGOs is extended by various ministries and departments in the form of grants-in-aid, subsidies, government loans/bank loans, stipends, honorarium and cash awards etc. Depending on the nature of the project and type of activity, the government provides financial assistance to voluntary organizations in the form of both recurring, non recurring grants, such as administrative grants, maintenance grants, grants for purchase of land and construction of buildings, extension and repair work, paying rent, purchase of equipment/ furniture and meeting the expenses of teaching/learning materials,

Table 5.7 : Institutional and Non-institutional Sources of Funding to Voluntary Organizations

Level	*Institutional*	*Non-institutional*
1. National funding		
(a) Private	— Socio-cultural bodies —Religious bodies —Trusts —Trade Unions —Corporate Bodies —National level NGOs	Internal Sources Membership Contributions Sponsorship Fees, Sales, Interests, Community Philanthropists and Individual Donations
(b) Government/Semi government	—Ministries/Departments —Autonomous	
(i) Central Government	Government Bodies e.g. CSWB, KVIC, etc. National Funds e.g. Rural Development Fund National Children Fund National Cultural Fund	
(ii) State Government/UT Administration	Ministries/Departments	
(iii) District Level Administration	—e.g. District Rural Development Agencies —Zilla Parishad	
2. International Funding		
(a) Private	—International NGOs —NGOs of the North at the country level —Solidarity groups and trade unions —International corporate bodies	Philanthropists and Individual Donors
(b) Government/Semi-government		
(i) Bilateral Funding	Government to government e.g. USAID, British Aid	
(ii) Multilateral Funding	World Bank, ADB etc.	

salaries and allowances of staff workers, transport and travel costs, printing and copying postage, stationary, typing and telephone charges etc. Similarly, non-financial assistance takes the form of technical resource support, training, goods and services whenever required, depending upon the type and nature of the project.

The government of India is now concerned with the rationalization and simplification of procedures of grants-in-aid to VOs for effective utilization of resources. In response to the recommendations made by the Krishnaswamy Committee in 1988, the Department of Administrative Reforms, Public Grievances and Pensions in the Ministry of Personnel had produced a Study Report (1997) entitled, "Monitoring of Government Aided AGO Projects" which primarily focused on issues relating to the methods and procedures adopted for the release of grants-in-aid to NOGs. In this report, the department recommended that the central ministries/departments should adopt more open and transparent procedures for release of grants-in-aid to voluntary organizations.

In order to overcome the problem of delay in recommendation of the state governments and timely relase of the grants to the NGOs, the Ministry has designated agencies for carrying out the inspections of the NGOs working with the assistance provided by this Ministry. It has proposed to designate the Schools of Social Work, the National Institutes for the Handicapped, universities and other institutions to regularly inspect the NGOs and send their reports and help in release the instalments of grants.

Funding of NGOs: Patterns and Mechanism

Since independence, funding has come mainly from government and foreign agencies. Private, non-government support of social development has not grown commensurately with need, though in the pre-independence period, voluntary action was almost entirely funded by private indigenous, non-governmental contributions. The reasons are three-fold (Sampradan, 2001) :

(i) Government became the predominant player in development because of centralized planning;
(ii) Taxes were increased heavily for the purpose, leaving both a disinclination for charity as well as a smaller surplus in individual and corporate hands; and

(iii) The availability of foreign funds reduced pressure on private charity.

Government recognized the potential of voluntary action for supplementing and complementing its efforts. In the First Five Year Plan itself it stated:

> "Any plan for social and economic regeneration should take into account the services rendered by these agencies and the state should give them maximum cooperation in strengthening their efforts. Public cooperation through voluntary service organizations is capable of yielding valuable results in channelling private efforts for the promotion of social welfare."

In the Seventh Plan, an allocation of Rs.1500 million was made for NGOs, and it is estimated that presently around Rs. 4000 million flow to NGOs from a variety of ministries like social welfare, education, health, urban development, environment and rural development. NGOs have also attracted funds from foreign donors. In fact, foreign funding of NGOs has increased manifold since the 60s when foreign funds first became significant in the wake of several natural calamities.

Most of the NGOs in the developing countries depend on the NGOs of the developed countries for funding. The major sources of funding through which the NGOs of the South receive aid from the North are:

(a) *Private grants from Northern NGOs directly from their own resources.*

(b) *Bilateral aid which is channelled through:*
   (i) Northern NGOs' funding,
   (ii) Direct grants by DAC countries to Southern NGOs,
   (iv) Aid Missions or embassies in the recipient country, and
   (v) National governments.

(c) *Multilateral aid which is channelled through:*
   (i) Directly by the multilateral agencies or their cofinancing projects, and
   (ii) National governments.

Multilateral and bilateral funds go through government, and are, therefore, included in government funding. But funding by private foreign donor organizations has itself become quite substantial and is much larger than government funding of NGOs. In 1984, 3,612 NGOs received private foreign funds to the tune of Rs. 2,530 million. By 1999-2000, the last year for which figures are available, the amount had increased to Rs. 38,100 million. About 20,000 organizations were registered with the FCRA division of the government. Through all of them may not have received the funds, it indicates the maximum number of organizations who do, or can, receive money from foreign donors. However, since the number of voluntary organizations in India are said to run into a million, (there are no reliable estimates available), it means that a large number are dependent on funds from other sources. There is an urgent need to build up an alternative third source for three major reasons (Sampradan, 2001):

(i) Government funding is beset with a lot of red tape and inflexibility, moreover, government is often itself the problem against which NGOs are fighting;
(ii) Foreign funding is often governed by geopolitical considerations and can, therefore, be unstable. Also, unless the agendas are set locally, it can be divorced from local needs and perceptions; and
(iii) To provide choice and ensure independence of action and sustainability of the NGO sector.

Many of the official funding agencies are interested more in resource transfer than in issues of participation and empowerment for sustainable development. The result of large scale transfer of funds without creating the right conditions for their productive use has seen a sapping or destruction of the local governance structures and local sources of funds, creating dependency, financial and non-financial. The funding practices of government and foreign donors such as either too large (generally foreign donors), or too small (mostly government) grants; inflexibility in use of funds; preference for project rather than programme or core support; unwillingness to give endowments; frequent shifts in funding preferences and agendas etc., have all led to a concern, both among donors and recipients either about creating dependencies among beneficiaries or about sustainability of organizations and their work in the long-term.

There are many factors that affect the ability of indigenous NGOs to attract foreign aids. These include the track record of local NGOs and their credibility with the donor, their management systems and administrative capacity, the extend to which their priorities, activities and methodologies are compatible with those of donors and the level of support of their government, etc. All donors have priorities, procedures and specific requirements, etc. geographical and target group priorities are set by the aid donors. From a developing world perspective, indigenous NGOs have complex relations with governments, sometimes cooperating and sometimes conflicting. However, in India, NGOs derive much support and encouragement from the government and both work in close collaboration.

Funding Patterns of Bilateral and Multilateral Agencies

Most of the social development works in India are funded by bilateral and multilateral foreign agencies, countries and world organizations. The authorization and utilization of external funding by different sources is given in Tables 5.8 (a) and (b).

The foreign assistance of all forms to India has never been great in comparison to the quality and quantity of problems India has been facing. But foreign financial assistance has been playing important role in many forms of socio-economic and infrastructural development programmes. An observation of the pattern of foreign financial assistance does not give a promising picture. During the period 1999-2000, India received more grants (Rs. 2603.8 crore) in comparison to that of 1998-99 (Rs. 205.2 crore). But it is still less than what it got in 1996-97 (Rs. 2773 crore), which happens to be the highest total foreign grant it ever received.

Foreign grants mostly depend on the geo-political situations. Global premium was on to India during the first phase of liberalization, which started in 1991. But after 1996-97 it seems the attention of external source on India's social development has been either reduced or stagnated. May be the global perception is that after 10 years of liberalization, India must have generated enough indigenous economic-political and infrastructural mechanisms to pursue its own sustainable development. It is the impression that is given by the fact that foreign financial assistance in form of loans has been reduced drastically.

Table 5.8. (a) : Authorization and Utilization of External Assistance by Source (US $ millions)

Source and type of assistance	*Authorization of External Assistance (Grants)*					*Utilization of External Assistance (Grants)*				
	1995-96	*1996-97*	*1997-98*	*1998-99*	*1999-00*	*1995-96*	*1996-97*	1997-98	1998-99	1999-00
1	2	3	4	5	6	7	8	9	10	11
1. Consortium Members Country-wise Distribution	338.4	780.7	319.1	48.8	601.6	265.5	200.0	173.8	172.8	173.8
(i) Austria	–	–	–	–	–	–	–	–	–	–
(ii) Belgium	–	–	–	–	–	–	–	–	–	–
(iii) Canada	–	21.5	8.6	1.7	9.6	0.4	1.2	2.0	1.4	1.5
(iv) Denmark	–	105.5	17.4	11.6	11.0	7.0	6.3	6.0	7.1	12.4
(v) France	0.9	0.6	–	–	–	0.7	1.1	0.6	0.8	-1.0
(vi) Germany	55.9	55.9	89.8	–	39.6	4.5	6.6	10.1	31.0	23.9
(vii) Italy	–	–	–	–	–	–	–	–	–	–
(viii) Japan	61.1	18.2	24.6	32.3	1.3	26.6	31.4	32.3	27.5	8.3
(ix) Netherlands	87.9	135.0	97.6	2.9	–	110.3	33.6	33.1	12.5	19.4
(x) Sweden	57.7	133.2	6.4	–	–	20.0	27.7	12.3	9.7	7.1
(xi) U. K.	23.9	274.5	44.0	–	471.7	84.5	85.3	52.6	61.1	68.2
(xii) U.S.A.	41.8	15.9	30.7	–	66.5	11.3	6.5	14.2	14.9	17.2

Contd... (Table 5.8)

(US $ million)

Source and type of assistance	*Authorization of External Assistance (Grants)*					*Utilization of External Assistance (Grants)*				
	1995-96	*1996-97*	*1997-98*	*1998-99*	*1999-00*	*1995-96*	*1996-97*	1997-98	1998-99	1999-00
1	2	3	4	5	6	7	8	9	10	11
2. East European Countries										
Country-wise distribution	–	–	–	–	–	–	–	–	–	–
(i) Russia Fed.										
3. Others	60.6	44.9	274.2	1.1	2.7	53.5	105.6	74.8	40.2	–
(i) Switzerland	0.3	3.9	11.9	–	2.7	3.1	7.6	1.9	1.7	–
(ii) EEC	60.3	36.8	221.9	1.1	–	40.8	87.8	61.3	29.1	–
(iii) Kuwait Fund for Arabic Economic Dev.	–	–	–	–	–	–	–	–	–	–
(iv) Spain	–	–	–	–	–	–	–	–	–	–
(v) Norway	–	–	13.4	–	–	–	4.3	4.4	2.8	–
(vi) Australia	–	–	–	–	–	–	–	–	–	–
Grand Total	408.6	845.9	840.5	50.7	605.1	362.7	405.0	305.6	239.8	157.0

Source : Ministry of Foreign Affairs, Govt of India, 2001.
Economic Survey, 2000-2001

Table 5.8 : (b) Authorization and Utilization of External Assistance

(US $ million)

Source and type of assistance	*Authorization of External Assistance (Grants)*					*Utilization of External Assistance (Grants)*				
	1995-96	*1996-97*	*1997-98*	*1998-99*	*1999-00*	*1995-96*	*1996-97*	*1997-98*	*1998-99*	*1999-00*
1	2	3	4	5	6	*7*	*8*	*9*	*10*	*11*
1. I.B.R.D	-	20.4	-	0.4	-	0.2	0.3	8.0	3.0	5.1
2 I.D.A.	-	-	-	-	1.9	-	-	2.3	3.7	7.0
3. OPEC	-	-	-	-	-	-	-	-	-	-
4 IMF Trust fund	-	-	-	-	-	-	-	0.2	-	-

Source: Economic Survey, 2000-2001.

Private Sector Funding: Increasing Participation

In recent times, particularly after the liberalization phase began in 1991, the map of Indian industry has gone through complete restructuring. Industry in private sector has taken a complete positive turn around in all aspects, i.e., operation, strategy, quality, export, size, profit, sales, production, etc. The new corporate movement in the course of its development took up social responsibility of participating in the overall social development of the country. This is not a completely new attitude as far as Indian private industry is concerned. In the beginning phase of industrialization in India, and continuing well into the post-indepencence decades Indian private corporate houses were involved in socio-cultural-religious development of the society. They were mostly doing a lot of charitable and philanthropic activities, i.e., art, culture, education, religion, infrastructure, etc. But the current practice of corporate social responsibility is more pragmatic, professionally strategic, personally more committed and politically matured. Corporates now feel it is their duty to see the people across the whole country must prosper and grow in socio-economic and political aspects of life. They also seek for people's participation in this new endeavour, thus making people realize their right to ask, not only for corporate's participation in removing their basic problems, but also their responsibility of providing right kind of support and opportunity to the corporate sector, so that the latter can carry on social development work. Corporate social responsibility is a powerful performance parameter for the successful coalition of democracy and market economy. It has taken place and contributed to the democratic development of society in many other countries in the world. Indian corporate sector seems to be modeling itself after the more successful corporate social responsibility pattern of the developed countries.

The atmosphere for intersectoral cooperation is promising. Implementing joint efforts of the government, business and the voluntary organizations in social, economic and political sectors has become a global strategy. To ensure adequate budgetary allocations to social sectors, financial resources will have to be mobilized by both the Centre and the States. Furthermore, available resources need to be better targeted and effective safety nets need to be designed to protect the poor and vulnerable sections against income fluctuations and market failures. In this context, public efforts and resources need to be supplemented by private sector participation and support from NGOs for the development of different social sectors.

The aim of the industry is not to support but supplement efforts of the government by forming partnerships. Subsequent to the launching of Second Five Year Plan, tremendous growth and expansion has taken place in the corporate sector. The increased socio-economic demands of society accelerated the pace of expansion. Diverse types of industries with different produce are coming up and demand for skilled labour is increasing. The government alone cannot achieve the onerous task of eradicating various social and economic problems in the country. Though many NGOs, civil society group and individuals are involved in this, yet much more needs to be done. Corporate sector can play a major role in improving current scenario in the social sector.

Many business corporations today accept that it is in their interest to be more socially aware and to engage in programmes for the benefit of the community. However, the number of corporations actually undertaking social development programmes is still very small. Mostly, companies prefer to undertake development projects themselves or to contribute cash on request. There are fewer instances of companies building up sustained relationships with NGOs. For many, the lack of motivation is partly due to a lack of information about and exposure to community problems and social development projects, and NGOs working dedicatedly for the country (CII, 1998). Corporate support has gradually moved from one time charitable giving to a more long-term relationship based on a perception of mutual relevance and benefit. This trend can be referred to as 'from charity to social investment'.

The above analysis on the funding pattern for social development provides a clear picture of the slow decline in the external assistance for social development. The empirical data for this study also supports this analysis which is discussed in the following chapters. There has been substantial discussion of the government's major role in social sectors. However, there is an urgent need to fill this crunch in fund that has resulted because of the declining trend in multilateral and bilateral funding. The corporate sector could be the driving force in funding for social development as an investment. The business has a vast pool of resources in terms of men, functional expertise and money. With these resources at its command, business is in a better position to work for social goals towards long-term sustainable development.

6 Paradigm Shift of Corporate Sector Participation in Social Development

A large section of the society is by-passed by the process of development. The models of 'development from above' with the basic assumption that the benefits of economic growth would trickle down to the poorer sections of the society did not succeed in achieving expected goals. Similarly, the models of 'development from below' with an equitable, need-based approach are not experienced to achieve the desired outcomes. The international forces have influenced the economic and social forces at the national and local levels as a result of increasing globalization, liberalization and de-regulation, thus leading to an increasing dis-empowerment and powerlessness of the people, particularly among the poor and marginalised sections of the society. There is a greater need for empowerment of these groups, economically, socially and politically. Development of people's organizations, i.e., the organizations, which are controlled by the people, is an effective means of the process of empowerment. In this changing global and market-oriented economy, a diminishing role of the State, on the one hand, and the special significance of the voluntary sector, on the other is witnessed. The greatest challenge before the NGOs today is building the civil society and to articulate themselves in projecting the importance of civil society *vis-á-vis* the state and the market.

A people-centred sustainable development with the central concerns to enhance equitable human growth and well-being of late has become an alternative development paradigm. India faces the greatest challenges in the front of socio-economic development, education, health and welfare of the masses. The unprecedented population growth, an unbalanced regional development and widening rural-urban disparities, increasing rate of unemployment and underemployment, malnutrition, under-nutrition, a widespread of diseases and an inadequate health and family welfare services, an inadequate availability of safe drinking water, sanitation and a poor quality of life, increasing incidences of violence against women, growing environmental degradation, pollution and the resulting Eco-crisis, growing health hazards such as AIDS, place the country in a pathological state. In addition, the frequent communal strife and terrorism in the recent decades, a growing regional consciousness and a threat to the national integration are fast eroding away the social fabrics of the country.

Financing of development on a sustainable basis needs to be primarily and largely a domestic effort and it has been so in India. External assistance has not financed more than 10 to 12 per cent of domestic investment on a gross basis. Such assistance has covered a wide range of areas from sectoral approach to build up institutional capacities, from direct poverty alleviation initiatives to developing debt-servicing instruments. As socio-economic problems in the country intensify, social development has become a recognized priority in the agenda of the Government of India. In India's domestic economy, despite increasing level of urbanization, the predominance of rural perspective has forced the planners to formulate the basic development objectives in such a way that allocation for the rural sector has been very high.

In the case of external assistance, the budgetary constraint in the donor countries, specially the OECD countries, and, with the limits to multilateral agencies lending and the additional claims from new entrants on their resources, official and multilateral lending will most likely continue to decline on a net basis. At a given level of the development of a country, the funds that it can mobilize for investment are determined largely by three factors, viz. domestic savings, the ratio of taxes to the Gross National Product (GNP) and the net inflow of capital from external sources. However, social reality in India is a complex issue. Government alone cannot tackle developmental problems. The vast majority of our population needs help to improve their lives. This indicates that one of the major initiatives to raise adequate funds could be the untapped and expected resources from in-house including the corporate sector. Corporate sector funding for social development is the paradigm shift and this trend for increasing private sector participation is substantiated with empirical findings in this study. In this chapter, it is attempted to analyze the significant contributions made by the corporate sector and NGOs in social development. An attempt has also been made to study different perspectives on the issue of social development to have a better understanding of the concept of corporate social development and streamline the focus on the need for corporate sector participation in social development funding.

Sustainable Development: Introspect and Prospect

Sustainable development is a process of simultaneously ensuring continuation of the economic, social and ecological basis of human life. To ensure the sustenance of the trinity, the economic, social as well as the ecological conditions and requirements are to be kept in mind. We cannot have ecological conservation even at the expense of degradation of the social or economic basis of human life or the other way round. Existing literature has carefully documented the circular relationship between ecological destruction and socio-economic deprivation. Sustainable development is thought of as involving increases in the quality of life which are equitable. Sustainable development is a process interface between political, economic, ecological and cultural systems, contextualised in North-South transactions, for preserving, protecting and sustaining all life forms and environmental resources. Sustainable development compromises two elements: ecological practices resulting in the protection of environmental resources, and equity in their utilization, combining environment and economy. It is this combination that makes it a paradoxical paradigm. Sustainable development would not only involve ecological practices that enable meeting the needs of future generations, but a change in production and consumption patterns in an equitable manner whereby resources, which are currently being wasted, are saved and re-channelled to meeting the needs of everyone today as well as the needs of future generations.

Equity, social justice, self-reliance, biodiversity, respect for indigenous knowledge systems, decentralization, and participation: these are the core values that constitute the organizing principle of sustainable development. From an institutional point of view, sustainable development requires building local institutions that would mobilize the resources of the poor, build on existing horizontal and cross-sectoral linkages among development-related organizations, and facilitate vertical linkages that allow grassroots influence on relevant policy-making. In the Indian context, social movement and NGO interface is not strong. Links between progressive groups in academic institutions, the civil service, and the judiciary, on the one hand, and the NGO-social movement categories, on the other, converging of these could be a great source of strength, although this has not been adequately explored by the key actors. Pretext of this, it may be cited that the Human Development Report (1997) emphasizes the need for partnerships: "The success of political mobilization against poverty hinges on winning broad and diverse support. Poor people alone, however, well organized, cannot force the policy shifts for poverty eradication. Alliances, partnerships and compromises are the only viable vehicles for peaceful sustained reform." Sustainability, as espoused by the UNDP, has become a route to empowering people by enhancing their capabilities and enabling their participation in local self-governance. The sustainable human development paradigm of the UNDP focuses on four major areas: poverty alleviation, advancement of women, productive employment and creation of jobs and protection and regeneration of the environment. One good example of people's participation and sustainability is the Forest Department's collaboration with Ford Foundation to initiate Joint Forest Management programmes involving the government, local community and NGO, for the afforestation and protection of degraded forest lands. This inter-relationships between people's participation and sustainable development are brought out in the following Figure 6.1.

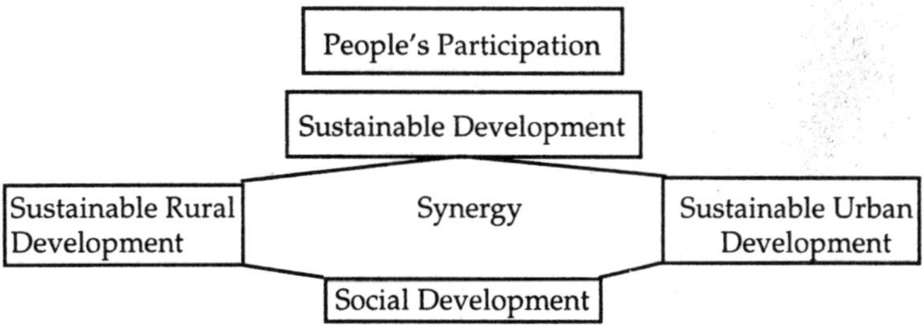

Fig. 6.1 : Inter-Relationships between Participation and Sustainability

Therefore, the fundamental requirement for a community to be sustainable is that the locus of power lies within it. By the late 60s, everybody realized that empowerment was a more desirable goal than relief. The word 'development' was coined as something distinctly different from 'relief,' as it involved introduction of the concept of empowerment. Gradually, institutions like NGOs, VOs, developed further specialization and evolved into organizations that were contributing to development. It is in this context that specialization and evolution of roles and responsibilities resulted in the creation of different stakeholders, co-operating with each other for promoting development. Clearly distinct entities can be identified as role players or stakeholders in the process of development. These include the elected representatives of the people forming the Central and State Governments, responsible wings of the government involved in implementation of development policies and measures decided by elected representatives of people such as government departments, civil servants, state officials, the Planning Commission, etc. The role of the private sector remains increasingly important in economic and social systems. Private sector is powerful enough to foster the changes needed to ensure sustainability.

Participatory Development: Some Insights

Participatory development is a process through which stakeholders can influence and share control over development initiatives and over the decisions and resources that affect themselves. Lessons from experience show a variety of potential benefits from participation (Asian Development Bank, 1995). These include:

(i) More appropriate development interventions that fit the needs of the community and users of the facility;
(ii) Better implementation and sustainability of development initiatives;
(iii) More complete utilization and increased ownership of services provided;
(iv) Greater efficiency, understanding and better planning, based on the concerns and ideas of a wide range of participants;
(v) A better match between human capabilities and capital investments;

(vi) Improved institutional performance because of greater transparency and accountability;
(vii) More efficient functioning of markets because of improved information flows;
(viii) Increased equity and empowerment through greater involvement of the poor, women and other disadvantaged groups;
(ix) Strengthened capacity of stakeholders to initiate other development activities, as a consequence of their involvement; and
(x) Increased commitment for policies and projects, including a willingness to share costs and an interest in sustaining the benefits.

Participation needs to be seen as a scale, ranging from token participation, on the one hand, to full participation and empowerment, on the other. Participation at a large scale rather than a local scale cannot occur without the involvement of large-scale institutions, be the national government, NGO, donor agencies, or others. But for a large institution to support increased and higher quality participation in more places means more than focusing on communities, it also means changing the institutions themselves. Whereas large institutions like governments have an advantage of scale over local groups, and also have the disadvantages in it that they are usually not very participatory.

Foreign donor agencies and banks also started playing a significant role in raising and making available financial resources and specialized technical expertise for promoting the well-being of people in developing countries. Thus, donor agencies also play a critical role in fund raising for promoting developmental interventions. Other players in social development include registered societies, charitable trusts, foundations and community based organizations such as Mahila Mandals (or women groups), and Credit and Thrift Societies. Research and academic institutions are also playing a vital role by addressing the issue of developing people-friendly hardware and software technologies for human welfare or modifying and adapting existing technologies for their application in development. The business sector is also increasingly realizing the responsibility of ensuring the development of the common men, especially those affected. Last but not the least, important are the target communities, the deprived or the marginalised, forming the most important stakeholder in the process of development.

This chapter will show how the corporate sector is developing programmes of social investments that have made a significant difference in developing strategies that are more economically vibrant, have social stability, and a healthier, more engaged citizenry. Now there is the need for the corporate sector in India to develop innovative and sustainable funding mechanisms, mobilize core competencies, develop partnerships, and undertake community capacity building efforts. The changing role of the corporate sector is outlined here:

From Philanthropy to Social Investment

1. *Money: from cash donations to innovative funding mechanisms;*
2. *In-kind support: from ad hoc approaches to mobilizing core competencies;*
3. *From public relations to building partnerships; and*
4. *From charity to community capacity building.*

The social performance of corporations has garnered considerable attention from scholars and industry observers alike. Such focus has helped raise awareness among those in the business community that a firm is dependent upon the goodwill of society—which can either sustain or impair a company's existence. Corporate Social Performance (CSP) or Corporate Social Responsibility (CSR) as the extent to which an organization meets the needs, expectations, and demands of certain constituencies beyond those directly linked to the firm's products and markets.

The corporate sector cannot replace the government or community organizations as funders or policy designers but they can bring special capacities to a partnership in social development. They possess a focused energy and goal orientation that can help galvanize their other partners. Corporate can 'make a difference' in areas of social development such as local enterprise development, improvements to the environment, contributions to rural development, to unemployment problem, to health, to education, etc. The following section outlines 16 case studies from the corporate sector, 16 from NGO's and 4 case examples of Corporate-NGO Partnership. Apart from this, a 'Rolling Plan' by company for social development is given here to establish the rationale of paradgim shift of corporate sector participation in social development.

Corporate Social Development in Practice : Case Studies

Case 1. Bajaj Auto Ltd.

Bajaj Auto Ltd. is the two and three wheeler giant in India. The company is known for its ethical business practices and good corporate citizenship. Bajaj Auto Ltd. has a long tradition in CSR. It supports a large number of community development programmes in Maharashtra (where it has three manufacturing plants) through the Jankidevi Bajaj Gram Vikas Sanstha. Bajaj Auto is also a member of Prince of Wales Business Leaders Forum.

Areas of Operation: Bajaj Auto carries out social development activities mainly at two levels:

(i) Through Samaj Seva Kendra by providing loans to its employees from nearly rural areas for lift irrigation schemes.
(ii) Through Jankidevi Bajaj Gram Vikas Sanstha {JBGVS), a trust formed in 1987.

Community development activities are carried out in both Pune and Aurangabad districts of Maharashtra. The following activities are carried out for social development:

(1) Agriculture and dairy development;
(2) Health and family welfare;
(3) Educational programmes;
(4) Environmental sanitation programme;
(5) Women and child development; and
(6) Income generation programmes.

JBGVS and Samaj Seva Kendra have been able to establish partnership between the community, government agencies and local industries in Pune and Aurangabad districts. This partnership has opened up new opportunities for the poor to come out of poverty and live a healthy and productive life, as responsible citizens of the country.

Bajaj Electricals Ltd. of the Bajaj Group is also carrying on developmental works in the field of women's welfare, rural development, rural healthcare and other welfare activities. Public expectations from business have changed. It is reasoned that the institution of business exists only because it satisfies the valuable needs of society. Therefore, if business wishes to remain viable in the long run, it must respond to the society's needs and give the society what it wants. Objective is carried forward by this corporate house successfully

Case 2. Glaxo & Wellcome India Ltd.

Glaxo and Wellcome India, a premier pharmaceutical company, is actively involved in community development and related activities in social development. Since the 1970s, the company has been implementing various social responsibility programmes. These are earned out through its social work unit situated at its Head Office in Mumbai.

Areas of Operation: The programmes undertaken by the social work unit are:

1. Community Development
   (i) The Shishukalyan Snehi Swayamsevak Sanstha, which operates in the Koliwada area of Worli, Mumbai.
   (ii) Quality Streets Circle, which promotes a healthy civic environment in the neighbourhood.
   (iii) Gramin Arogya Vikas Sanstha, which works in Dhondbar village in Sinnar taluka, Nashik district.
2. Promoting health awareness,
3. Support to voluntary bodies,
4. Medical education, and
5. Charitable and community support by Glaxo Wellcome plc. UK.

The Shishukalyan Snehi Swayamsevak Sanstha is a registered charitable trust started by Glaxo in 1979, the International Year of the Child. It aims at promoting the physical, intellectual, emotional and psychological development of needy persons, especially children who are deprived of opportunities such as basic education, healthcare and recreation. The Arogya Kendra of the Sanstha provides medical aid, a nutritional supplement programme for 70 children attending the local Balwadi and educational sponsorship for needy and deserving students, especially girls. Quality Streets Circle is an association of over 25 business establishments located around the company headquarters in Worli with an objective to maintain a clean and healthy civic environment in the neighbourhood. The company has been the employer of large number of disabled persons in all its four factories, has won awards from voluntary bodies, and has got recognition from the government for the same.

The company supports needy organizations by way of cash donations, advertisements in publications and medicines. Registered voluntary organizations, which are recognized for their developmental work revolving around disadvantaged population, are the recipients of such support and donations. The Jayaben Mody Hospital in Ankleshwar, the Aparna Trust in Haryana, and the Cancer Patients Aid Association in Mumbai are some of the recipients of financial support from Glaxo. In selecting projects to support, priority is given to those, which improve healthcare and promote scientific and medical education. Initiatives in the field of visual and performing arts are also supported. Thus, the firm, which is most responsive to the improvement of community quality life, will as a result have a better community in which to conduct its business.

Case 3. Hero Honda Motors Ltd.

Hero Honda's approach towards development is through assimilation of the rural sub-systems of the country to the main stream of development. The company believes in community participatory approach of development by creating awareness about health, education and removal of poverty.

Areas of Operation : The company, pertaining to community development, undertook the following programmes:

(1) *Employment Generating Programme* : A vocational training centre was started in February 1993 with the view to train the rural women for gainful employment.

(2) *Education Programme* : The company started a school in July 1992 called Raman Munjal Vidya Mandir to cater to the educational needs of the children of the company employees/its ancillaries/surrounding areas in Dharuhera in Rewari district of Haryana.

(3) *Rural Health Project :* The company runs a medical centre situated in the factory premises in Dharuhera. It launched the mobile clinic project in 1991 to provide comprehensive healthcare at the doorstep of the rural masses.

(4) *Promoting Health Awareness :* The company has been carrying out HIV/AIDS awareness programme at work place for over 3 years now in conjunction with CII.

(5) *Donations :* The company has made donations to various developmental activities in Rewari.

The basic approach towards development of the company in a large agrarian economy like India has been through the involvement and assimilation of the rural sub-systems of the main stream of development. By doing so, the company can increase rural income, generate employment and can provide basic amenities in the rural areas.

Case 4. ITC Ltd.

The core emphasis of ITC is to promote art and culture, education, sports and environment, apart from developmental activities in the areas it operates, that is across the country.

Areas of Operation : The area in which the company is involved are the following :

(1) *Community Development :* At ITC's factories in Saharanpur, Munger, Bangalore and Kolkata, involvement with the community is through various welfare schemes including immunization programmes, creation of awareness on family planning, vocational guidance courses, construction of bus shelters, providing for the handicapped, setting up libraries, organization of blood donation and eye camps.

(2) *Art and Culture :* ITC's unique contribution has been the establishment of the Sangeet Research Academy to revitalize and preserve Hindustani classical vocal music. The *Guru-Shishya parampara* is the institutional framework of the academy.

(3) *Education :* ITC units support local educational institutions with funds, infrastructure development and equipment. At Tiruvottiyur near Chennai, the Nehru Matriculation Higher Secondary School, supported by the Packaging and

Printing Division, began in 1967. Today it has 1150 students and 50 staffs. The Tribeni Tissues Vidyapith in West Bengal, which started as a primary school for employees' children in 1962, has grown to be a Council for the Indian School Certificate, affiliated institution with 50 per cent of the students coming from adjoining areas.

(4) *Environment* : The 'Green Guntur' project is now a model case study. Working in tandem with municipal authorities, government departments and local organizations, ITC has planted 50,000 avenue plants and distributed 175,000 fruit saplings in Guntur, Andhra Pradesh. Preserving and recycling natural resources, planting saplings and anti-pollution drives are among its initiatives.

The Farm Forestry programme is being scaled up by the company in partnership with the government of Andhra Pradesh. Select NGOs and ITC Bhadrachalam carry the potential of creating 40,000 jobs in the backward tribal regions of Andhra Pradesh. This programme also provides an alternate remunerative opportunity to the farmers, now increasingly relevant in the context of the overflowing granaries.

(5) *Sports* : ITC is the largest sponsor of sports in India. It has brought to the country international sporting fixtures like the Wills World Cup in 1996, the Gold Flake Open Tennis Championship and the Wills Golf Tour.

The company's model of contribution to rural India in the tobacco sector encompassing the entire value chain from seed to smoke is being aggressively replicated in other crops. Over the last decade, the company has been engaged in linking the Indian farmer to world markets through the agri-exports of the International Business Division. The company is now engaged in imparting a new dimension to its rural partnership by leveraging information technology to elevate the Indian farmer to a much higher order of empowerment. This strategic initiative has already become one of rural India's largest internet-based interventions, reaching out to more than 1,20,000 farmers in one thousand villages through 235 *choupals* in the states of Madhya Pradesh, Karnataka and Andhra Pradesh.

Case 5. Larsen & Toubro Ltd.

Larsen & Toubro has for the last 25 years engaged in extending welfare services to a large number of people both within the outside the organization.

Areas of Operation : Some of the major activities undertaken by the company are outlined below :

(1) *Vikas* : The Village Improvement Knowhow and Skills is a project committed to improving the quality of life in a cluster of villages around L&T's cement plant at Awarpur in Maharashtra. Vikas undertakes activities in the field of agriculture, community welfare, health, etc.
(2) *Health Centre, Mumbai* : The company's health centre, located at Andheri, Mumbai, is a landmark for safe family planning service as well as services in the areas of mother and child care, immunization, leprosy and tuberculosis eradication, preventive health education, etc. The Health Centre is renowned and widely recognized in Mumbai for the extensive professional services being rendered for the last 25 years. It also runs a TB clinic in collaboration with Bombay Municipal Corporation (BMC), at Andheri, Mumbai.
(3) *Education* : L&T set up the L&T Institute of Technology (LTIT) in Mumbai in 1983. The company provides active support for funding and operating the Indian Institute for Production Management (IIPM) at Kansbahal in Orissa, which has been jointly promoted by ICICI (promoter), L&T and Government of Orissa (copromoters) and Usha Martin and Steel Authority of India (Associate promoters).

The company also provides welfare services to all its employees and their families at various locations. Activities through other NGOs supplement the work of the welfare departments. For example, L&T patronizes KRIPA Rehabilitation Centre for services to alcoholic and for close follow-up by the social counsellors from the company.

Case 6. Ranbaxy Laboratories Ltd.

Ranbaxy, one of the largest pharmaceutical companies in India, extends its business motives to social development through its sincere efforts in various developmental activities. Ranbaxy flagged off its first mobile healthcare van in 1980 to take healthcare to the doorsteps of the unprivileged communities in rural or urban slum areas of Punjab. This philanthropic mission was an express manifestation of Ranbaxy's concern and the sense of responsibility towards those who had little or no access to even basic health care. Ranbaxy Community Healthcare Society (RCHS), an independent registered society (in effect it is a company-promoted NGO), was created in 1994 with a corpus sponsored by Ranbaxy with an aim to carry on the initiatives on a long-term basis.

Areas of Operation : Currently, the society operates nine mobile health care units, which include a team of 38 representatives (11 doctors and 15 paramedicals), is located in the states of Punjab, Himachal Pradesh, Haryana, Madhya Pradesh and Delhi. The vans are equipped to provide a range of services and diagnostic checkups, especially for women. This emphasizes the importance of creating awareness and promoting community participation. RCHS works together with the government who provides vaccines, family planning material, iron/folic acid tablets, etc.

RCHS has also joined hands with CASP-PLAN (Delhi), an NGO working in Sangam Vihar, which is an unauthorized slum colony, and therefore does not receive government support. Healthcare being an important need, the two organizations have decided to pool their resources—CASP-PLAN will provide the premises and lab technicians, while Ranbaxy will pay the capital and running costs. The company also works with a number of other NGOs. In Punjab, the Maharaj Jagat Singh Medical Relief Society provides office premises for three of its mobile healthcare units besides sharing half of the revenue cost of running these vans. It also supports the health programme of Navjyoti Development Society and Environment Society of Haryana through RCHS. These organizations help mobilize the community and provide the much-needed healthcare.

The company contributes some money every year to a corpus fund of RCHS, depending on its own profits. The company also provides the Society with the following support :

(1) The company gives some medicines free of cost (the balance requirements are bought from the market).
(2) The personnel department of the company facilitates all personnel-related work of the Society, including payrolls, attendance, recruitment, etc.

(3) The company handles the Society's accounts.
(4) In five locations, the van is parked at the company's premises. The company also gives office and storage space.
(5) The company pays for the running costs of these offices and has provided furniture as well.
(6) The Socieity also uses the company's computers to compile data generate reports.

Ranbaxy has multiplied its efforts by cooperating with other NGOs and the government. The company focuses on healthcare which is synergistic with its own business.

Case 7. Steel Authority of India Ltd.

In line with its objective of prosperity with social development, Bhilai Steel Plant (BSP) has undertaken peripheral development activities since 1963.

Areas of Operation : The major categories of peripheral development works are :

(i) *Augmentation of drinking water supply* : This includes installation of hand pumps, sinking of wells, deepening of tanks, construction of Pachari Ghats, etc.
(ii) *Education* : This includes opening of Adult Education Centres, construction of school buildings, etc.
(iii) *Civil Construction* : Construction of approach roads, culverts, electrification of roads, construction of passengers waiting halls, community halls are some of the activities under this category.
(iv) *Health Facilities* : Under this category comes construction of buildings for health services, organizing general health check up camps, organization of eye camps, providing vaccines and health tablets, etc.
(v) *Cultural* : Activities in the area includes running of community services including literacy and cultural activities, promotion of folk art and cultural troupes, organizing sports programmes, etc. BSP has provided support for construction of community centres and cultural halls in several villages. It has also organized a rural festival of folk art and culture.

The planning and implementation of the peripheral development works and carried out in close association with the people's representatives of the area. Meetings on peripheral development are held with the Member of Parliament and the Members of the State Legislative Assembly whose constituency comes within a radius of 16 km of Bhilai and the mines. These specific works required in their areas are carried out after detailed discussions and all MLAs individually.

Major construction works done under infrastructural development schemes in the last four years include borewells for drinking water supply, construction of veterinary hospital in Sirsakala village, cultural hall in Newai village, construction of classrooms in schools for deaf and dumb and in school for mentally retarded children, installation of 45 hand pumps, etc. BSP gives support to Yogashram, Bhilai and Kishore Kirti Sabha.

Case 8. Tata Engineering & Locomotive Co. Ltd. (TELCO)

In Jamshedpur, TELCO's community development works get off to a modest start in seven slums in 1965. The initial thrust was on healthcare, education and on building roads to link the remote villages, which could only be approached by walking over the railway tracks. Currently the company's Community Services Division is made up of the Gram Vikas Kendra, the Parivar Kalyan Sansthan, the Nav Jagrat Manav Samaj and the Shiksha Prasar Kendra. While the Gram Vikas Kendra is in charge of integrated rural development focusing on the agriculture, water management, self-employment and afforestation programmes, the other societies specialize in healthcare, family welfare, rehabilitation of leprosy patients cured and education for the blind.

Areas of Operation : The major social development programmes of Telco are described below:

(1) *Revamping Agriculture :* The old age methods of cultivation followed by the farmers on the Chhotanagpur plateau are being totally revamped under the company's agri-development programmes through multi-cropping system.

(2) *Water Management Network :* Telco has collaborated with the government and constructed a vast network of ponds (249), Check Dams (5), Lift Irrigation Projects (9), Tube wells and wells (100) over the last few years. Over 12,000 families have been benefited from these projects.

(3) *Resurrecting the Forest* : Depletion of forest resources in the Chhotanagpur plateau has been massive. A huge amount has been so far spent on the programmes to resurrect forest cover by the company, the government, and the local community.

(4) *Parivar Kalyan* : Parivar Kalyan Sansthan has been a remarkable success in implementing its comprehensive family planning programmes, which include counselling and the distribution of birth control aids. The company's Mother and Child Care Centres have also set the target to bring down the maternal mortality rate and reduce the net fertility rate from 2.4 per thousand to one by the year 2000. The Sansthan's new projects include anti-drugs campaign targeting vulnerable school children, AIDS awareness programme for adults and community based rehabilitation of the blind.

(5) *Leprosy Eradication* : For the eradication of leprosy, which is endemic in the Sighbhum region, the company has formed the Nav Jagrat Manav Samaj. The Samaj takes care of 4000 leprosy patients in Jamshedpur. The company is also doing rehabilitation of these patients through various self-employment schemes. In addition, the Samaj is implementing the government's leprosy eradication programme, called SET (Survey, Education, Treatment), in 214 villages in the Ichagarh and Nimdih blcoks of Singhbhum.

(6) *Health Services to Rural Communities* : Telco's Community Development Department, Mobile Medical Society and the Department of Industrial Health work together to run a Mobile Medical Hospital providing health services to a group of 16 villages situated in the remote region of the upper basin of river Bhama in Khed Taluka, near Pune, Maharashtra.

(7) *Social Awareness in Villages* : The Community Development Department has set up primary education and vocational training centres and training staff to man these centres, harnessing alternative sources of energy, improving rural sanitary conditions in Pune.

(8) *Rural Development* : Telco's rural development project has been successful in stemming the flow of migration of rural

youth from the rural areas to urban centres in Pune. It has set up Vocational Training Centre at village Pimpri, Budruk for this purpose. The Shiksha Prasar Kendra has funded the infrastructure development project of various schools. Telco has several programmes for the development of tribal people.

Case 9. The TATA Iron & Steel Company Ltd. (TISCO)

The Tata Iron and Steel Company (TISCO) first established a social welfare scheme in 1916 to provide assistance in the rural areas surrounding the town of Jamshedpur, Bihar. The Tata Steel Rural Development Society (TSRDS) itself is an NGO with a strong business ethos focusing on education and literacy, health and medical activities, agriculture and irrigation, drinking water, vocational training, and income generation.

TISCO's multifarious social service programmes are implemented through three formally institutionalized and professionally structured departments, viz. Family Initiatives, Community Development & Social Welfare and the Tribal Harijan Welfare Cell.

Areas of Operation : TSRDS has made rapid progress in strengthening the socio-economic fabric of rural community by adopting and designing programmes in over 700 villages in the vicinity of the company's business operations in Bihar, Orissa and Madhya Pradesh. After 10 years of operations, the Society's managers decided to change the way they work. These changes include participatory development, accountability, top management support, etc.

The company has a formal, written policy on corporate social responsibility. It has identified social responsibility as a 'key business process' equal to the other seven business processes that define the way the company works. Its welfare departments are equal to the personnel or marketing departments of the company. The Society has become sustainable because it has achieved the very difficult task of ensuring that the local community is a stakeholder in these projects. It has involved the people so that they have to contribute money, labour, or kind (material goods).

Corporate social responsibility at TISCO is, therefore, not a peripheral activity that could be taken up "if resources permit" but a key to business process.

Case 10. Titan Industries Ltd.

Titan industries is a joint venture between the House of Tatas and the Tamil Nadu Industrial Development Corporation. Titan has evolved a written policy to guide its development work.

Areas of Operation : The major area of involvement of the company are the following :

(1) *Employment for the Disabled* : Titan employees several disabled persons in its factories in Hosur, Tamil Nadu. The ability to perform a task is given priority over desired rate of output. In its Hosur and Dehra Dun plants, the company provides employment to a total of 198 disabled persons, 154 of whom are hearing impaired, 6 are visually impaired and 38 are movement impaired.

(2) *The Titan Scholarship Scheme* : The scholarship scheme was started in 1989 with the objective of providing assistance on a non-denominational basis purely on criteria of merit and need to deserving students in the Dharmapuri district of Tamil Nadu to pursue undergraduate and postgraduate courses in various fields.

(3) *Other Developmental Activities* : Under the aegis of the Tata Council of Community Initiatives, Southern Regional Council, Titan has participated in various community development programmes including a pilot waste management project in association with an NGO group in Bangalore. In association with NGOs, a community based rehabilitation unit providing physiotherapy services to the disabled in thirty villages has been established. The company has implemented a scheme for the outworking of watch strapping and dispatch operations through Myrada, a voluntary organization, thus generating work for rural youth and stemming migration. It was associated with a project to raise funds for Child Relief and You (CRY) making rupees 8,00,000 available.

Titan works through NGOs and not by itself because the core competence of such agencies is community development. The company uses certain criteria to select an NGO :

(1) Working in the same fields as listed in the company's guidelines;

(2) Working in the geographical region where the company has its operations (mainly, the Dharmapuri district of Tamil Nadu);
(3) A well-established NGO with a clearly defined and well-conceived project; and
(4) Having a good track record and a clean images.

Case 11. Dabur India Limited

Sustainable Development Society (SUNDESH), set up by Dabur India Limited with its managerial, technical and financial support in 1993, is a registered voluntary organization. The organization is pledged to integrated development through carrying out research and welfare activities to make community self-reliant, self-governed through healthcare programme and other need based development activities in the operational area.

The important programmes areas of its activities cover health with special concern for mother and child, non-formal education, income generation (training on-tailoring, bee keeping, mushroom farming etc.) and the community organization to bring stability. Its operates in 11 villages of Dholana block of Gaziabad District of Uttar Pradesh. The company implements various social welfare activities with an aim to minimize the persisting imbalance in different sectors of the society.

Areas of operation : The focus areas of the company are briefly described below :

(1) Health : a mobile clinic has been running in coordination with Chunni Lal Medical Trust in 5 villages of Nidhwali, Chouna, Basatpur, Parpa and Nagla Gaju for providing preventive and curative services to the villages.
(2) Education : Non-formal education centre was started on 14th November 1994, in village Piplera with strength of 32 students. Children are attending classes between the age group of 6-14 years. Health checkups of students are being done on a regular basis. Total enrolled students are 150 and out of these, 31 students were admitted in the formal school.
(3) Income Generation : Tailoring Training Centres are running at villages Shoulana and Samana. Women successfully completed the training programmes on tailoring. All the

trained women are now engaged in production of uniforms through a self-help group.

(4) *Self-help Group* : The self-helped group was established in 1997. Trained women from a tailoring centre formed this group for their economic development.

(5) *Bee-keeping* : The bee-keeping project, which started in 1995, gives training to beneficiaries. The beneficiaries are already doing division by making boxes with local available material. It is excepted that for project area the bee-keeper will be opting for boxes which will give a high yield.

Dabur India Limited has committed itself to the task of providing value for money healthcare products to its consumers.

Case 12. ICICI Limited

ICICI has played an enabling role in the development of the commercial sector in India and has also extended this role to the social sector. For many years now, ICICI has invested capital and human resources in providing support and catalyzing various development initiatives in healthcare, rural advancement, aiding the physically and mentally challenged as well as providing management and technical assistance to the social sector.

Areas of Operation : Most of ICICI's attention will focus on identifying and supporting initiatives in :

(i) Universalizing primary education,
(ii) Reduction of infant mortality rates,
(iii) Micro-finance, and
(iv) Application of information technology and other technologies to facilitate the above faster.

The main aim has been to identify and support initiatives, which are designed to improve the capacity of the poorest of the poor to participate in the larger economy. These initiatives must be cost effective, measurable in impact, capable of large-scale replication and should have the potential for both near and long-term impact. Some of the initiatives supported by ICICI are :

(1) *Education* : *'Pratham'*—a primary education programme designed to tackle the problem of urban illiteracy, has

addressed the issues of scale successfully as is testified by its coverage of nearly 100,000 children per day in the city of Mumbai.

(2) *Eklavya Foundation* : Eklavya in Madhya Pradesh has been actively involved in designing innovative curriculums, teaching methodologies and educational material for science, social science and primary education.

(3) *Mass Media* : ICICI has explored the opportunities offered by different media for the purpose of universalizing primary education.

(4) *SEARCH, Gadchiroli, Maharashtra* : The Society for Education, Action and Research in Community Health has been working on various aspects of community health, especially women and child health, for the last few years. It has designed and implemented several interventions in around 53 villages in Gadchiroli district.

(5) *Micro-finance* : Bharatiya Samruddhi Finance Limited (BASIX) is an innovative micro-finance institution that meets the credit needs of the poor in districts of Andhra Pradesh and Karnataka. Samruddhi reaches the poor through its customer service representatives who function on an incentive based on the recovery of loans and the amount of loans. The loans are given against personal background and the ability of the borrower to repay rather than a collateral or a security.

Case 13. Infosys Technologies

Infosys Technologies is one of India's fastest growing information technology (IT) companies. Commitment to society is among the core-values of Infosys. Towards its social initiatives, the company set up the 'Infosys Foundation' in the year 1996. The company has committed one per cent of its after-tax profits to the Foundation, whereby Rs. 36 lakh will be available in quarterly instalment. So far, the Foundation has not needed to hire any full-time people because its work needs are met through the services of a retired executive.

The money is distributed in two ways : The first gives 30 per cent of the funds to old people, the destitute and the handicapped; 15 per cent for rural development ; 30 per cent for the education of brilliant but poor children; 15 per cent for cultural activities like plays, music and drama; and 10 per cent for medical relief, both in villages and cities. The second method of distribution is as follows. Infosys has offices in four states : Karnataka (Bangalore), Maharashtra (Pune), Orissa (Bhubaneshwar) and Tamil Nadu (Chennai). The Foundation's money is distributed according to the tario of employees working in these four states. The Foundation prefers to give money to smaller NGOs, who are equally deserving but do not have the public image and hence the access to funds that larger agencies have.

Areas of Operation : The Foundation functions under a Board of Trustees and undertakes projects such as healthcare, education, community development, preservation of art and culture, etc.

(1) *Education* : The Shalegondu Granthalaya (a library for every school) programme has been helping schools in villages set up their own libraries. The Foundation has donated five lakh rupees for the construction of Shisuvihar for the Vidyalaya Gurukula which works to improve the lot of destitute children.
(2) *Healthcare for the poor* : The Foundation has built a brain fever ward for the children in Bellary, called the "Infosys Infant Ward", a cancer hospital in Kanchilpuram, Tamil Nadu, and an OPD for poor patients in Aurangabad, Maharashtra.

Infosys has a three-floor main office on a 100-acre campus outside Bangalore. This is cleaned by 25 poor women who come from the local community. The otherwise hi-tech company has deliberately hired these cleaning women to generate employment. However, the company has restricted its social work to giving money through the Foundation. Each annual report of the company has a theme. For 1996-97, it was 'Social Responsibility of the Corporate Body.' Five pages were devoted to talking about why companies in general should be involved in social development and the role of Infosys in this regard. Infosys demonstrates the importance of organizing a company's socially responsible activities in the same systematic manner that companies organize their normal business processes.

Case 14. Mahindra and Mahindra

The Mahindra and Mahindra Limited, one of the largest private sector companies in India, set up the K.C. Mahindra Education Trust in 1953. It was established for promoting education among Indians at all levels.

Areas of Operation : During the last 40 years, 600 meritorious students have been the recipients of the renowned K.C. Mahindra Scholarships for Post Graduate Studies Abroad in subjects that would benefit our country. In 1983, the Mahindra Search for Talent Scholarships was envisaged and since then has been established in 34 education institutions, including schools and colleges in India to encourage and enthuse the students and reward their excellence in academics. The K.C. Mahindra Education Trust established the Mahindra All India Talent Scholarships in 1995 to award scholarships to students belonging to lower income families with good scholastic record pursuing job-oriented diploma courses and vocations in various polytechnics in India.

Deprived girls at Ramakrishna Mission in Kolkata receive scholarships from the Trust every year to enable them to undergo nurses' training and secure lucrative jobs. Keeping in mind the deplorable status of a large percentage of female children in India with general lack of access to opportunities, the Mahindra Girl Child Project—Nanhi Kali was launched in 1996. Through this scheme, the Trust sponsors the primary education and the general welfare of 100 underprivileged girls across the rural and urban parts of the country. The Trust reaches out of these children through various voluntary agencies and organizations and regularly assesses and monitors their activities. To take the project more participatory and involving, individual sponsorship is encouraged wherein individual donors 'adopt' the Nanhi Kali's education and give them a fighting change in life. There are numerous NGOs and voluntary agencies that are doing extensive community-based development work through which the Nanhi Kali sponsorship project is extended to the girl child.

Case 15. Lupin Laboratories

Lupin Labortories launched an integrated rural development programme on October 2, 1998 in 35 villages of Alwar and Bharatpur district in Rajasthan. This programme was run by a company-sponsored NGO called Lupin Human Welfare and Research Foundation. The main objectives of the programme are :

(1) To provide an income of Rs. 1000 a month to each working

person by increasing the resources available to people through better use of the government's various schemes.

(2) To improve social indicators of the villagers by increasing access to health and education. Also, to change the social attitudes of people by removing social ills like dowry, denial of education to women, negative attitudes to family planning, etc.

(3) To improve rural infrastructure such as roads, school buildings, water bodies, etc.

Areas of Operation : The company collaborated with the government, local NGOs, banks and the beneficiaries to come up with an integrated approach. The government has the infrastructure and the resources. The corporate sector could provide the management skills and scientific temper. NGOs are closer to the people and know their needs. Therefore, an integrated approach combining all three sectors was considered ideal. Lupin asked the villagers to organize themselves and appoint a 'Lupin Gram Vikas Panchayat,' which decides and prioritizes the village needs. It chooses the appropriate government scheme and helps the villagers to get the government to pay its share. Finally, if there is a shortfall, the Foundation pays the balance.

It is the firm belief of the organization that economic and social development should go together not sequentially but jointly at the same time. The organization is working since its inception in 1988 for the fulfilment of national goal on primary education and health.

Case 16. Indian Aluminium Company Limited (INDAL)

INDAL is known for its commitment to the welfare of the communities that live in proximity to its plants. Working for the weaker sections of communities forms a part of the company's core values. INDAL social projects are now carried out under the aegis of the Aditya Birla Centre for Community Initiatives and Rural Development.

Areas of Operation : The main focus of the company is on healthcare, spreading literacy and sustainable livelihood.

(i) To provide healthcare to people in extremely remote areas, INDAL organizes medical camps in the interiors of Lohardaga, Muri in Jharkhand, Belgaum in Karnataka and Radhanagari in Maharashtra. On project work, INDAL partners with the local NGOs, district level government bodies and primary health centres.

(ii) INDAL espouses adult education and support balwadis which are non-formal education centres. Adult literacy programmes are conducted at several locations at INDAL's Adult Education Centres.

(iii) One important project in terms of social importance and wide coverage has been the Women's Empowerment programme undertaken at Radhanagari, Maharashtra, near the company's bauxite mines at Durgmanwadi. The programmes are being implemented in partnership with a local NGO, which runs the INDAL sponsored Skills Tranining Centre, Yashogami. Yashogami has encouraged women to start selling their handmade articles in village fairs organized for the purpose. It can be expected that 50 per cent of the women who have been imparted skills training can utilize the same for income generation.

(iv) To create sustainable employment for the local communities, the company has taken two major measures. Firstly, the company encourages income generating schemes, which include dairy development projects, mushroom cultivation, pisciculture, piggery and carpet weaving. INDAL also provides extensive training to village women in various skills such as tailoring, candle making, weaving and knitting.

For the year 2000-2001, INDAL has invested around Rs. 8 million towards social welfare and community-oriented projects. The company's involvement has made a palpable difference to the lives of the inhabitants where the company operates.

The above 16 case studies of the corporate sector suggest that social development can be an integral part of the business ethics. Employee involvement and top management commitment can make a significant difference. Therefore, corporate involvement in social causes can be executed with the same degree of care and planning as in the case of business interests. Social development can be an integral part of the business ethics at all times. And it is also a good idea to involve the local communities and beneficiaries in CSD for a better synergy. The more the companies and NGOs harness available government schemes and funds, development would get a real fillip.

Corporate responsibility as depicted by these companies is to adhere to ethical and environment friendly practices. Companies are inclined to stick to the triple bottom lines—of economic, social and environmental responsibility towards workers, the shareholders and the community. The aim here was to assess the existing practices of the companies towards social responsibility to support the empirical findings. Important means of assessing social needs and expectations relative to these companies include social forecasting, opinion surveys, issues management, social scanning and social audits. Assessment of the social impact of a company's activities, an evaluation of programmes specifically aimed at achieving social goals, and a determination of areas in need of organizational action has been key to the sustainability of various social developmental programmes cited in the above case studies.

6.4 NGO Case Studies

Case 1. CINI (Child in Need Institute)

Established in 1976, CINI is an implementing NGO located in West Bengal. The main focus of activity includes various areas of child welfare. Resources are mobilized from government sources, both central and state, and from donations.

Objectives

(1) To promote health and nutrition programmes for children; and

(2) To undertake programmes for street workers' children and children prostitutes.

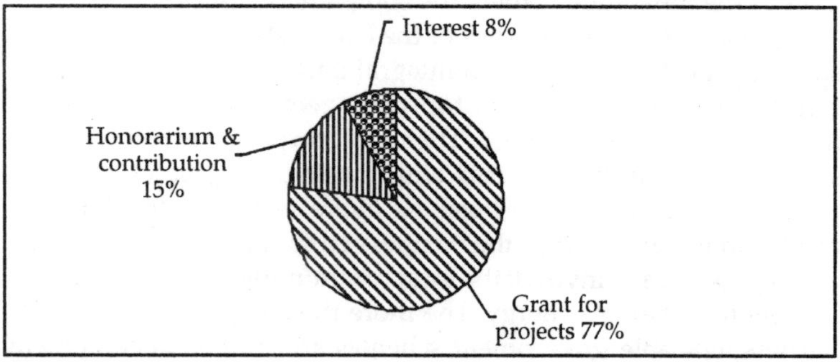

Fig. 6.2 : NGO Case -1

Programmes

1. Awareness generation about child welfare.
2. Education and training programmes for poor children.
3. Need-based programmes to improve the quality of life in terms of basic living standards.

Case Example-1

Jahangir, a male peer educator, has been working for the past two and a half years in two villages of Kamarpole and Lakhapara area in Diamond Harbour. He discusses reproductive health issues like ante-natal, post-natal and child care, sharing workload during pregnancy, importance of male participation in child care, maintaining personal hygiene, adoption male methods of family planning (both temporary and permanent methods), counselling on prevention of sexually transmitted diseases and HIV infection and safer sexual behaviours. Jahangir himself had undergone vasectomy to convince his peers in the villages concerned. After intensive counselling on the need of discussion between the partner regarding family spacing, men voluntarily asked condoms from him and also advises on permanent method of male sterilisation. He was able to dispel their myths and misconceptions regarding vasectomy. Jahangir has become a role model for the entire community through his tireless work towards increasing gender sensitisation of men.

Case Example-2

Manobesh Duari, a boy from South Amgachia village, a remote village in South 24 Paraganas District, was sponsored by SAHAY Child Sponsorship Programme. The poor economic conditions of his family forced him to discontinue his studies after reaching class XI. His parents were unable to support him in his pursuit of higher studies with their meagre monthly income. The programme provided him with financial support and special guidance (private coaching) to help him continue his education. Manobesh passed his Higher Secondary examination with flying colours and enrolled himself in Mathematics Honours course. He is now doing B.E. in Electronics and Telecommunication at Jadavpur University after getting through the Joint Entrance Examination. Manobesh believes that he will definitely reach his goals with his sincere efforts and support of the Sponsorship Programme, which has helped him dream about his future.

Case 2. UNNATI Organization for Development of Education

Unnati, a support and implementing agency active in Gujarat, was set up in 1990. It is active all over Gujarat and some part of Rajasthan. The main theme of this organization is development.

Objectives

1. To promote the practice of participatory principles, gender and social justice in the process of social development;
2. To create a support base for individuals engaged in rural development; and
3. To strengthen, support and facilitate grassroots initiatives in diverse spheres such as health, education, income generation and awareness building.

Programmes

1. Education and training.
2. Policy advocacy and advice.
3. Research and surveys.

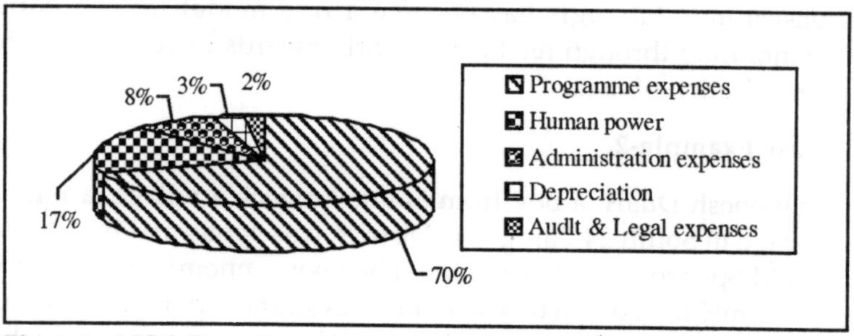

Fig. 6.3 : NGO Case -2

Promotion of Community Based Livelihood Activities

In an ongoing effort, UNNATI extended support to promote community participation in programmes for ten clusters of villages—six clusters for on-farm livelihood and the remaining four clusters for off-farm livelihood—in the desert region.

The support for community participation in planning and

execution of programme was extended in these villages to local voluntary organisations. These were : Magara Mewar Vikas Sansthan (MMVS), Godward Gramin Vikas Sansthan (GGVS) in Pali, Shanti Maitri Mission (SMM) in Bikaner, Shrijamyaham in Jaisalmer, Research Institute of Plenary Rural Development (RIPROD) in Jhalore, Gramin Vikas Sodh Evam Takniki Kendra (GVSTK) in Tonk, Artisans Alliance Jawaja (AAJ) in Ajmer, Kalakar Vikas Samiti (KVS) in Nagor, Prakruti Foundation in Banswada, and Society for Sustainable Development (SSD) in Karouli.

The Case of Naverabera

Discriminatory practices in schools against dalit students continue to prevail in Rajasthan. In Naverabera village of Balotra block, teachers of a primary school used to address dalit students as 'dheriyas', an abusive word. When parents of these children with the support of the village committees, objected, the school expelled the students. After waiting in vain for four days for the school authorities to retract the expulsion, the parents first lodged a complaint with the Collector and with the support of one of the associate member (IDEA) of the Dalit Adhikar Abhyan, they went public and narrated the incident at a press conference.

Following this, an inquiry team comprising of the District Education Officer (DEO) and Tehsildar visit the school and found that discriminatory practices were definitely prevalent in the school. They chided the teachers and asked them to apologise to the villagers. The committee then requested the dalits to compromise and sort out the situation amicably. But later in its written report, the committee rejected the complaint, stating that no instances of discrimination were found in the school.

The case was again put up to the SDM, Balotra with support of NGOs. The SDM's report did acknowledge the presence of discriminatory practices and a First Information Report (FIR) was logged against the school principal and teachers. It was for the first time in government records that discrimination against dalits at public places was publicly accepted. But again a compromise took place on the assurance that the department would punish the teachers and the Collector would take responsibility of this.

However, the story did not end here. The atrocities against the dalits continued, first a dead crow was thrown inside the drinking water tank so that the dalit students would not be able to drink water. Then upper caste Hindus and Muslims decided that none of the provision stores of the village would sell anything to the dalit forcing the latter to travel 18 km to get provisions. The Panchayat functionaries also did not take up the issue. Representatives of dalit communities from nearby villages gather at the DRC and highlighted the matter in the media. This pressurized the district administration to take action. Finally, the teachers apologized in a village meeting attended by 200 people from the area and the case was withdrawn.

Although the case was not legally pursued, and it ended in a compromise, it was for the first time that discrimination against dalits was acknowledged and the upper caste publicly apologized.

Case 3. Myrada

Myrada, an implementing NGO, operates in Southern states of Karnataka, Andhra Pradesh and Tamil Nadu. It is an old organization, set up in 1968 and is active in the area of socio-economic development. Majority of funds come from foreign sources and some percentage is from government sources.

Objectives

1. To raise one million poor people above the poverty line by the year 2007 AD;
2. To shape an alternative vision of sustainable, humane development with equal rights to life;
3. To create awareness among the youth, women and the poor people; and
4. To initiate community-based motivational and socio-economic programmes in rural areas.

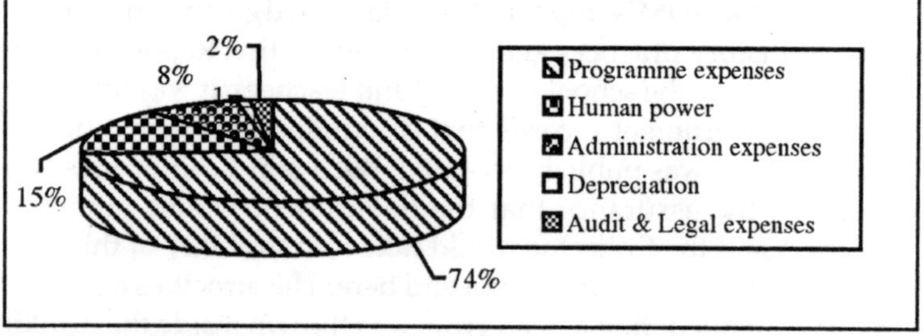

Graph 6.4 : NGO Case-3

Programmes

1. Education/training in the field of wasteland development, watershed development in the Southern states.
2. Awareness generation in health, nutrition and population issues.
3. Research and surveys in disaster management.
4. Project in technology development and assistance in rural technology and appropriate technology.
5. Income generation in rural areas through livestock management and enterprise development.
6. Micro-credit projects in rural areas of South India.

The agency believes in participatory approach of project implementation, which includes the population concerned, other NGOs, policy makers, industry and specific ecosystems.

Support to Local Initiative (SLI)

The programme on support of local initiatives aims at capacity building or/and support to civil society institutions and their leaders in respect of basic rights, livelihood and governance with a key thrust on people's participation, social and gender justice and accountability. Under this programme, people work during the year in close association with voluntary and people's organisations and community leaders.

Case 4. Sahbhagi Shikshan Kendra (SSK)

Established in 1990, SSK is active all over Uttar Pradesh. It is a support and implementing NGO, and 90 per cent of its funds come from foreign NGOs and funding agencies.

Objectives

1. To strengthen and develop capacities of organizations and people who are engaged in social change process;
2. To provide documentation and information in support of social action;
3. To promote cooperation and understanding among voluntary agencies working for rural communities; and
4. To impart education and training to young men and women for managing income generating and development activities.

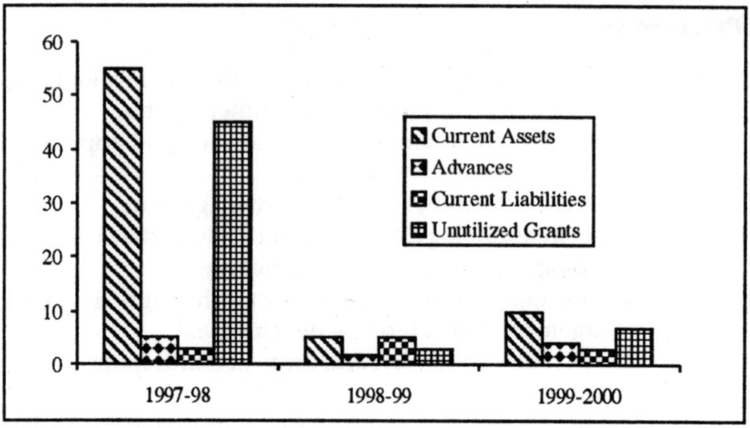

Graph 6.5 : NGO Case-4

Programmes

1. Educational and training programmes all over Uttar Pradesh, especially in rural areas.
2. Action-oriented research with people's participation.
3. Income generation programmes.
4. Programmes focusing on environment.

Target areas for these programmes are rural communities and backward communities. Successful implementation of these programmes is carried out through effective association with other NGOs engaged in social activities at the grassroots level. These projects are often long term in nature.

Case 5. SEARCH

SEARCH is an implementing agency based in Karnataka. It is an old organization in the field of social development and was formed way back in 1978. The main focus of activity of SEARCH is women and child welfare.

Objectives

1. To carry out welfare programmes for women and children;
2. To play a role in promoting practical programmes in areas of literacy and health; and

3. To improve the pace and quality of economic development, especially relating to the village and backward sector.

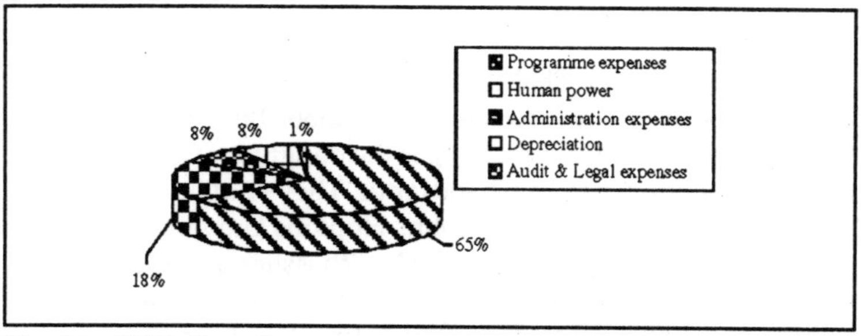

Fig. 6.6 : NGO Case -5

Programmes

1. Education and training programmes.
2. Provision of mobile creches.
3. Facilitating adoption programmes.
4. Project for women shelter.

The success for implementation is through women's participation and also the target groups. For the sustainability of these programmes diversified social issues are tackled in a focused area.

The Move to Gadchiroli

SEARCH was established in 1985 by a doctor couple, Abhay (physician) and Rani Bang (gynaecologist). They moved the following year from Wardha to the headquarters of Gadchiroli District to contribute to healthcare in the most underdeveloped part of the state. SEARCH envisaged the application to health problems of technical and managerial solutions that would emerge from community-based interaction and research.

Since their arrival with "an ambulance, three workers, two small children, and lots of ideas" [25] in 1986, SEARCH has seen a tremendous growth. From a warehouse provided by a prominent tradesman in 1986, by 1994 it had moved to its own complex ("Shodhgram", i.e. 'Search Village') 16 kms. from Gadchiroli town, the district headquarters. SEARCH now has 10 doctors , in addition to the Bangs themselves; 7 nursing staff; 115 Village Health Workers

(VHWs) and Supervisors; and around 15 administrative staff and social workers.

The Bangs and SEARCH

Abhay Bang's father Thakurdas is a prominent Gandhian. His family has been closely associated with Vinoba Bhave and Gandhi's Ashram at Wardha. Dr. Rani Bang is the daughter of a well-known medical practitioner from Chandrapur. They studied medicine at Nagpur, and have been to the Johns Hopkins University, USA for research. Their innovative work on health issues in Gadchiroli has been published in leading professional journals in India and abroad such as the Lancet, International Journal of Gynecology and Obstetrics, World Health Forum, WHO Bulletin, and the National Medical Journal of India, as well as general periodicals such as the Economic and Political Weekly and Manushi. Both have old family associations with some of the Governing Board Members.

SEARCH's contribution to tribal health has been recognized by the Maharashtra Government, which conferred the 'Adivasi Sevak' ('one who serves tribals') Award on Abhay Bang in 1989. Both the Bangs have been honoured by prominent Gandhian organizations.

The prime movers of SEARCH are the Bangs. This is formalized in their position as Director and Co-Director. Ostensibly, decisions are ratified or finalized in discussion with the staff. In effect, the ultimate decisions are theirs not merely by virtue of their formal positions and as founders, but by sheer force of personality. Although the strong hand of the Director in all that happens in SEARCH is palpable, there is constant dialogue and leadership by example. The Administrative Officer is Vijay Khati, a more recent recruit with a background in the voluntary sector elsewhere in Vidarbha.

Funds

From 1986 to 1991, SEARCH received around Rs. 4.5 million from various donors, mainly the Indian Council of Medical Research and the Ford Foundation. Funding increased three-fold to Rs. 15.5 million in the subsequent period upto 1994. External donors—chiefly Misereor and the MacArthur Foundation—provided the bulk of these funds. Other donors have included the World Health

Organisation (WHO), Oxfam, the Ashoka Foundation and some individuals. The complex's hospital generates some revenues through user charges. SEARCH is now well-established, and funding does not seem to be a constraint.

The development of community-based management of childhood pneumonia, which claims a million children, or one-third of all child deaths each year in India. in controlled trials reported in Lancet in 1990, rural parents were taught to suspect pneumonia and refer cases to the VHWs/Dais, who have been trained to treat it without further referral. Pneumonia deaths in the 58 catchment villages declined by 84 per cent in 2 years, with consequent reduction in infant mortality by 34 per cent. This was achieved at a greatly reduced cost in terns of medicines. A 'Breath Counter' device enables even illiterate Dais to diagnose pneumonia. WHO is promoting replication of this approach in other countries. Locally, in a reverse referral, some private practitioners are sending children with pneumonia to SEARCH's VHWs and Dais.

Case 6. VANI (Voluntary Action Network India)

VANI is a membership-based umbrella body for the voluntary sector, formed in 1988. The membership has increased to 236. These include several state and national level networks. VANI is concerned with voluntary organizations safeguarding and highlighting voluntarism and voluntary action.

Objectives

1. To strengthen voluntarism;
2. To provide fraternal support and strength to voluntary workers and organizations;
3. To provide a common platform for those concerned about various issues of development affecting the poor and the marginalized;
4. To be forum for sharing perspectives and analysis of local, national and international forces, laws, policies, programmes and structures;
5. To promote the values of democracy, gender equality and secularism in voluntary action;
6. To advocate on issues of concern; and
7. To coordinate campaigns on emerging issues.

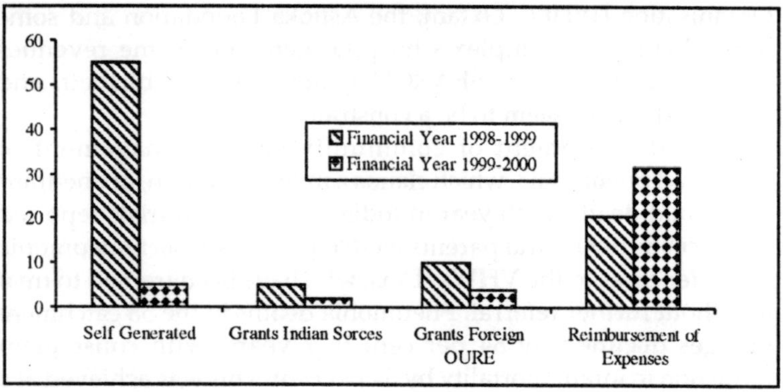

Fig. 6.7 : NGO Case-6

Programmes

1. Protection and promotion of political space for voluntary action—three task forces working on the Income Tax Act, Societies Registration Act/Public Trusts Act and FCRA, supported by regional and zonal level meetings.
2. A common platform for development issues—strengthening local self-governance through a series of workshops in different parts of the country on Panchayati Raj and the role of voluntary organizations.
3. Structural adjustment programmes—documentation includes a list of resource persons, series of workshops and seminars.
4. Low-priced publications in English and Hindi—task force reports, leaflets on communalism, etc. VANI News provides monthly updates on a wide range of voluntary activities.

ROLE VANI acts as a platform, network and association of voluntary action in India:

(i) As a platform, it promotes voluntarism and engenders political space for voluntary action.
(ii) As a network, it attempts to bring about a convergence of common sectoral issues and concerns for building a truly national agenda of voluntary action in the country.
(iii) Also as a network, it facilitates linking up of various efforts

and initiatives in the country for a multiplier effect, to create and sustain the process of change in an organic manner.

(iv) As an association, it works towards fostering value-based voluntary action and long-term sustainability among its members.

(v) Ever since its inception, VANI has been working constantly to promote voluntarism and for critical image building of the sector. It has been highlighting good, innovative work of voluntary activists, positive and negative developments in the voluntary sector, etc. through the VANI Newsletter, mainstream media, booklets, leaflets etc. various publications for debate and countering propaganda against voluntary sector was brought out after thorough research and analysis of information and data.

(vi) VANI has adopted the document "Guiding Principles for the Voluntary Development Organizations". The Guiding Principles would help the voluntary sector to firmly establish its creditability and effectively combat the misinformation campaign against it.

Case 7. NFI (National Foundation of India)

NFI is a national development support agency. It was registered as a non-profit charitable trust in 1992 by a group of concerned citizens drawn from the corporate sector, development organizations, community initiatives and research institutions that would mobilize public opinion and generate resources for supporting development action. The founders recognized the right of every Indian to lead a life of dignity and self-respect in a just and equitable society; and the need to improve the capacities of individuals and communities to improve the quality of their lives and enhance their ability to negotiate from the position of strength. A strength that would come from being educated, in good health and having the capacity to be engaged in productive work.

In the last few decades, voluntary organizations and community groups have emerged as strategic players on the development scene. Many of them base their work on the emerging needs of the community. However, unlike other organizations which focus their efforts on sectoral programmes, the foundation supports long-term development initiatives that arise out of the felt needs of the people. The foundation recognizes that the process of

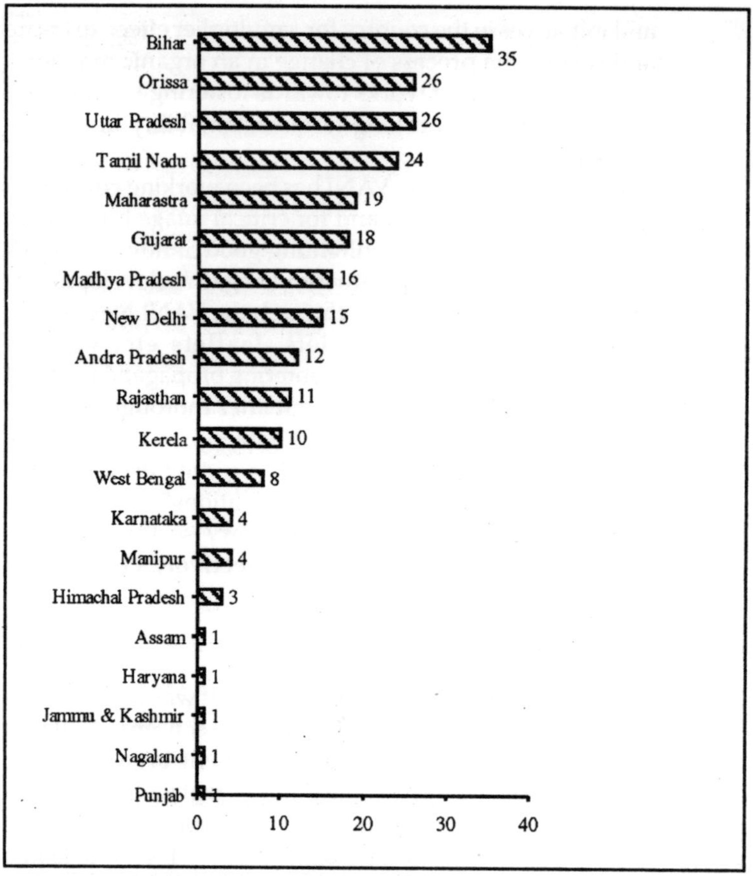

Fig. 6.8 : NGO Case-7

development is as important as the outcome. Within the above framework, the foundation is committed to work towards a synergy of different inputs as being necessary for a people-centred development strategy. It is a professionally managed body which identifies opportunities for financial support, monitors activities and provides systematic feedback.

Objectives

1. To work towards a synergy of different inputs as being necessary for a people centred development strategy; and

2. To mobilize public opinion and generate resources for supporting development action.

Programmes

1. Support to NGOs working in the fields of gender justice and equity, for example, supporting the Community Services Guild (CSG) project for the 'Eradication of Female Infanticide' in Salem district, Tamil Nadu.
2. Grant to National Law School of India, Bangalore for setting up 'The Child and the Law Centre' in partnership with UNICEF.
3. Public Affairs and Urban Governance, e.g. Support to SPARC, Mumbai for 'Strengthening Community Action for Improved Urban Governance in Maharashtra.'
4. Sustainable livelihoods, e.g. PARIVAR, a forum of grassroots NGOs in Udaipur.
5. Initiatives in the North East, e.g. supporting AVARD-NE for a project entitled 'Documentation and Development Initiatives on Majuli Island' in Assam, the largest riverine island in the world.
6. Media exchange programme provides for eight fellowships a year for journalists from the North East to be seconded to a national newspaper/television network.

The main achievements of the organization have been in the area of capacity building and education. The organization also promotes philanthropy through new ways of approaching philanthropy by reaching out to untapped groups within the society.

Programmes

The National Foundation for India perceives development as a people-centred process of empowerment of the poor and marginalized based on democratic values that ensures gender equity and justice, encourages pluralism and diversity in the society. The foundation looks at development from a rights perspective and firmly believes that the civil society bodies, and particularly the non-governmental (NGOs working closely with the communities), have a significant role in bringing about such transformation in the society.

NFI Innovations Fund: The foundation has housed a programme on innovation, particularly in three areas: Health, Volunteerism and Community Foundations in collaboration with Centre for Innovation in Voluntary Action (CIVA) and OXFAM-India.

Case 8. VHAI (Voluntary Health Association of India)

VHAI was founded in 1970 as a secular, apolitical, non-profit, registered, NGO, federating 24 State Level Voluntary Health Associations (SVHA) in the country. It is linked to over 4500 member institutions, affiliated to the SVHAs. It is a networking NGO.

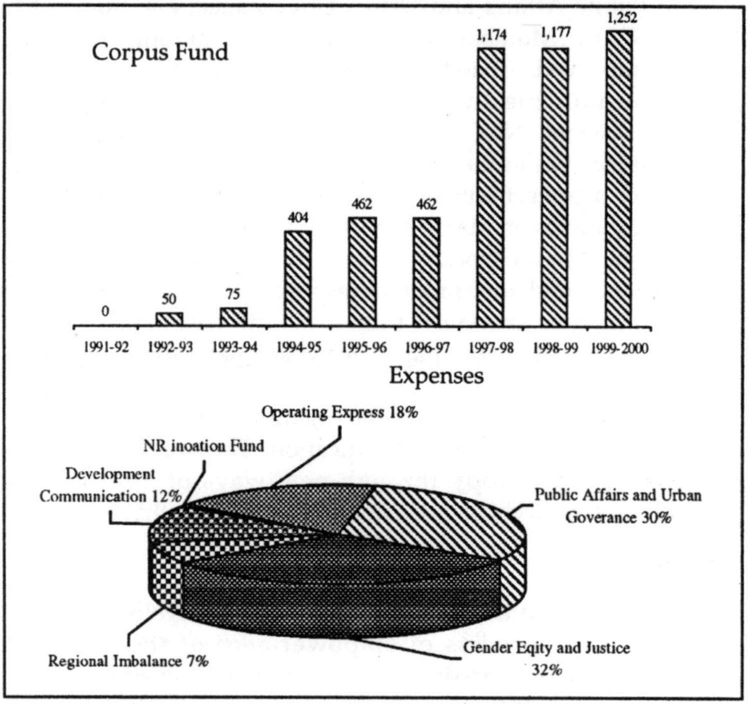

Fig. 6.9 : NGO Case-8

Objectives

1. To promote social justice, equity and human rights in the provision and distribution of health services;
2. To strengthen a people's health movement in the country; and

3. To advocate congenial policies and programmes aimed at improving the health status and quality of life of the people.

Programmes

1. Aparijita Orissa, a long-term rehabilitation of the cyclone victims.
2. Aparijita Gujarat, a relief and rescue operation of earthquake victims.
3. Networks proactively working with national and international development agencies, health activists, grassroots level NGOs.
4. Empowerment of the rural poor for better health in Shivpuri district of Madhya Pradesh and Sewapuri district of Uttar Pradesh.
5. Nine monographs for ICHI.
6. The KHOJ experiment was launched about 8 years ago in some of the least developed and difficult areas of the country.
7. The Greater Noida Project, a semi-urban health and development project.

These model programmes aimed at empowering marginalized communities through health and development interventions are becoming self-reliant and sustainable initiatives. Desired goals are achieved through campaigns, policy research, advocacy, need-based training, media and parliament interventions, and running of health and development projects in some difficult areas for evolving a sustainable health movement in India. The outreach of VHAI has steadily grown over the years to make it the apex voluntary organisation in the field of health promotion in the country. Presently in VHAI network, there are 24 State VHAs with total membership of more than 4000 NGOs. Besides, there are over 100,000 village workers in its fold.

Khoj Project Activities

Khoj projects were started as model projects in remote and most backward pockets of some of the Nothern and North-eastern States as well as Orissa, in view of their critically poor health and development status. The projects have an integrated approach with health as a major component. Presently, there are 17 Khoj projects which have made a significant positive impact on communities they have been serving.

The projects which receive constant technical support and guidance from VHAI are emerging as models which can be emulated by other developmental agencies across the country. To supplement visits from VHAI senior projects, a Khoj partners' meeting was also organized at VHAI. TB emerged as a major concern in all the projects. A SWOT analysis, discussions on future sustainability of the projects and an EZE-VHAI's study "Basic Needs: People's Perceptions" were some of the important outcomes.

Case 9. PRIA (Society for Participatory Research in Asia)

It is a research organization involved in training, information dissemination and networking which commenced activities in 1982. Its target groups are grassroots organizations, NGOs, people's, organizations and their networks, other support organizations; trade unions, cooperatives and other associations, consumer groups, institutions of local self-governance, national and state governments, academic institutions, private sector enterprises and international agencies.

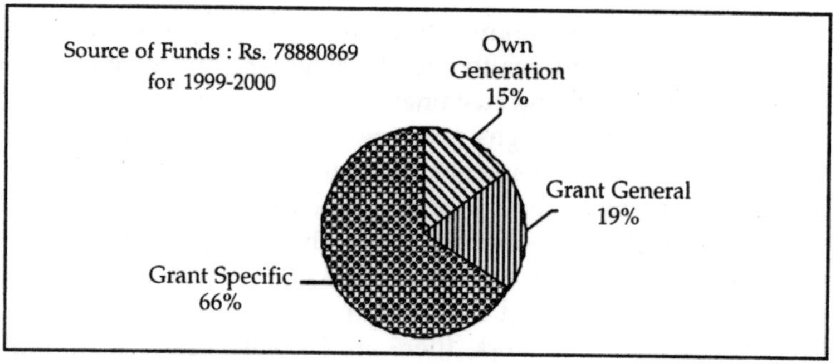

Fig. 6.10 : NGO Case-9

Objectives

1. To promote people-centred, holistic and comprehensive evolution of society characterized by freedom, justice, equity and sustainability;
2. To create opportunities and sharing, analyzing and learning among formations of civil society;

3. To engage in independent and critical analysis of societal trends and issues, development policies and programmes; and
4. To enable dialogue across diverse perspectives, sectors and institutions.

Programmes

There are four programme areas:

1. Centre for participation and governance promotes people-centred management of national parks and sanctuaries; promotion of participatory research and development through local grassroots groups and development agencies; to promote Panchayati Raj Institutions.
2. Centre for Occupational and Environmental Health focuses on health hazards at work places and those affecting communities. Computer database on occupational and environmental health within India and worldwide are being built.
3. Centre for Institutional Development had established the first ten-week development management training programme for senior staff of South Asian Voluntary Development Organizations in collaboration with Regional Support Organizations (RSOS) in areas of participatory training, planning and evaluation.
4. Centre for Global Alliance provides networking, monitoring and advocacy functions at regional, national and global levels.

Study on Civil Society in the New Millennium

The Commonwealth Foundation-sponsored study on Civil Society in the New Millennium was completed during the last year and an India country report was finalized and published. The findings of the India report were presented in a national seminar in Delhi in August 1999. These were widely reported in the media as well.

The 'Citizens and Governance' report, presenting findings of the study in 44 Commonwealth countries, was presented and discussed in Durban, South Africa, during the Third Commonwealth NGO Forum in November 1999. The report was also tabled during the Commonwealth Heads of Government Meeting (CHOGM) held at Durban in November 1999. Based on the commendations of the CHOGM, follow-up implementation of study findings is being planned in South Asia.

Financial Summary, 1999-2000

Grants	Amount (Rs.)	%
FCRA grants	39,545,600.00	92.50
Indian grants	3,206,400.00	7.50
Total	42,752,000.00	100.00
Total income	Amount (Rs.)	%
Core grants	11,995,267.05	22.89
Project grants	30,992,603.97	59.15
Other earned income	9,412,878.10	17.96
Total	52,400,749.12	100.00
Total expenditure	Amount (Rs.)	%
Programme expenses	38,115,386.28	81.97
Administrative expenses	3,523,596.03	7.56
Capital expenditure	4,860,238.25	10.45
Total	467,499,220.56	100.00
Programme Centre-wise Expenditure	Amount (Rs.)	%
Centre for Civil Society Development	9,027,003.02	19.41
Centre for Participation in Development	5,624,499.31	12.10
Centre for Environmentally Sustainable inds. Devlt.	5,694,681.71	12.25
Centre for local self-governance	15,961,917.54	34.33
Information Resource Centre	10,191,118.98	21.92
Total	46,499,220.56	100.00

Case 10. SAMPRADAN—Indian Centre for Philanthropy (SICP)

Indian Centre for Philanthropy is a networking organization set up in 1996 with a mission to re-establish philanthropy as a way of life in Indian society. It attempts to promote a philanthropy movement in the country, which encourages organized, informed, effective and regular giving of time, talent and other resources to meet important societal needs. And its mission is also to secure and maintain an environment conducive to philanthropy to increasing awareness and appreciation of its role by people, corporations and the state.

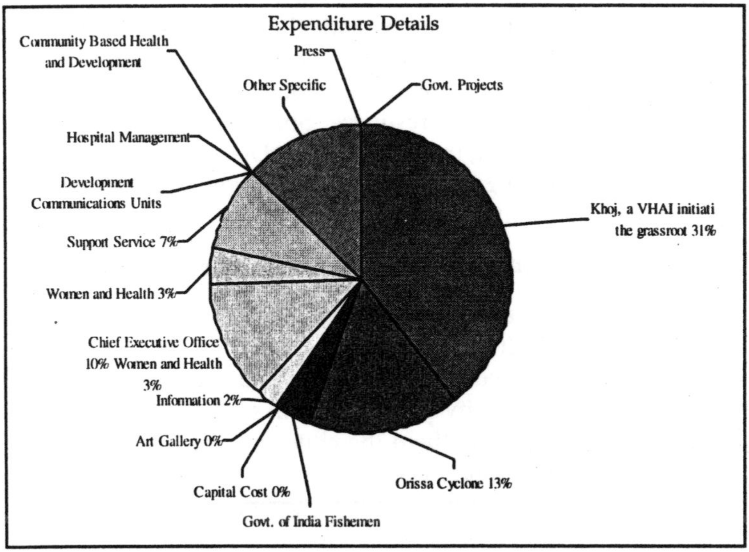

Fig. 6.11 : NGO Case-10

Objectives

1. To foster cooperation between the state, corporate sector and civil society organizations for purposes of philanthropy;
2. To encourage and promote networking among donors and between donors and NGOs;
3. To secure and maintain public policy supportive of philanthropy by advocacy before the government, the media and the public;
4. To act as a clearing-house of information of national and international philanthropy; and
5. To act as a catalyst for promotion of like-minded organizations in the country.

Programmes

1. Research and documentation of several foundations, viz. NFI, CIF, Ashoka Foundation, Bhoruka Charitable Trust, etc. and also many publications in the form of monographs.
2. National survey on household giving in urban India.
3. Case studies in fund raising.
4. A study on religious philanthropy in India.

5. Community Foundation Reader being published and sold.
6. Promoting and organizing meetings and seminars on philanthropy and community foundation concept.

SICP is emerging as a resource. Sustainability is achieved through conceptualizing the NGO-Donor Dialogue which would bring about greater alignment in thinking on identified issues and foster greater mutuality.

Case 11. CYSD (Centre for Youth and Social Development)

CYSD is a secular and non-political voluntary organization established in 1982. It operates in Orissa. The main focus of the organization is socio-economically disadvantaged people who are resource-poor and capacity-poor, people in slums, rural and tribal communities, and among them the children and women are the focus of direct participatory action.

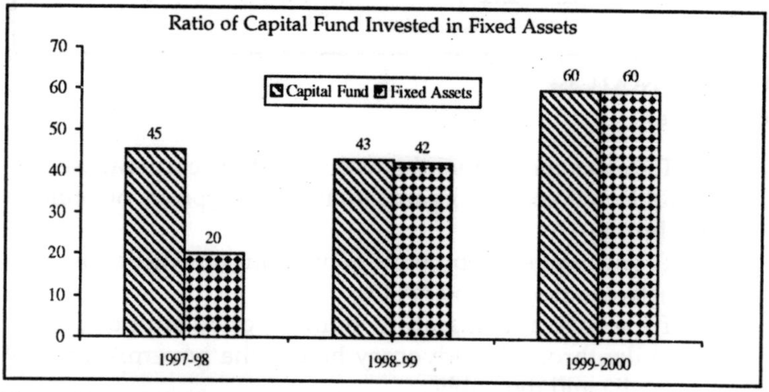

Fig. 6.12 : NGO Case-11

Objectives

1. To enable the poor to analyze the social dynamics of deprivation and to organize them into interest groups for collective action;
2. To collaborate with other organizations for strengthening their productive/entrepreneurial abilities, facilitate through participation, technology enhancement and skill development;
3. To enable the poor to play an assertive role in the governance system (starting with the Panchayati Raj system) and a decisive role in the development processes affecting them;

4. To integrate principles of gender sensitivity and justice among all—empowering women and the poor communities in the society;
5. To initiate participatory action to improve quality of life and facilitate self-reliant growth of the deprived; and
6. To promote professional competence in development action through training and consultancy services.

Programmes

The programmes are organized thematically into four programme centres:

1. Centre for Sustainable Human Development (CSHD), along with building up community organizations, pursues water harvesting and eco-agricultural activities, community health and sanitation, education and income generation in collaboration with local communities.
2. Centre for Policy Research and Advocacy (CEPRA) engages itself in issue-based policy research.
3. Development Resource Training Centre (DRTC) extends training support for management efficiency and skills development in relevant areas of people's organizations, NGOs at local, national and international levels.
4. Alternative Banking and Small Enterprise Development Centre (ABSED) provides credit support, financial management skills to self-help groups and also to producer's cooperatives.

Case 12. CRY

CRY is a national resource mobilization and support organization established in 1979. The main focus is support to small and

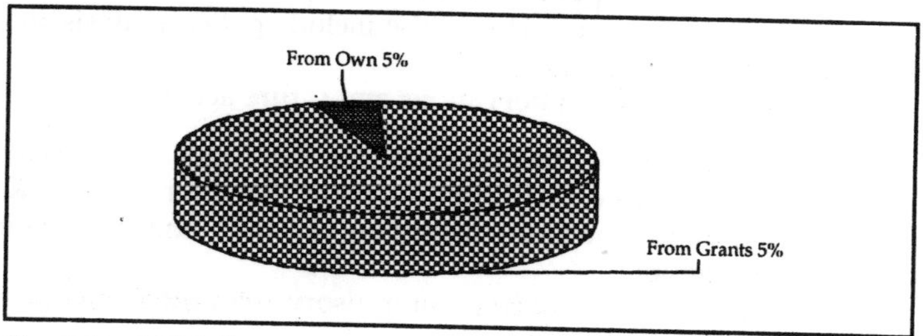

Fig. 6.13 : NGO Case -12

medium-sized NGOs working with socio-economically disadvantaged children, including those suffering mental and physical disadvantages and child abuse.

Objectives

1. To provide resources of funds, material, skills and information to field projects, individuals, networks and action-research programmes engaged in the development of children;
2. To emphasize on education, child labour and the girl child; and
3. To involve Indian citizenship, youth and other sector in taking responsibility for the situation of needy children by providing diverse resources and other relevant supports.

Programmes

1. Programme Support Division supports projects financially as well as with training, information, development of communication material, consultancy and networking opportunities; priority given to education, health, vocational training, income generation and community development.
2. Rippan Kapur Fellowship Programme encourages more social workers to work full-time with children.
3. Public Awareness and Fund raising works with over 200 schools and colleges all over India, sensitizing and motivating youth to be aware of and take action for children; stimulating and increasing awareness on child related issues through press, radio and hoarding.
4. Developing partnerships with the corporate sector, including Tata Group of Companies.

The organization plans to continue expanding the scale and scope of programme support and also include policy analysis and lobbying on children's rights.

A Glimpse of CRY's intervations and future action

1. Strengthening and generating the fund mechanism strategic system through corporate intervention of PRI institutions for implementation of health and education programme.
2. Implementation of free, compulsory, relevant elementary education and healthcare.

3. Building a gender focus into every intervention.
4. Strengthening a goal oriented focus on prevention and promotion in interventions.
5. Facilitating community involvement/particularly through corporate sector, Panchayati Raj Institutions, in water, sanitation and income generation projects to ensure community participation and control.
6. Building up a pool of knowledge through educational interventions and empowering communities to take affirmative action for children's development.
7. Corporate sector involvement with the new dimension to the programme which can be more oriented towards capacity building through training, strengthen indigenous system of production and marketing, which ultimately give a shape of sustainable floor for integrated child development.
8. Ensuring a corporate community institutional focus in training of educational and medical personnel.
9. Building relevant data base for planning, policy formulations, implementation and monitoring of child development service.
10. Constitute a strong and vibrant "National Commission for the Child", which, should be a conglomerate platform of corporate sector, government and NGOs. This can be a standardised regulatory body for national child development programme *vis-a-vis* service.

Case 13. Action Aid India

Action Aid is an international development organization spread across many developing countries in Asia, Africa and South America. Its India operation commenced in 1972. It is dedicated to

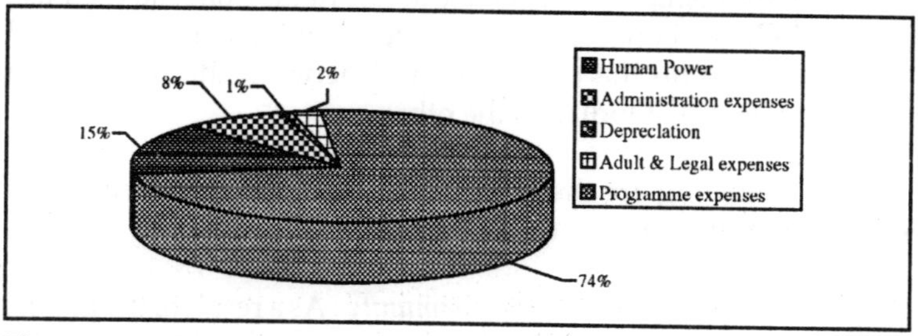

Fig. 6.14 : NGO Case-13

help children, families and communities overcome poverty and secure lasting improvement in the quality of their lives through support to NGOs and direct operational work.

Objectives

1. To provide financial, managerial and technical support for long-term integrated rural development;
2. To work with the urban poor;
3. To support disaster relief;
4. To work with disabled people; and
5. To influence policy-makers at national and international level.

Programmes

1. There is a special interest in promoting Participatory Rural Appraisal (PRA) and in meeting educational and primary health care needs and, wherever possible, government and other local resources are tapped.
2. Disability Division's focus is towards developing community-based rehabilitation (CBR) services for people with disabilities from socially and economically underprivileged sections of society. More than 15,000 disabled people have been assisted through 16 CBR projects in about 900 villages.
3. Development Support and Research Division—Health, Education and Livelihood Systems Units—carry out research on thematic issues, provide technical support to project partners.
4. Corporate Partnerships Division actively builds bridges between the corporate and the development sectors. Donor Partnership Unit created to access funds from and establish linkages between various support and donor agencies and NGOs, on the one hand, and between the former and Action Aid India, on the other.

The following are the areas where Action Aid is focusing to achieve its thrust objectives of community intervention :

A. *Potential autonomy of the community* : As a result of the project interventions, the community is supposed to be empowered and to assess that one should look into the progress made by the community towards self-reliance, the degree of independence achieved by the community from the project implementing agency, the ability to organise themselves without the interference of the project authorities, the capacity to mobilise resources and harvest extended benefits.

B. *Membership base of the community organisation:* When a community organises itself to form a group, some of the important aspects one should always address are the solidarity of the group, the habit of knowledge sharing, the self-confidence of the members, the growth rate in membership, the various reasons for group formation, and the steps taken to ensure effective leadership.

C. *Knowledge base of the community:* Every community possesses a certain knowledge base, the idea is to assess if the community has an experimental approach in its functioning, so that they are able to self-evaluate themselves, and have the capabilities to monitor and evaluate their developmental programmes.

D. *Networking and sustainability* : If any development programme has been successful in an area, one must look if the community has made efforts to spread the programme to other areas, whether they were able to develop linkages within and outside the programme, what are the linkages of the community with other local organisations, the level of support given by the community, the ability of the community to resist pressures from outside, and the ability of the community to sustain the development activities upon withdrawal of the programme.

Case 14. CSE (Centre for Science and Environment)

Since 1996, there has been a change in the Centre's activities. For the first 16 years of its existence, it had largely concentrated on creating awareness about environmental problems, and, of course solution. But it had waited for this awareness to sink into the nation's consciousness with the hope that one day it will result in action. But, as is common with so many things in India, action takes a long time to come. It was great for Lord Krishna to tell Arjuna, the warrior, in the venerated *Gita, Karmanevadhikaraste ma phaleshu kadachana* (your right is only to your actions, not to the results), but, being common mortals with desires and ambitions, all of us to want to see the results of our actions.

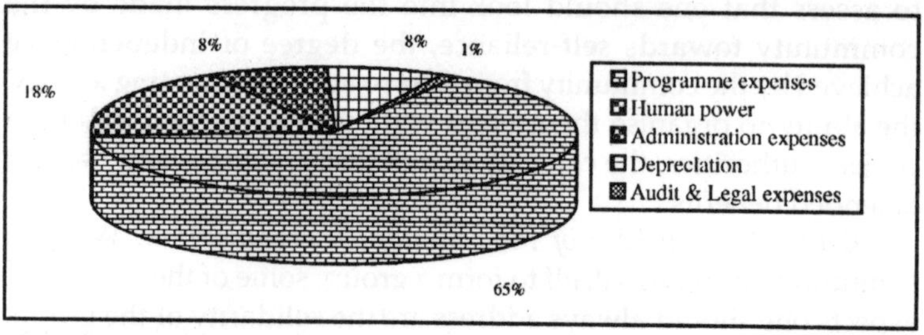

Fig. 6.15 : NGO Case -14

CSE's strength has been in producing books and other publications. So what could CSE do to change the society? Gunnar Myrdal, the famous Swedish economist, had once said to CSE, "Books are like time bombs. If the ideas contained in them are of value, they will explode one day. It is hard to predict when that will happen". For some unknown reason, these wonderful words uttered some 25 years ago, remained in CSE's mind.

This was 1996 and CST was in the process of producing two books—one on the growing air pollution in Indian cities and another on India's community-based traditions in water management. As both these books had clear messages, they thought to myself, 'How can they actively promote the messages in these books and not wait passively for people to internalise them and then hopefully take some action.

Over its 15 years of work, CSE had accumulated a considerable amount of "social capital" within certain key segments of the Indian society, in particular, the civil society, the political world and the media. These are important opinion-makers and decision-makers in democratic India. Therefore, they ask: How can we bring this 'social capital' and our knowledge together?

Within a few weeks, Justice Kuldeep Singh of Supreme Court took *suo moto* notice of the press publicity and ordered the Delhi Government to file an affidavit on how it intends to control pollution. Our message had gone home to one of the most powerful institutions of democratic India: the Supreme Court. It gave them great faith in Indian democracy. This development swept them off their feet. In 2001, just four years later, people are saying Delhi's air is indeed cleaner even though the city continues to add an unbelievable 200,000 vehicles every year.

In March 1997, CSE was ready to release a book, *Dying Wisdom*, a massive ten year exercise to document India's traditions in water management using the technology of rain water harvesting. Though rainwater harvesting was till then an unknown water management paradigm, with only few people like P.R. Mishra, Anna Hazare and Rajendra Singh working on it, isolated and with little impact on policy, it was clear to us that this traditional paradigm was relevant today and in the future as it was in the past. This was also something that people could get involved with without waiting for the government to get them water. A few islands of irrigated prosperity.

This pre-launch phase is very important. Firstly, it helps CSE to understand the issues in depth, get good grasp of the state of art they have realised that nobody would listen to us if people do not have confidence in what we are talking about. Secondly, it helps create a tool for spreading the message. Thirdly, it helps CSE get in contact with the civil society working in the field and build network of people already active or interested in it.

Lending a Helping Hand

CSE started its volunteer programme on a regular basis in 1996. Since then, they have consolidated the programme and they now have many requests from people willing to contribute their services and expertise for the cause of environment. Between 1996 and 1998, volunteer contribution has gone up to around, 3,500 days. This equivalent to almost 14 regular employees.

The magazine, *Down to Earth* and the CSE website offer a very effective medium to source volunteers. Volunteers range from students to retired persons, data entry operators to qualified scientists, and computer professionals to film-makers. For the volunteers, this is an opportunity to get to use CSE as a means to work for self fulfilment and to satisfy the urge to serve the cause and the country. For young students, this stint gives them rich working knowledge in environmental issues and a first hand experience in undertaking research, communications, advocacy and documentation.

For CSE, the system serves as a nursery that gives us chance to spot and train potential recruits and induct them into the CSE culture before they can be recruited. For instance, at least seven volunteers were absorbed as CSE's regular staff in the year 1999-2000. The system also provides a monetary benefit apart from fulfilling the primary aim of strengthening our constituency. Assuming a monthly expenditure of Rs. 5,000 per month as salary to a regular employee, CSE was able to save approximately Rs. 8.4 lakh through voluntary involvement.

Case 15. Gram Vikas

Gram Vikas has its origins in the visit to Orissa of activists from Madras University belonging to the Young Students' Movement for Development (YSMD) as volunteers for CARITAS-India and CRS-USA in the wake of a cyclone and tidal wave in 1971. Some made Orissa their base. They initially undertook standard rural development activities. In 1976, the group moved to Ganjam district in southern Orissa at the encouragement of Ramnath Das, then Chairman of the District's Central Cooperative Bank and a prominent figure, who would later join Gram Vikas Board; and S.K. Patnaik, the local Project Officer of the Small Farmers' Development Agency (SFDA), a government official working under the District Collector.

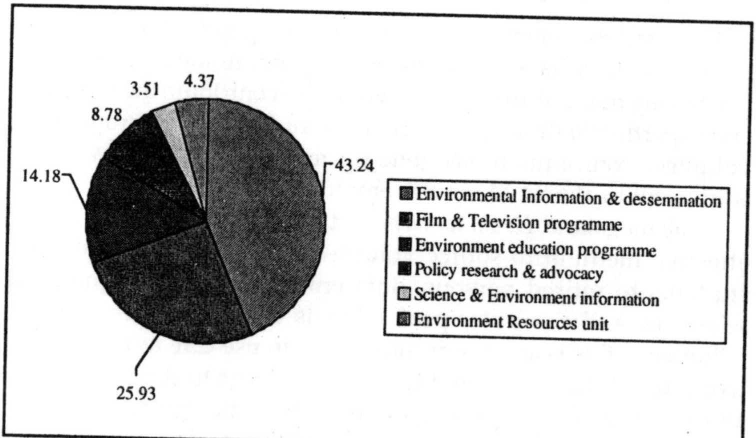

Fig. 6.16 : NGO Case-15

Gram Vikas was established in 1979 with Joe Madiath, a founder of YSMD, as Executive Director. His wife Anthya was prominent among the organizers in her own right. Its headquarters were at Mohuda, near the district's main trading town of Berhampur, where it now has a large complex. The area abouts the

Kerandimal hills, much of whose population consists of Khond tribals. Village settlements are small, often poorly linked, and the population dispersed. Although Gram Vikas' activities would eventually extend further, the Kerandimals continue to be the crucible for experimentation.

Prople's Organizations

Gram Vikas seeks to promote the empowerment of local communities for their own development, particularly the tribal groups which face special problems of marginalization and exploitation, and whose traditional sources of livelihood and socio-cultural sustenance are being severely undermined. Its programmatic activities are, therefore, subordinate to the goal of catalyzing local people's organizations on which the effectiveness of the programmes depend. The first such organization—the Kerandimal Gana Sangathan (KGS) (Association of the People of the Kerandimals)—was initiated in Kerandimal hills where Gram Vikas began its work. It has become a powerful organization and a model for other project areas. Catalyzed by Gram Vikas using health (particularly the control of endemic malaria and TB) as an entry point, it was able to break the exploitative hold of outside liquor merchants and contractors, redeem mortgaged assets and prepare the community to interact more confidently with the local agencies of the state within its first few years.

Finances

Gram Vikas has assets and liabilities of nearly Rs.130 million—large by NGO standards—and spends around Rs.25 million annually. A revolving fund-cum-corpus of Rs. 80 million generates interest income. Several foreign donors have funded Gram Vikas, including, most recently, EZE (Germany), Bread for the World (Germany), the Inter-Church Coordination Committee for Development Projects (Netherlands), Community Aid Abroad (Australia) and the Ford Foundation. As a matter of principle, Gram Vikas has also striven to access funds from governmental and other domestic sources to the extent possible. In 1998-99, it obtained Central Government funds from the Council for the Advancement of People's Action and Rural Technology (CAPART), the National Wasteland Development Board and the Ministry of Human Resource Development; from the State Government through the Orissa Renewable Energy Development Agency (OREDA), various

Integrated Tribal Development Agencies (ITDAs), the State Scheduled Castes and Scheduled Tribes Development Corporations and the District Rural Development Agencies (DRDAs) of Ganjam and Kalahandi; and from Rajiv Gandhi Foundation, New Delhi.

Impacts

'To those unfamiliar with the context, the 1986 order might appear to be of little import. We have sought to show that it was less innocuous than it seems. Even with the new policy in operation, Gram Vikas has on occasion faced difficulties in obtaining land of its choice on various grounds, so the situation prevailing prior to it can be imagined. Community forestry by several NGOs in Orissa has been facilitated by easier access to public lands. From small and slow beginnings in the mid-80s, Gram Vikas alone had prompted afforestation on a considerable area of around 3,200 hectares (8,000 acres) of revenue wastelands until 1999, 40 per cent of which was undertaken in 1998-99 alone. Nevertheless, NGO (including Gram Vikas) contribution to afforestation in Orissa remains small relative to the work of state and other agencies.

CASE 16. CDF : The Cooperative Development Foundation

Genesis: The Multi-Coops Association

CDF was established at Hyderabad, the capital of Andhra Pradesh, in 1982 with Mr. M. Rama Reddy as Secretary and Ms. Shashi

Programme and Activity-wise Expenses for the Financial Year 1999-2000

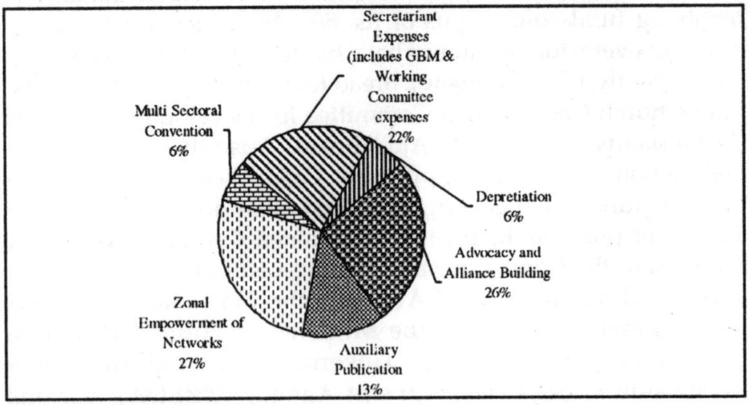

Fig. 6.17 : NGO Case-16

Rajgopalan as Director. It was originally called "Samakhya", by which name it is better known even today. CDF was promoted by another membership organization, the Multipurpose Cooperatives Association (MCA).

M. Rama Reddy founded MCA in 1977. In the mid-70s, he was Chairman of the Rajendranagar Panchayat Samiti, a Block-level local authority in what is now Ranga Reddy District. His father was a State legislator, and District Council and State Cooperative Union Chairman. Most of the 54 primary agricultural cooperative societies (PACs—grassroots multifunction mainly credit, cooperatives at the base of a three-tier structure, also known as multicoops) in Rajendranagar, as in the rest of the State, were virtually defunct. Rama Reddy took some farmers and extension workers to study the Mulkanoor cooperative in Karimnagar district, which had a reputation for solidarity and performance. Mulkanoor was headed by A.K. Vishwanath Reddy, a prominent cooperative leader. They began to apply the lessions learnt from Mulkanoor, encouraged by Rama Reddy. The 54 Rajendranagar cooperatives also reorganized themselves into 15 more viable bodies. After leaving office, Rama Reddy involved himself more fully with them. He went on to establish MCA in 1977 as its Secretary, with Vishwanath Reddy as President, and the 15 cooperatives as its initial members. At its peak, MCA had nearly a hundred member-cooperatives. Although few in comparison with the total number of cooperatives, its active user-members accounted at one stage for 10 per cent of the credit and 50 per cent of the non-credit business of all PACs in the State.

In 1984, some of these principles were incorporated in the Multi-State Cooperative Societies Act, the Central legislation applicable to cooperatives which are not confined to a single State—a feature absent in most State-level cooperative laws. (ICA has reformulated and added to these principles recently, somewhat in elegantly and without much change in substance).

In 1977-78, the Andhra Pradesh Government embarked on a reorganization of cooperatives through compulsory mergers.

It consequently postponed elections to the cooperatives' managing committees and appointed its own nominees, even in the 15 Rajendranagar cooperatives which had reorganized themselves earlier. Whereas the Rajendranagar adjustments had been member-driven, the general cooperative reorganization was

Ratio of Heads of Funds (Our Own)

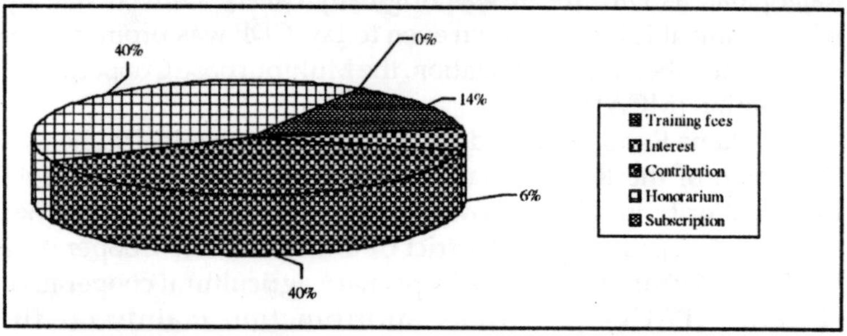

Fig. 6.18 : NGO Case-16

Government directed, and militated against the right to freedom of association. MCA representations and legal challenges drew the charge that its members, cooperatives themselves, were motivated by political self-interest. Although MCA's capacity-building through training and consultancy of its members was useful, sustained achievement was often affected by interference, sanctioned by law, from bureaucrats and politicians. Another constraint MCA faced was that it could not provide financial services to its own members in terms of the Societies' Registration Act under which it had been established. Ultimately, C. McKone of the Plunkett Foundation for Cooperative Studies, Oxford was commissioned to review MCA's functioning.

CDF's Features

One outcome of these events was the establishment of CDF (as Samakhya) in 1982. Firstly, unlike MCA, CDF had no member-cooperatives, and would extend its services beyond MCA's membership. Secondly, CDF would undertake the financial part of MCA's development programme (mainly through a 'Cooperative Revolving Fund'). Thirdly, MCA and CDF were organizationally linked through reporting by MCA's Executive Committee and General Body to CDF's Board of Trustees. MCA's President and Secretary were on CDF's Board, and the latter's Secretary and Director were members of MCA's Executive Committee. Last but not least, CDF was expected to promote an environment conducive to the development of cooperatives in line with cooperative principles, including training, consultancy and related services.

Funds

CDF's external funders have included Oxfam, the Ford Foundation, the Friedrich Naumann Foundation, BFW-Germany, Misereor, CRS World Neighbours, War on Want, ActionAid and Christian Aid. Revenues from consultancy and training fees, and bank interest on the Cooperative Revolving Fund support its staff expenditure of around Rs. 1.5 million and various reserves such as a 'Cooperative Education Fund'.

CDF's Activities and Programmes

CDF is engaged in cooperative development finance and advocacy.

1. CDF has promoted
   - (i) 235 women's thrift groups with more than 12,000 members. Group funds total Rs. 6.8 million. Rs. 10.3 million were loaned to members in 1994-95. Defaults have been less than 5 per cent. As the thrift groups gain experience and capability, CDF expects that they will cover 100,000 women within 5 years, with cumulative savings of around Rs. 78 million and disbursements of Rs. 250 million—large amounts by any standard.
   - (ii) Paddy farmers' cooperatives (Andhra Pradesh is a major rice producer) brought together in a Paddy Farmers' Federation. They provide paddy storage capacity of 2,000 tonnes, as well as processing and marketing services to around 1,000 members.
   - (iii) A Cooperative Thrift and Credit System (CTCS) in the States of Andhra Pradesh, Karnataka, Tamil Nadu, Goa and Pondicherry. CTCS has around 200,000 members in 300 primary thrift cooperatives organized into 14 Regional Associations and an apex federation. Regional Associations' funds exceed Rs. 25 million.
   - (iv) Training and consultancy services to dairy, agricultural and other cooperatives and their networks, as well as to various cooperatives development and financing institutions.

2. CDF's Rs.13 million Cooperative Revolving Fund (CRF)

finances working and fixed capital (godowns, rice mills, etc.) requirements of paddy and other agricultural cooperatives for processing and marketing, and has assisted the women's thrift groups and the CTGs network to acquire equipment. With National Cooperative Development Corporation (NCDC) financing of cooperative infrastructure in Andhra Pradesh being affected by the State Government's reluctance to put up its share because of recent budgetary difficulties, the CRF's utility has increased.

3. Supporting these activities and its advocacy efforts, CDF has published extensively: booklets and pamphlets, posters, press articles, seminar papers, training and management material, discussion papers for policy-makers, reports and audio-visuals.

CDFs Role

CDF was able to inform, organize and articulate these diverse forces and exploit the room for manoeuvre within the state apparatus. To paraphrase the Minister, it is difficult to establish a simple, one-to-one correspondence between the policy change, in which several complex forces were at play, and the actions of CDF as a single entity. However, he would acknowledge that CDF was one of several important catalysts whose individual contributions are difficult to isolate. Moreover, CDF contributed to galvanizing and enabling these forces to be effective. Within these terms and given a conjunction of fortuitous circumstances CDF had, in the Cooperation Secretary's view, directly through devices such as the Ramkrishnayya Report, which was "a landmark", and indirectly through other means, an "overwhelming influence" in the adoption of the new law. CDF critical in the process by which reform of the cooperative law came to be seen by many cooperators, politicians and bureaucrats alike as an idea whose time had come.

6.5 Corporates-NGOs Partnership: Successful Case Studies

Because of the variable nature of the tasks and the characteristics of the actors in each context, it rejects the idea of a common blueprint and suggests that, for interventions which include participation, the design of contextually appropriate methodologies must itself be an integral part of organizing the participatory process. To complement the empirical status of this study, a few cases of successful private sector-NGO participation are outlined in the following boxes.

Box 1. Arvind Mills-SAATH Partnership

Public-Private Partnerships for the Urban Poor: Slum Networking Project, Ahmedabad, India, is an innovative corporate sector initiative that was started by the Arvind Mills in partnership with the Municipal Corporation of Ahmedabad, and SAATH a local NGO. The project was the brainchild of Himanshu Parikh, an environmental and infrastructure professional who convinced Mr. Sanjay Lalbhai, Managing Director of Arvind Mills, of the value of slum upgrading through a slum networking strategy. Lalbhai and his team saw the project as an excellent way to improve the quality of life in Ahmedabad. With this a pilot project was initiated with the above partners with the following objectives: improving the basic physical and non-physical infrastructure facilities within the selected slum areas; facilitating the process of community development; and building a city level organization for slum networking and infrastructure development.

The project has been successful in implementing the physical component of the pilot project at Sanjay Nagar, a two-hectare plot of land owned by the Municipal Corporation. Sanjay Nagar has about 181 households and a population of 1,200 people. Improvements included building of new pathways with storm water drainage, installation of sewerage lines with manholes and inspection chambers, and water pipe connections to each household. This has been a significant achievement with Arvind Mills providing the leadership in both implementing and managing the project.

One of the strengths of the project was the participation of the community in the decision-making process from the design of the infrastructure to the payment of bills. Some of the shortcomings were that being a pilot project the basic idea of networking the infrastructure among different slums was not possible. Also, there has been a low level of community development activities as part of the project.

(Contd.)

Further, the aim of this project was to mobilize and galvanize participation of other business and industries for slum upgradation and networking projects. But this has not been possible simply because of the bureaucratic hurdles that had to be surmounted in carrying out the project. Nevertheless, the experience learned by the participants will go a long way in mobilizing future support for corporate sector participation in urban development in Ahmedabad.

Box 2. United Phosphorus and Janarth

United Phosphorus is a Mumbai-based producer of agricultural inputs such as pesticides. Janarth is an NGO working with farmers in Aurangabad district of Maharashtra. For the last three years, they have been working together successfully to deliver the latest pesticides and know how to poorer farmers—teaching them ideal techniques and the correct usage of implements, etc. United Phosphorus has appointed Janarth as its distributor, who in turn sells these fertilizers to farmers through a network of shops and warehouses that it has built up. Janarth was selected as a distributor without the usual conditions (e.g. putting up a deposit or providing sales targets) because it is an NGO. The company made these concessions as part of its commitment to be socially responsible. The company also allows Janarth to use imported machinery, provides knowledge on advanced crop protection and production technologies.

Janarth is deriving certain benefits out of this partnership. It uses the distributor margins to cover the cost of running the shops, making this a better alternative to raising funds from other sources. And the farmers benefit by getting need-based pesticides and access to the latest crop production technology. United Phosphorous has the technology and Janarth has the reach with the farmers.

Box 3. HMT and Amar Jyoti

HMT Limied is an engineering public sector undertaking. Amar Joyti is a Delhi-based NGO that works with disabled children. Amar Joyti works to train the poor, disabled adults in some skill that would enable them to earn a living. HMT gave advise to Amar Jyoti on the equipment needed to repair watches. Amar Jyoti approached Action Aid and the British High Commission to pay the capital cost by buying the machinery. As Amar Jyoti was not in a position to solicit enough watches for repair, HMT arranged for some watches that come to its dealers to be sent to Amar Jyoti for repairs. Currently Amar Jyoti is handling 25 per cent of the repairing of these watches in and around Delhi. HMT also provides quality spare parts to Amar Jyoti on a consignment basis which also reduces working capital of Amar Jyoti and also ensures that quality parts are used.

Amar Jyoti has trained a number of disabled people in watch repair. They have now set up their own small watch-repair shops in local colonies. This increase in the number of trained watch repairers was the primary objective of MIT. Amar Jyoti has also succeeded in its primary objective to create skilled employment for disabled people. This partnership has led many disabled people getting jobs, economic security and dignity

Box 4. Hindustan Lever and Ramana Maharishi Academy for the Blind

Hindustan Lever's rural development programme at Etah is well known. But it has an extremely innovative partnership with the Ramana Maharishi Academy for the Blind in Bangalore which was started in 1972. The Academy has a blind school, hostels for blind boys and girls, and a job-training centre. This job-training centre has had a long association with Brooke Bond Lipton which has now been merged with Hindustan Lever.

The Academy found that the blind could work with hand-operated assembly tools, which could be used to make

(Contd.)

corrugated boxes for packaging. In 1976, Brooke Bond gave them a preliminary order to make corrugated boxes. In 1983, Brooke Bond further assisted the Academy by supporting its work in dairy development and it also agreed to pay the variable cost of a few cows for the Academy to keep in its backyard, the milk from the cows was used in the hostel and the surplus, if any, was sold nearby houses. Brooke Bond also paid for raising poultry at the Academy and also the infrastructure.

The Academy now supplies other smaller companies with corrugated cardboard boxes, but its largest buyer remains HLL. The Academy earns Rs. 75,000 a month by supplying corrugated boxes to different companies. HLL gives no financial contribution to the Academy, but by merely buying most of its products it ensures a market.

6.6 An Ideal Case of Corporate Social Responsibility: Hindalco Industries Limited

Hindalco, a flagship company of the Aditya Birla Group, has established a full-fledged Rural Development Department manned by qualified rural development professionals. The framework of Hindalco's socially responsible activities is outlined below.

Goal: The three year rolling plan has been prepared with a goal — "Overall sustainable Socio-Economic Development of the community in the operational villages."

Objectives

(i) To develop the inherent skills of the community through capacity building programmes;

(ii) To develop and adapt a sustainable and profitable agricultural system and other income generation activities and actualize the potential through active participation of the community;

(iii) To spread the knowledge of hygienic living and family planning to ensure better health status of the community;

(iv) To ensure sustainable resource generation and encourage adaptation of modern and appropriate technology; and

(v) To develop and empower village development committees to ensure ownership of the community to development projects.

Focus Areas : The key focus areas of development for the three years rolling plan consists of :

- Education
- Sustainable Livelihood
- Health and Hygiene
- Family Welfare
- Agriculture and Watershed Management
- Infrastructure Development
- Social Projects.

Operational Area Profile : The rolling plan has been formulated for 86 selected villages out of 334 villages spread in the vicinity of Renukoot, Renusagar Power Plant—Renusagar, Mines Division—Lohardaga, Mines Division—Samri and Wheels & Foils Division, Silvassa. The operational area profile is given in the following table.

Table. 6.1 : Operational Area Profile

Sl. No.	*Division*	*Total no. of existing operational villages*	*Demographic status of Three-year Rolling Plan*		
			No. of selected villages	*No. of households*	*Population*
1.	Hindalco, Renukoot	187	45	12508	75991
2.	Renupower Division, Renusagar	32	12	2845	15758
3.	Mines Division, Lohardaga, Jharkhand	73	18	2840	188.58
4.	Mines Division, Samri, Chhattisgarh	40	09	1599	9465
5.	Wheels & Foils Division, Silvassa	02	02	1736	7624
	Total	334	86	21537	127696

The salient features of this rolling plan include identification of village; participatory approach in planning and implementation of programmes; social mobilization; and monitoring and evaluation. The main thrust of economic activities is to generate additional employment opportunities through mobilizing human resources and optimum utilization of available natural resources such as land, water and forest for enhancing additional income.

This chapter has discussed elaborately the individual case studies selected for analysis from a qualitative perspective. The main purpose for this review was to highlight the major contributions to social development by the different stakeholders and how there could be an effective link between these stakeholders to attain the goal of social development. To make a valid conclusion, a special reference is also being made of the three-years rolling plan of the Aditya Birla Group which is the first ever attempt by a corporate house to carry forward social reponsibility in a unique way. At the same time, in a small way the vibrant examples on paradigm shift of corporate sector participation in social development are in reality today.

7 Current Approaches to Funding in Social Development

The corporate sector could be a viable funding agency for social development in association with the government, NGOs and the civil society as a whole. Funds for social expenditure by the corporate sector depends upon the availability of resources, i.e., it depends on the profits of the corporates. Most corporate houses set apart a fixed amount for donations annually. Well known business houses have set up their own foundations for channelling corporate resources to respond to the needs of social sector projects and organizations. While Tatas have set up nearly two dozen public charitable trusts for funding NGOs and individuals, other known and successful corporates like Infosys, Wipro, Birlas, Reliance, Godrej, etc. have set up at least one public charitable entity for channelling fund or directly undertaking social sector activities. Certain other corporates have created separate divisions within its business operations for social sector interventions. Such examples are Housing Development Finance Corporation, ICICI, ACC, etc.

The Indian corporate sector is large and highly diversified. It is the source of most organized industrial activities. The aggregated sale of the companies was 62 per cent of India's Gross Domestic Product in the year 1997-98. The overall picture of the vast corporate sector of India is given in Table 7.1.

Economic prosperity is directly linked to social prosperity. Appropriate economic climate is essential for social development to be realized. Economic policies in India have undergone much change over the last few years (since 1991), and more changes are still happening. According to Sen (1995), the central approach underlying these reforms, initiated during liberalization in 1991, involves a greater reliance on the market mechanism, and this

Table 7.1 : Summary Indicators of All Companies

(Rs. in crores)

Indicators	*1995-96*	*1996-97*	*1997-98*
Sales/Income	754137.6	837647.7	881974.4
Growth in Sales/Income (%)	22.1	12.9	7.2
Profit After Tax (PAT)	37002.5	29701.9	30649.5
Growth in PAT (%)	13.1	-16.1	4.2
Total Assets	1578489.7	1821030.0	2081918.3
Growth in Total Assets (%)	15.9	14.2	14.6
No. of Companies	6519	6771	6193

Source: CMIE, May 1999.

translates into a class of public policies including deregulation and reduction of governmental controls, greater autonomy of private investment, less use of the public sector, more opening of the economy to international trade, less restrictions on the convertibility of the rupee, etc. Nehru (cited in Sen, 1995) once pointed out that the elimination of ignorance, of illiteracy, of remediable poverty, of preventable disease, and of needless inequalities in opportunities must be seen as objectives that are to be valued for their own sake. Economic growth is important, but it is valuable precisely because it helps to eradicate deprivation and to improve the capabilities and the quality of life of ordinary people.

According to the U.N. Secretary General, Mr. Kofi Annan, "Globalization is perhaps the most profound source of transformation since the industrial revolution began to turn external trade into a routine feature of international life." He further notes that "Globalization, and the liberalization that produced it, have generated a sustained period of economic expansion and a rapid configuration of international geography."

In the classical oriental thought, the idea of human progress dates back thousands of years while economic growth, on the other hand, is a very recent human preoccupation. Its arrival had to await the development of an indicator, the measure of gross national product. Its spread across the globe awaited the concept of economic development and the establishment of development agencies. Economic systems exist to provide for people, not *vice versa*. Markets would be tuned to reach socially determined ends and not promoted *per se*. The scope of markets would match the scope of effective governance. The gains to capital from globalization must not be at the expense of communities and effective governance. Economic justice is as important as individual economic freedom. Economic freedom should not be pursued to the detriment of other freedoms (Norgaard, 1999).

Based on the primary data source, this chapter attempts to study the need for an adaptive Social Development Management through the initiation of multiple, deliberately diversified projects that are sustainable. It looks at the implications of the social development projects that could be strengthened by strategic mobilization of funds from the corporate sector to achieve larger goals more effectively. Any and all support, which strengthens and sustains the mission of a development initiative, usually manpower, material and financial forms which are the core areas of corporate giving competencies. Some common forms of CSD are consulting services in the areas of management, advertising, marketing, promotion, legal, taxation, financial, strategic planning, project design, system development, etc. Corporates can also offer financial support (capital costs, costs for feasibility studies, small business start-up costs, credit facilities for purchase of assets, sponsorships, travel grants, deficit finance, etc.), donate equipment (machinery, furniture, computers, office equipment and other infrastructure), donate land and infrastructure, give products (educational, healthcare, construction, raw materials, etc.), and offer employee volunteer services to train people from the less fortunate community, and to help run the NGOs more effectively. Other forms of support could be technical assistance such as use of corporate services, viz. facilities (financial and administrative support services, meeting space, mailing services, computer services, printing and duplicating, etc.), provision for extending dealerships of corporate products to NGOs, having marketing link up for NGO products, event sponsorships, cause-related marketing, and social investing. Corporates are also found to be sponsoring salaries of NGO professionals during the promotional period of the NGO or any of its new programme. However, these forms of corporate involvement are considered strategic citizenship building for social development where each citizen, namely, NGO, corporate and the community, benefits mutually.

The Corporate Sector

Corporate India has actively participated in development issues, along with its economic goals. Major corporate houses like Tatas, Birlas, the Godrej family, the Bajajs, the TVS group, the Mahindras are contributing to the cause of social development. A 1999 survey by Social and Rural Research Institute (SRI) of the Indian Market and Research Bureau (IMRB) showed that 69 per cent (414 out of 600 companies surveyed) provide various kinds of support for social development (SRI, 2000).

It was the Tatas who first introduced many welfare measures for the benefit of their employees and several years later, the government made them compulsory of other business houses to follow. The Tatas spent an all time high of Rs. 136 crores in 1999-2000 as compared to Rs. 100 crores in 1998-99 in developmental projects, out of which Rs. 40 crores were pure funding. Twenty-eight major Tata companies that comprise the critical mass of the Tata group have come together to carry out corporate social responsibility through a common direction by bringing out the Tata Guidelines for Community Development. The companies now have a specific policy on CSR.

In India, there has been very clear thinking on the issue of CSR since the 1st Five Year Plan. At the conceptual stage itself, the steel industry was envisaged to fulfil much more than the basic economic role of producing steel. It had the additional responsibility of developing the backward regions of this country by creating opportunities for employment and better standards of living for the inhabitants. This is a responsibility which Hindustan Steel Limited and, thereafter, SAIL, have consistently tried to fulfil.

With the intervention of Partners in Change, more than 60 corporates have entered into agreement with NGOs for partnering in social sector projects. It is reported that about half of the partnership projects have already started functioning. Tata Infotech helped setting up a full-fledged computer training for slum children in partnership with Each One Teach One Charitable Trust, Mumbai. HMT in partnership with Deepalaya set up a service centre for HMT watches to be operated by the disabled. Citi Bank has been actively supporting micro credit initiatives of a number of NGOs in different cities. Such examples are growing rapidly (Garain, 2001). Involvement of TISCO and Bajaj Auto are examples of personal involvement of CEO in CSR.

The involvement of the corporate sector in providing financial, manpower, material and infrastructural support to projects carried out by the NGOs has a variety of corporate benefits. Certain direct and indirect benefits to the corporate refer to improving corporate relations with surrounding community, enhancing public image, developing cooperation and good relations with community leaders and opinion makers, improving employee attraction, recruitment and retention, building a cohesive and motivated workforce, strengthening skills of and helping prepare future workforce, adding to employee morale, reducing absenteeism and promoting teamwork, reducing isolation of employee from community, increasing effectiveness of CSR, helping maintain a healthy community, and demonstrating to employees that the corporation is committed to the community. Business leaders need to play their role and understand what were the issues and the priorities in being a good corporate citizen *vis-a-vis* responsible and responsive businesses.

The study covering 16 corporate houses in various regions (constituencies) of India is portrayed in Table 7.2. Companies selected for the study caters to the four regions of India, i.e. North, South, East and West.

Table 7.2 : Region-wise Distribution of Companies

Region	*Frequency*	*Cum. Freq.*	*Percentage*
North	5	5	31.25
South	2	7	12.5
East	3	10	18.75
West	6	16	35.5

Corporate funding for social development could be directly linked to the industrial performance, growth and other economic factors. To assess the resource volume and its possible impact on social development, various economic indicators like sales turnover and profit after tax for the period 1998-2000 are taken into consideration (Table 7.3). The indicators chosen here are to bring out the positive relation between the level of availability of resources and the support which could be generated from these vast resources available in the corporate sector.

Table 7.3 shows that 1 per cent of PAT of the 16 companies in a given year is generating approximately Rs. 53.15 crores. The commitment and motivation of NGOs if it could matching with the corporate specialised knowledge and financial resources that

Table 7.3 : Sales Turnover and Profit after Tax

Names of the Company	*Year*	*Rank*	*Sales Turnover (in Rs. crores)*	*Profit after Tax (PAT) (in Rs. crores)*	*1% of PAT (in Rs. crores)*	*Area of Operation*
Bajaj Auto	1998-1999	11	3526.91	552.84	5.53	Pune
	1999-2000	10	3705.15	634.86	6.34	Maharashtra
Glaxo India	1998-1999	30	885.50	71.06	0.77	Mumbai,
Ltd.	1999-2000	68	934.62	70.54	0.70	Maharashtra
Hero Honda	1998-1999	33	1532.03	121.37	1.21	Haryana
Motors	1999-2000	9	2248.17	192.08	1.92	
ITC	1998-1999	3	7579.17	623.42	6.23	Kolkata
	1999-2000	6	7953.06	792.40	7.92	
Larsen and	1998-1999	14	7291.44	468.39	4.68	Maharashtra
Toubro	1999-2000	21	7423.80	339.49	3.39	
Ranbaxy	1998-1999	26	1559.83	193.89	1.94	Delhi
Laboratories	1999-2000	18	1745.90	180.50	1.80	
SAIL	1998-1999	32	14993.85	1573.66	15.73	Bhilai, MP
	1999-2000	50	16250.16	1720.02	17.20	
TELCO	1998-1999	21	6599.61	97.85	0.98	Pune,
	1999-2000	34	8789.91	92.75	0.93	Maharashtra
TISCO	1998-1999	23	6126.67	282.23	2.82	Bihar
	1999-2000	25	6720.85	422.59	4.2	
Titan	1998-1999	196	634.34	19.20	0.19	Karnataka
Industries	1999-2000	129	643.35	19.28	0.19	

Contd. ..

Contd. ...

Names of the Company	*Year*	*Rank*	*Sales Turnover (in Rs. crores)*	*Profit after Tax (PAT) (in Rs. crores)*	*1% of PAT (in Rs. crores)*	*Area of Operation*
Dabur India	1998-1999	82	914.77	50.13	0.50	Uttar
	1999-2000	54	1042.59	77.66	0.78	Pradesh
ICICI	1998-1999	34	633.09	63.36	0.63	Maharashtra
	1999-2000	NA	1046.92	105.30	1.05	
Infosys	1998-1999	16	508.89	135.26	1.35	Karnataka
Mahindra &	1998-1999	42	4025.09	225.91	2.26	Mumbai,
Mahindra	1999-2000	16	4290.45	263.48	2.63	Maharashtra
Lupin	1998-1999	162	715.73	23.50	0.24	Rajasthan
Laboratories	1999-2000	NA	543.72	30.62	0.31	
INDAL	1998--1999	NA	1152.00	76.40	0.76	Bihar
	1999-2000	87	1180.77	83.93	0.84	

Source : Companies Annual Reports.

could make havoc to achieve the sustainable development of the nation. Therefore, if the corporate sector sets aside a percentage of PAT, there would be greater involvement in the source and use of funds.

Another study was also conducted to understand the trend of corporate participation in social development. For this purpose 300 companies were contacted through e-mails by sending a structure set of 7 questions (see Appendix). The companies were selected randomly from available sources. The majority of the respondents were Indian private companies. The areas of business were varied and there were multiple areas of business for a fairly large number of companies. From the analysis of the answers given by the company personnel contacted through e-mail, the following general information could be gleaned out:

(1) At least 70 per cent (N = 300) of the companies are found to be involved in social development.
(2) Most of the companies adhere to multiple aspects of social development though one or two aspects are at the focus.
(3) Almost 80 per cent of the companies agreed that poor, deprived, disabled, landless farmers, destitute, poor and illiterate women, child labourers should be the target population for social development.
(4) Nearly 75 per cent of the companies agreed that social development should be sustainable, and 50 per cent said it to be participatory.
(5) 60 per cent of the companies said the company management should be directly involved in the developmental programmes.
(6) 75 per cent said that only through a genuine involvement in social development that business could realize its ethical character. It will be a learning experience to not only the business house but also to the people as a whole.
(7) Almost 85 per cent confirmed that corporates are as responsible as the government in the sphere of overall social development. Industry is the real strength of the government. So the broader duties and responsibilities are, to some extent, duties and responsibilities of the industry.

The responses of the companies contacted through e-mail of

their involvement in the following areas are given in Table 7.4. These 300 companies were asked to provide details for more than one significant social development activities in the last two years. The following table summarizes the exhaustive list of issues that are more salient for respondents as ways to fulfil their social responsibility.

Table 7.4 : Corporate Participation in Various Categories of Social Development

Social Sectors	*Companies (N=300)*	
	Number	*Percentage*
Education	195	65
Health, Hygiene and Sanitation	165	55
Social Forestry and Environment	114	38
Community Development and Social Welfare	210	70
Employment Generation and Skill Development	186	62
Women Empowerment	150	50
Animal Husbandry	66	22
Rural Development	165	55
Youth Development	117	39
Girl Child and Primary Education	105	35
National Crisis	180	60
Micro Planning	144	48
Rural Infrastructure	138	46
Art, Culture and Crafts	120	40
Agricultural Development	96	32

The e-mail responses show that almost all the companies contacted are engaged in multiple social development activities. The highest number of companies are involved in community development and social welfare (70%), followed by education (65%).

The Role of Corporate Associations

Confederation of Indian Industry (CII), in 1995, set up a Social Development and Community Affairs Council (SDCA) whose mandate is to motivate industry, help members integrate social development activities into corporate plans, to network with government and NGOs and to create a data bank of useful information. To promote primary education in the country, CII is promoting an 'education campaign' targeting the underprivileged children who lack formal education. This campaign needs people's support and commitment. The long-term objectives of SDCA are to improve the quality of life in both urban and rural areas, to provide the benefits of reforms and industrial growth to people living in poverty and unemployment; to ensure the image of industry as a 'concerned' group about community and to establish and strengthen social development. The major developmental activities organized by CII in the last two years include AIDS Workplace Programme which is in line with the objectives of the National AIDS Control Organization, Ministry of Health & Family Welfare; income generation programmes in Delhi — these are recycling waste paper, detergent making and chalk making; and initiative on wasteland development. Following the drought situation in Rajasthan, Gujarat and Andhra Pradesh, CII took the initiative of bringing out a "Guide to Rain Water Harvesting" in cooperation with the Central Ground Water Board, Ministry of Water Resources.

CII has been promoting issues such as corporate values, corporate governance, investing for the long term, accountability and responsibility, transparency, tackling corruption, human rights, employee relations and environment. Globalization and economic liberalization have brought in their wake many opportunities for development and increased prosperity, but also the danger of marginalizing the vulnerable sections of the society. The United Nations Secretary General, Kofi Annan, presented to the world business leaders assembled in Davos in January 1999 the concept of a Global Compact of shared values and principles. Citing the fragility of the mostly business-led globalization process, he called on business leaders to embrace, support and enact a set of nine universal principles in the areas of human rights, labour rights and the environment. CII has agreed to be the co-partner in the India Partnership Forum with UNDP. Partnership activities could include:

(i) Demystification of gender stereotypes and the use of technology;
(ii) Addressing information/communication needs of women;
(iii) Gender sensitive training programmes in computer literacy, knowledge and skill building;
(iv) Gender sensitive recruitment and workplace policies; and
(v) Training in gender impact assessment.

In view of International Year of Volunteers (2001), corporate commitment to the community could manifest through the following :

(i) Policy structure for volunteering;
(ii) Identifying volunteers;
(iii) Evolving programmes through volunteers;
(iv) Training and orientation;
(v) Evaluation and documentation; and
(vi) Exchange and dissemination of best practices.

CII has been organizing 'Social Summit' every year since 1998 to bring together all the stakeholders — industry, NGOs and government to create awareness about corporate social responsibility and the viable partnership between the stakeholders. A CII-CBC (Commonwealth Business Council) Round Table on Corporate Citizenship was organized on 8th March, 2001 in New Delhi to share views on issues such as corporate values, corporate governance, the role of government, civil society and industry, accountability and responsibility etc.

Similarly, ASSOCHAM's objective is that of a long-term vision of economic prosperity to ensure the future of the underprivileged and the poor, and insure them against the vicissitudes. The broad objectives of the association are the following:

(i) Controlling population;
(ii) Continuance of economic reforms and liberalization;
(iii) Streamlining and simplification of procedures;
(iv) Decontrol and removal of administrative hurdles to form the way for free and market-driven enterprise;
(v) Boosting exports, improving balance of payment position and consolidating reserves;
(vi) Modernization and strengthening of core infrastructure;
(vii) Upgradation and making available state-of-the-art technology in all spheres of the economy; and
(viii) Making India into a vibrant and market-driven economy compatible and comparable with the economic super powers.

To achieve the above objectives that are an inherent part of the 'Vision of India' of ASSOCHAM, the foundation is laid by:

(i) Managing population growth;
(ii) Improving productivity and employability through education;
(iii) Providing a healthy environment;
(iv) Creating security through housing; and
(v) Infrastructure.

Management of the strategic framework is what is governance. ASSOCHAM strongly believes that the management of strategic framework for achievement of Vision must be within the policy framework of the government. This would facilitate focused attention and immediate intervention for quick results.

Multilateral and Bilateral Agencies

Public spending has long been considered one of the main channels through which foreign aid influences development outcomes. Most aid (over 65 per cent of the total) to developing countries is given in the form of sectoral investment projects that are intended to supplement recipients' own resources in those sectors. Among developing countries, India continues to be one of the largest recipients of foreign aid. The average annual disbursement of aid to India in the first half of the 1990s was close to US$ 2.9 billion. On a yearly basis, it financed over 4 per cent of the combined spending of the Central Government, State Governments and public sector enterprises. The Indian Constitution mandates that all external assistance (including funds earmarked for state projects) accrue to the Central Government, which is also liable for any repayments. In turn, these funds are pooled with a portion of domestic resources to finance 'Plan Outlays' which are various development projects, programmes and schemes includes in the country's annual plan. Development expenditure has been in the seven subcategories or sectors—agriculture, irrigation, energy, industry, transport and communication, social sector, and others. The understanding of the whole issue of multilateral and bilateral funding has already been discussed exhaustively in the preceding chapters.

Extensive survey of secondary sources reveal that grants from all bilateral and multilateral sources have either declined or remained constant in the post-liberalization period. The sources support the hypothesis of the study that funds have in fact declined if the figures are compared to the pre-liberalization period (Table 7. 4.). The ratio of grants to total disbursement have declined in the post-liberalization period although marginally.

Table 7.5 : External Assistance Grant Position

(Rs. crores)

Year	*Total Disbursements*	*Grants*	*Grants/Total Disbursements %*
1985-86	2862.14	2428.22	15.16
1986-87	3442.13	3022.17	12.20
1987-88	4853.50	4396.30	9.42
1993-94	10115.52	9229.90	8.76
1994-95	9529.74	8613.70	9.61
1995-96	8709.63	7646.07	12.21

Source : 'External Assistance' 1991-92 and 1995-96, Department of Economic Affairs.

For this study, seven organizations have been selected in both bilateral and multilateral sectors each to analyze the funding pattern of these organizations. The 14 multilateral and bilateral organizations have been selected purposively, as these have been the major funding agencies in India's developmental programmes.

It is evident that funding by multilateral agencies declined by approximately 34 per cent from $ 2280.21 million during 1990-91 to $1495.14 million in 1999-2000.

Table 7.6 : Multilateral Agencies Funding (US $ millions)

Organization	*1990-91*	*1994-95*	*1998-99*	*1999-2000*
World Bank	1991.4	843.8	688.40	85.0
ADB	212.4	N.A	600.00	1300.00
ILO	0.15	0.025	1.52	1.04
UNICEF	40.83	64.76	41.00	73.00
UNDP	24.55	19.70	18.54	16.5
WHO	9.98	8.81	16.45	19.00
FAO	0.90	0.56	0.35	0.60
Total	2080.21	937.66	1366.26	1495.14

Source : Respective India offices confirmed by UNDP.

Table 7. 7 : Bilateral Agencies Funding

(US $ millions)

FAO	*0.90*	*0.56*	*0.35*	*0.60*

Organization	1990-91	1994-95	1998-99	1999-2000
DANIDA	4.10	11.30	11.60	11.0
CIDA	N.A	5.10	1.70	9.60
SIDA	10.80	10.30	N.A	N.A
Germany	6.40	120.20	N.A	39.60
USA	21.00	N.A	N.A	66.50
UK	141.10	85.50	N.A	N.A
Japan	34.30	39.40	32.30	1.30
Total	217.60	271.80	45.60	128.00

Source : Respective Embassies confirmed by UNDP.

Bilateral assistance decreased by 41 per cent from $ 217.6 million in 1990-91 to $ 128 million in 1999-2000. Thus, both multilateral and bilateral funding have declined significantly during the last decade.

The Role of NGOs

NGOs in developing countries can be categorized as support organizations, policy analysis and advocacy organizations or grassroots implementing institutions. These three distinct categories of NGOs can further be subdivided on the basis of the thematic areas addressed by specific NGOs such as those working on health, education, environment, economic or agrarian developmental sectors. Support organizations are usually larger city-based organizations more often than not with 50 or more regular employees. They are well-equipped with technical manpower and equipment and are able to access the latest technical and financial information from donors, especially foreign funding institutions. They usually have a high level of expertise and skills in organizational development, training, documentation, communication, technical skills, etc.

Over the years, the role of NGOs in development has been very significant. In India, they are found in almost all areas of human activity. In the areas of welfare, education, health, sanitation, environment, human rights and social justice the sector has had done tremendous efforts. In fact, the works of the sector have influenced the government policies and programmes. Some NGOs have been successful enough to change the attitude of government towards the neglected sections. The recent trends in their activities in the country have been more of building sustainable partnerships with the corporate sector for social development initiatives, based not only on financial support but skills enhancement, access to markets, promoting NGO work in ancillary activities, providing work opportunities and access to the resources of the companies. Corporate funding for innovative projects in social development is very essential and crucial for the NGOs in India in the light of declining fund pool from other sources in recent years. Typically, companies have provided donations while NGOs have managed and implemented the projects. However, in the current scenario, the corporate sector could emerge as a strategic player in funding for social development. Various CEOs in different parts of the country are engaged in developmental projects.

Some small NGOs work only with volunteers, use participant donated space and equipment and do not need (or sometimes want) any funding for their activities. However, most NGOs, whether in a developed or developing country, need to raise funds for their very existence (to pay full-time staff, for rent, etc.), and for projects or activities. Some try to manage with very limited funding, but most require some degree of outside funding. The classification thus distinguishes as (Mencher, 1999):

(1) NGOs receiving foreign funds from the developed world, including bilateral funds, international agencies, NGOs in the developed world such as OXFAM, or various Church groups, marketing organizations such as Pueblo to People; or from individuals, foundations, special funds, etc.;
(2) NGOs only or also receiving partial funding from their respective national governments;
(3) In the case of South Asia, NGOs receiving funds from state governments or even local district governments;
(4) NGOs using only or primarily funds raised through group members' donations or small monthly fees, etc.; and
(5) Varied combinations of the above 4.

The case studies of NGOs have been selected from all the constituencies. The style and purpose of the case studies took into account geographical representation, field of study, and type of fund raising, to provide evidence to the trends in the funding pattern of NGOs. An attempt has also been made to study the pattern of resource mobilization and resource dissemination of the NGOs. There are 16 region-specific NGOs from various parts of the country who are operating in that particular region which include donor NGOs, support NGOs, networking NGOs and NGOs promoting philanthropy and mediating partnership building between corporates, NGOs and government. The geographical distribution of the NGOs for this study is outlined below:

Table 7.8-9 : Region-wise Distribution of NGOs

Area	*Number of NGOs (N=16)*	
	Frequency	*Cum. Freq.*
North	9	9
South	3	12
East	2	14
West	2	16
	N=16	

Category	*Frequency*	*Cum. Freq.*
Support and Implementing NGOs	6	6
Networking NGOs	4	10
Funding NGOs	2	12
Implementing NGOs	4	16

Source : Study Data.

NGOs vary in numerous ways including their (1) composition, (2) size, (3) mission or purpose, (4) sources of funding, (5) histories, (6) whether or not they focus on a particular arena, and (7) their manner of day-to-day functioning, including decision-making. The table above (Table 7. 9) analyzes the pattern of involvement of the selected NGOs in various areas of social development. The percentage of NGO participation in various social developmental activities (N = 16) is given in Table 7.10.

Almost all the NGOs contacted are found to be operative in multiple areas of social development activity. In an average, an NGO is active in at least two areas of social development. NGOs are flexible in their operation and mostly they take up genuine issues of social development. Three factors, i.e. money, areas of operation, government support, and the NGOs own experience capabilities, together decide their selection of developmental projects.

The supporters of NGOs have been individuals, corporate

Table 7.10 : Areas of Operation of NGOs

Areas of Activity	*Percentage*
Environment	42
Education	65
Children's Rights	45
Capacity Building	72
Gender Equity	60
Awareness Generation/Community Development	78
Anti-drug and Addiction Campaign	40
Natural Calamities	60
Development of Rural Technology	45
Animal Husbandry	45
Employment Generation	50
Skill Development and Training	58
Working for People with Disabilities	35
Sustainable and Participatory Approach	75
Health	70
Population Control	48

Source : Study Data.

sector, government and international organizations. The form and means of the participation or support varies not only between the categories but also within a category due to differences in policy, conditions, circumstances and beliefs. By having a cross-section of levels of giving and types of activities, NGOs have created a supportive network of contributors from various economic classes and professional backgrounds. For example, in 1995, CRY structured its fund-raising divisions into 'Corporate Partnership' and 'Individual Partnership' in order to be more focused on the two chief categories of donors being addressed.

Corporate support has gradually moved from one time charitable giving to a more long-term relationship based on a perception of mutual relevance and benefit. This trend can be broadly referred to as—from charity to social investment. There is the potential for innovative partnerships between the corporate sector and NGOs. The corporate sector could also make need-based grants in the areas of new initiatives and could contribute substantially to the corpus fund of NGOs. The study reveals the following break-up of sources of funding of NGOs given in Table 7.11.

The above break-up of sources of fund suggests that almost all the NGOs contacted generate their money from multiple sources.

Table 7.11 : Sources of Funding

Sources of Funding	*Percentage of NGOs*
Government	65
Foreign Bilateral Agencies	52
Foreign Multilateral Agencies	55
Corporate Sector	38
Others (Donation, etc.)	65

Source: Study Data.

Since NGOs operate in various categories of social development, they generate money by contacting funding agencies which have their priority area of operation matching their priority areas. Sometimes, they take up particular kind of social development projects if there is availability of money and they have flexible capabilities to do the new job. Sources of funding and the nature of development work the NGOs pursue are dynamically related and a whole of socio-political and economic factors are involved in it. Most of them, from small-scale single village ones to large multi-levelled national and international ones, see their main functions as offering help in one form or another. Often the same NGOs which are involved with issues of fundamental change also focus on diverse survival needs. There are many conclusions that can be drawn from the current status of NGOs, however, the functions of the NGOs can be summarized as:

(1) To educate people about laws, entitlements, etc.;
(2) To advocate for changes in society or in structured inequality;
(3) While providing credit and helping individual members improve themselves financially, also to empower women and the poor to stand up for themselves, to help create an alternative model of development;
(4) Making use of participatory research and participatory decision-making; and
(5) To start processes that can spread from village to village without help of NGOs but just through empowered people.

Beneficiaries' Outlook

There has been an increasing concern within the development

community to promote effective people's participation in order to improve the distribution of benefits of development and to re-emphasize development as a process concerning people. A real assessment of development can be made if we can assess participation in the development programme. Technically, such evaluations would have both a quantitative and a qualitative dimension; to date much work in this area has been reduced to the former. If the assessment is done with an objective that the results could be used to overcome shortcomings of those involved in the process, it has turned out to be a very fruitful and learning exercise about the people's stake in whole process.

One of the prerequisites to a successful assessment is sharing of information and consultations with the target groups who are to be assessed. This will help the community to self-evaluate themselves and visualize their participation in the project.

It is very important to identify the right indicators that can be used to show what progress has been made to incorporate people's participation and thereby develop their capacity. To assess people's participation in development projects undertaken by NGOs, CBOs and corporates in their respective areas of operation, a structured questionnaire was developed with a set of 12 questions considering relevant issues (Appendix). The idea was to reach an agreement over the answers or statements that best described its own position. Each statement is given a number, or a score to reflect progress. The scores are ranked on a scale of four, i.e. "0 to 3". A score of 3 is very satisfactory, 2 describes a satisfactory situation but with room for improvement, 1 is unsatisfactory with definite room for improvement, and 0 is very unsatisfactory with great deal of room for improvement. The four alternative rankings for each indicator provides judgements on the level of participation existing within the project. Each question adds up to a score of 480 in the cases of 160 NGO beneficiaries and 160 corporate sector beneficiaries.

The set of questions is divided into three categories, (a) Access and benefit assessment, (b) Community organization and activity assessment, and (c) Community self-reliance and empowerment assessment. There are 1, 6 and 5 questions in each category respectively. The total scores (out of 480) in each of the questions and their mean scores for the beneficiaries of NGOs and corporates is given below in Table 7.12. The NGOs beneficiaries' total scores are higher than that of corporate sector beneficiaries. This shows that the grassroots level operations of NGOs have made a more positive impact upon the selected area as compared to the corporate sector. However, there is a positive correlation if the total scores of both the NGO and corporate sector beneficiaries are compared, as there is not but difference in the average scores.

Table 7.12 : Beneficiaries Assessment

Questions	*NGO*		*Corporate*	
	Total score (out of 480)	*Mean score*	*Total score (out of 480)*	*Mean score*
A1	385	2.4	362	2.26
B1	350	2.1	353	2.2
B2	388	2.42	354	2.21
B3	334	2.09	290	1.81
B4	316	1.98	295	1.84
B5	313	1.96	240	1.5
B6	400	2.5	360	2.25
C1	332	2.08	320	2
C2	335	2.09	332	2.08
C3	375	2.34	315	1.97
C4	340	2.12	331	2.07
C5	330	2.06	318	1.99
Total	4198		3870	
Average	349.8		322.5	

Source : Study Data.

The average scores and the percentages are calculated in the following Table 7.13.

Table 7.13 : Average Score of Corporate and NGO Beneficiaries

Beneficiaries	*Average Score*	*Percentage*
NGO	349.8	72.87
Corporate	322.5	67.18

Source : Study Data.

Here we see that the percentage of beneficiaries is higher in case of NGOs. This may be attributed to the fact that the programmes conducted by the NGOs are people-centred in nature and hence the number of people benefiting are more. The individual

Table 7.14 : Comparative Scores of Corporate and NGO Beneficiaries

NGO Beneficiaries (160)		*Corporate Sector Beneficiaries (160)*	
Scores	*Percentage*	*Scores*	*Percentage*
10-14	3.33	10-14	3.33
15-19	0	15-19	10
20-24	6.66	20-24	20
25-29	56.67	25-29	46.67
30-35	33.34	30-35	20

Source : Study Data.

scores of 320 beneficiaries (160 of NGOs and 160 of corporates) are calculated as follows. The total scoring in case of one individual schedule adds upto 36.

While comparing the individual scoring of 320 beneficiaries, a marked difference is found. Between scores of 25 to 29, the percentage of NGO beneficiaries (56.67%) is much higher than that of corporate beneficiaries (46.67%). Therefore, it may be concluded that there is a strong need for a viable partnership between the NGO and the corporate sectors to reach out to the grassroots level.

The results presented in this chapter raise various issues regarding the determinants of social development and its funding. This study gives us the empirical evidence of the structure and declining nature of funding by multilateral and bilateral funding in recent years. The purpose of giving a picture of financial aggregates of the corporate houses like sales turnover and profit after tax is to look a little more closely at the evidence of the amount of resources available with the corporate sector. Various studies have been made on the issue of corporate social responsibility, but none attempted to bring out the linkage of corporate funding and the resource gap in developmental projects undertaken in India. Although the government sector is the single largest financier of social development, corporate sector participation in funding for social development is very essential in the light of declining trend in multilateral and bilateral grants to India. A parallel study was also carried out through e-mail to have a better understanding of the perception of social development among the corporates. Finally, in order to explore the implications of the different determinants of social development, the beneficiaries' viewpoint is taken into consideration to have a better understanding of the effectiveness of development programmes undertaken by the corporate and

NGO sectors towards a strong synergic and strategic partnership to achieve the mutual goal of sustainable development. Hence, the maim focus of this study to establish the logic on various stakeholders' convergence in social development and the new incarnation of corporate sector participation in funding for social development.

8 Analysis of Results

If business use their creativity and knowledge, they can provide a strong return for the stakeholders and grow their businesses—all while meeting the human needs of societies around the world and reducing the environmental footprint of their operations and products. This is the challenge to sustainable growth, and to meet it, the primary motivation for any company must be improved business performance. And environmental and societal benefits will follow, but the underlying rationale, which must always be in focus, is that in the global economy, sustainability will generate tremendous socio-economic value. To translate this concept into business practices, every business unit has to view sustainability as an opportunity for real growth, not just as a kind of corporate philanthropy. Businesses had to continually demonstrate that sustainable growth could indeed generate business value.

As a business practice, sustainable growth seeks to make more of the world's people as customers—and to do so by developing markets that promote and sustain economic prosperity, social equity, and environmental integrity. For a company to embark on a process of sustainable growth, its leaders and employees have to understand two critical things: what they value and how they create value, that is, a commitment to social development, integrity, and the fair and respectable treatment of people. For example, the Azim Premji Foundation (APF), whose vision is to "build the future of India through transforming the lives of millions of children by catalyzing universalization of elementary education" has launched a process of endurable growth. APF sees itself acting as a "change agent," influencing the key stakeholders in the universalization of elementary education. Unlike many private initiatives, APF has decided to work with the governments, mainly at the state level, because 90 per cent of Indian children study in government schools.

The objective of this study was to explore the determinants of social development, viz. the players in social development, changing pattern of funding for social development and to suggest how corporate participation in funding for social development would emerge as an alternative strategy in social development. Based on the study, certain trends emerged and some amount of variation was observed across the developmental contributors. The previous chapter has presented empirical evidence on the impact of various players on social development. Some suggestive evidence drawn from data was provided to support the hypotheses in the previous chapters. In this chapter, an attempt has been to further corroborate the elementary exercise conducted in Chapter 7.

The Corporate Sector Role

The activities in which the companies involve in social development broadly cover health, education, natural resource management, infrastructure, community support, livelihood and other activities. Some of the activities, however, transcended these main activities and involved more than one area. Even if some of the companies are not directly involved in any activities, but still they appreciate what others doing developmental works and they have expressed their inclinations to do the same provided they would get the necessary professional oriention. The following figure depicts the empirical evidence of corporate sector participation in support of the hypothesis undertaken for the study.

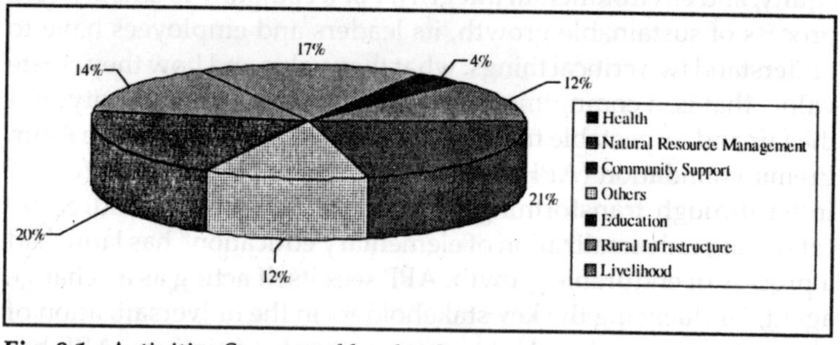

Fig. 8.1 : Activities Supported by the Companies

The figure presents that significancly higher percentage of activities are in the area of community support (70%) followed by health (55%), education (65%) and livelihood (55%). The trend has

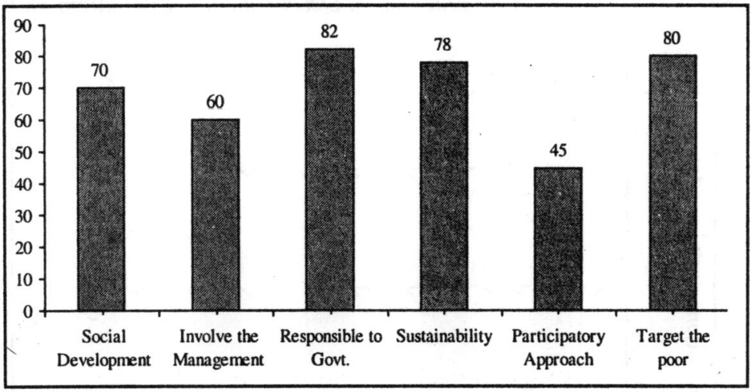

Fig. 8.2 : Belief in Corporate Social Responsibility

become such that more and more corporates are realizing their social responsibilities and commitment to government's developmental activities. More and more corporate houses in India are found to be pursuing developmental activities ranging from health, education to environmental issues.

The e-mail responses show that majority of companies believe that they have a major role to play in social development. It is also evident that the companies who undertake social development activities do have belief in efficacy of project in the long term. More than 65 per cent believed in sustainability of projects. The range of social programmes assumed by corporate sector has continuously expanded.

One of the significant findings from the e-mail responses is the higher percentage of corporates as responsible towards the Government. Analysis of both the e-mail responses and the case studies of 16 corporates houses convey similar results with respect to social development.

Linkage between PAT and Corporate Participation in Social Development

Today, corporations carry out a wide array of social actions. The span includes programmes for education, public health, employee welfare, housing, urban development, environmental protection, day-care centres for working parents and many others 'The fundamental reason why the concept and range of social responsibilities have expanded is that accelerating industrial

Table 8.1 : Relation between PAT and Social Developmental Activities

Name of the Company	*Year*	*Profit after Tax (in Rs. crores)*	*Health*	*Edu.*	*Enviro.*	*Infrastr.*	*Community*	*Art & Sports*	*Liveli.*
Bajaj Auto	1998-1999	552.84	√	√	×		×		√
	1999-2900	634.86	√	√	√		√		√
Glaxo India	1998-1999	77.06	√				√	√	
Ltd.	1999-2000	70.54	√				√		
Hero-Honda	1998-1999	121.37	√	√	×	×	×	√	√
Motors	1999-2000	192.08	√	√	√	√	√	√	√
ITC	1998-1999	623.42	√	×	×		√	√	
	1999-2000	792.40	√	√	√		√	√	
Larsen and	1998-1999	468.39	√	√			√	√	
Toubro	1999-2000	339.49	√	√			√	√	
Ranbaxy	1998-1999	193.89	√	√		√			√
Laboratories	1999-2000	189.50	√	√		×			√
SAIL	1998-1999	1573.66	√			√	×	×	
	1999-2000	1720.02	√			√	√	√	
TELCO	1998-1999	97.85	√		√		√		√
	1999-2000	92.75	√		×		√		√
TISCO	1998-1999	282.23	√	√		×	√		
	1999-2000	422.59				√	√		√
Titan	1998-1999	19.20		√			√		√
Industries	1999-2000	19.28		√			√		
Dabur India	1998-1999	50.13	×	√					√
	1999-2000	77.66	√	√					√

Contd. ..

Contd. ..

Name of the Company	*Year*	*Profit after Tax (in Rs. crores)*	*Health*	*Edu.*	*Enviro.*	*Infrastr.*	*Community*	*Art & Sports*	*Liveli.*
ICICI	1998-1999	63.36		√	×	×			√
	1999-2000	105.30		√	√	√			√
Infosys	1998-1999	135.26	√	√			×	×	√
Technologies	1999-2000	293.52	√	√			√	√	√
Mahindra and	1998-1999	255.91	√	√			×		
Mahindra	1999-2000	263.48	√	√			√		
Lupin	1998-1999	23.50	√			×	√		
Laboratories	1999-2000	30.62	√			√	√		
INDAL	1998-1999	76.40	√	√		√	×		
	1999-2000	83.93	√	√		√	√		

Source : From the study.

activity continuously changes society. The economic performance of the corporations also affects the kind of activities they are engaged in. In the following table an attempt has been made to see the relation between companies contribution of Profit After Tax (PAT) and social developmental activities.

Table 8.1 gives a picture that the PAT has marginally increased in the case of few companies. Since most of the companies enter into social development in a planned manner, they take time to decide the area and nature of their work. The time period considered in our study is for two years, it does not reflect the reality clearly. However, it could be observed that there is some linkage between the company's economic performance and its involvement in social development. The net profit of companies has certain role in companies' involvement in social development though it is not directly linked. However, the pool of fund in the corporate sector is very vast and if a small amount is diverted towards social development activities, undoubtly, it would give a positive impact on the socio-economic conditions of the country.

A Glimpse at NGO's Developmental Activities

NGOs play an important role to promote social development. The NGOs in our sample are categorized in a number of ways, depending on the nature of their work, their origins and income sources, for example, implementing NGOs, donor NGOs or funding agencies, support NGOs, etc. Data collected from 16 NGOs as part of our study provide a broad picture of how some of the active NGOs in developmental sector perform their activities. All the NGOs are found to have developed their own assessment of the situation, priority selection, performance structure, interaction with

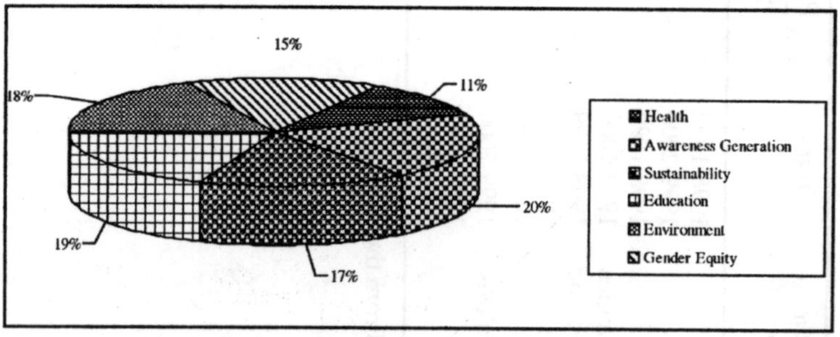

Fig. 8.3 : Broad Activities of NGOs

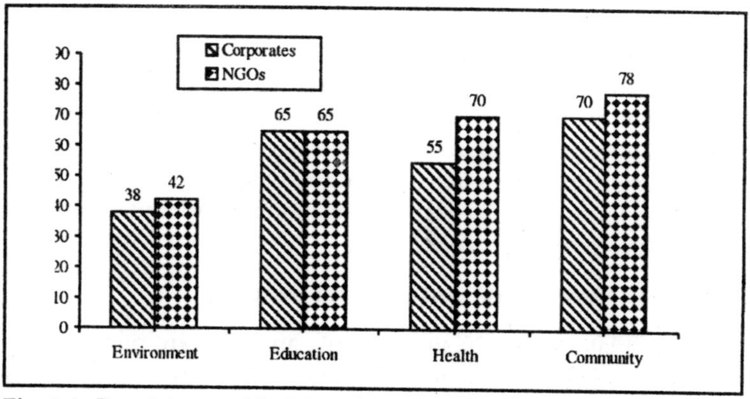

Fig. 8.4 : Broad Areas of Activity of Corporates and NGOs

people, field works etc. Most of them are very flexible in their operation and always try to involve people to get more success in their objectives. Many of them are engaged in awareness and knowledge ceation among the people. They also now adhere to clearcut methods and plans to impart their work. Broad activities undertaken by the NGOs are depicted in Fig. 8.3.

One of the interesting observations is that more and more corporates now-a-days prefer to work with NGOs in collaboration for their developmental activities while deriding how to implement their social responsibility programmes. For our purpose the broad areas of activities of NGOs have been categorized as health, education, environment, awareness generation, gender equity and sustainability. A comparative picture of the performance of the corporates and NGOs is given in the following Fig. 8.4.

Here four areas of activities (environment, education, health and community development) have been taken into consideration to make a comparison between the NGO sector and corporate sector performances in social development.

The study shows that the corporate sector account for 38 per cent in the overall funds generated by NGOs. The case studies reveal that more and more NGOs and corporates are willing to do social developmental work in partnership. NGOs through years of working at grassroots level with people of all strata of life and all kinds of government machineries and offices have acquired tremendous amount of experiences and work efficiencies. So corporates perceive that they will not only save time but also bypass whole lot of odds and difficulties in implementation of their developmental works by leveraging out lot of responsibilities to the NGOs. NGOs role in social sectors though has been limited. Current statistics reveal that their role is getting recognition by the government and also by the corporates. One of the major problems NGOs in India face is generating the required amount of funds for social developmental works.

Trends in Multilateral and Bilateral Funding

The multilateral and bilateral grants and aids are related to the geo-political situation at any given time. These grants and aids are not meant to grow progressively every year for a very longer period. They just initiate the developmental projects in a country and support its sustenance for a brief period of time expecting that the recipient country would pick up its own infrastructure and developmental strength in due course of time. Then gradually these funds start declining. It is almost 10 years since India entered into the liberalization process. So it is expected that India must have developed its own mechanisms to pursue the path of overall development.

The declining trend in external assistance in our case study is depicted in the following Fig. 8.5.

The secondary sources have also suggested the declining trend in the authorization and utilization of external assistance as studied

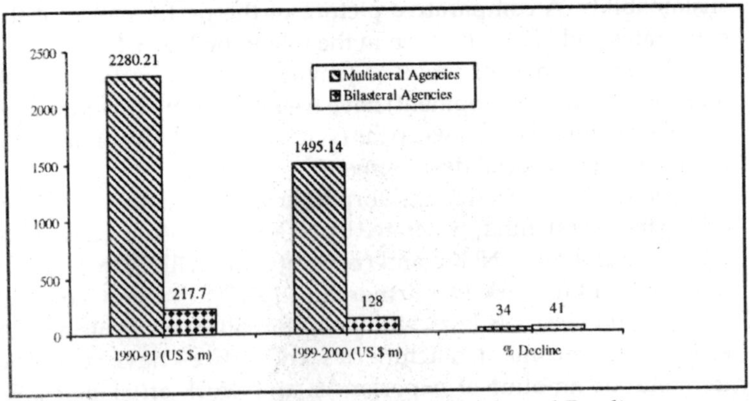

Fig. 8.5 : Declining Trend in Multilateral and Bilateral Funding

in earlier chapters. The sample of 14 multilateral and bilateral agencies was purposively selected, as they have been the major contributors of external assistance. These agencies' contributions towards India's social development purposes have been slowly declining. There are various geo-political reasons behind it. Most of the international agencies and the Western world started considering India to be among the fast developing economies. The general perception is that India has acquired competency and efficiency in various sectors of the economy. India has entered into mare than 10 years of post-liberalization phase. Also she has established its presence in various fields like IT, pharmaceutical, manufacturing, services etc. Therefore, most of the donor agencies think that India has already acquired some self-reliance and sustainability.

However, over the time, the contribution of external and in same areas of social sector expenditure has increased by the various donors and lenders including international organizations such as World Bank, several organs of the United Nations and DFID (the British department for international development). Table 8.2 shows that the share of external aid in sectoral spending on children in the Union budget has increased from 0.5 per cent in 1990-91 to around 29 per cent in 1997-98. On an average for the 1990s, out of every Rs. 100 spent on children around Rs. 20 came from external aid. The share of external aid is the highest for children in the health sector. More than 50 per cent of child health expenditure came from external sources.

Government's Social Sector Expenditure in the 1990

As a proportion of Gross Domestic Product (GDP), the share of social sector expenditure by both the Central Government and State Governments taken together has not increased during the reform period, except in 1999-2000 (Tables 8.3 and 8.4). The shares in the 1990s were lower than those of the 1980s. As a proportion of total public expenditure, the share for the social sector has definitely increased since the mid-1990s if both revenue and capital expenditures are taken together. The proportion was higher in the second half of the 1990s than it was in the late 1980s.

Since 1993-94, the share of GDP devoted to the social sector by the Central Government was higher than that in the base year 1990-91, although not very much different from the shares in the

Table 8.2 : Share of External Aid in Sectoral Spending on Children (Union Budget)

(Per cent)

Year	*Health*	*Child Development*	*Education*	*Total*
1990-91	–	–	1.4	0.5
1991-92	32.2	16.5	2.5	13.4
1992-93	53.3	13.4	4.9	17.1
1993-94	50.6	16.7	10.3	22.7
1994-95	53.2	13.1	20.6	26.2
1995-96	40.6	12.4	19.6	21.7
1996-97	33.6	21.6	13.6	19.5
1997-98	56.3	13.0	26.9	28.6
1998-99	79.0	9.9	22.5	25.3
1999-00	63.6	15.0	25.0	25.9
Average	51.4	14.6	16.4	20.1

Source : Ministry of External Affairs, Government of India, 2000.

late 1980s. As a proportion of public expenditure and as real per capita expenditure, there has been a significant increase in social sector spending since the mid-1990s. These figures were higher than those of the late 1980s. Over the years the number of centrally sponsored schemes has continued to increase, at the expense of the allocation from the overall plan outlay to the states.

The most significant change, visible both at the Centre and in the States, is a shift away from rural development, starting from 1996-97. Within the rural development outlay at the Centre, there is a shift away from rural employment schemes to rural housing, water and rural roads. We also have schemes on basic minimum services since 1996-97. In other words, there is a shift from the traditional ways of addressing rural poverty to human development or basic needs intervention. With regard to health, not much has happened. Neither the States nor the Centre increased their health expenditures considerably. The first half of the 1990s was especially bleak. In the second half of the 1990s, the per capita real expenditure on health by the states increased (but there was no increase in terms of proportion of GDP). Infra-sectoral allocation shows that there has been a shift towards public health and maternal and child health.

With regard to education, the share of education expenditure from all the departments declined from around 4.1 per cent in 1990-91 to 3.8 per cent in 1998-99. The picture on the share of

Table 8.3 : Combined Expenditure of Centre and States on Social Sector as Per Cent of Total Public Expenditure

Major Heads	*1990 -91*	*1991 -92*	*1992 -93*	*1993 -94*	*1994 -95*	*1995 -96*	*1996 -97*	*1997 -98*	*1998 -99*	*1999 -00 (R)*	*2000 -01 (B)*
1. Education sports, youth welfare	11.2	10.9	10.8	10.8	10.8	11.0	11.4	11.3	11.8	12.3	11.4
2. Public health and water supply	4.23	4.15	4.16	4.22	4.28	4.25	4.39	4.52	4.62	4.48	4.47
3. Family welfare	0.60	0.60	0.53	0.59	0.58	0.62	0.56	0.57	0.50	0.56	0.62
	0.99	1.07	0.97	0.90	0.92	1.04	1.40	1.44	1.50	1.66	1.56
4. Housing and Urban development											
5. Broadcasting	0.39	0.34	0.32	0.30	0.29	0.30	0.32	0.32	0.29	0.29	0.17
6. Social security and welfare	2.5	2.55	2.55	2.40	2.47	3.03	2.97	2.88	2.78	2.84	2.86
7. Labour and Employment	0.47	0.45	0.44	0.48	0.41	0.42	0.42	0.43	0.40	0.42	0.41
8. Other social services	1.15	1.14	1.10	1.09	1.18	1.18	1.29	1.19	1.18	1.09	1.23
9. Food subsidy	1.58	1.61	1.41	2.45	1.97	1.83	1.86	2.21	2.04	1.77	2.12
10. Total social services (1 to 8)	21.5	21.1	20.9	20.8	20.9	21.9	22.8	22.7	23.1	23.6	22.7
11. Rural development	3.32	3.13	3.17	3.80	4.10	4.08	3.69	3.48	3.47	3.32	3.02
12. Basic development services	–	–	–	–	–	–	–	–	–	–	–
TOTAL (10+11+12)	24.8	24.3	24.1	24.6	25.0	25.9	27.2	26.9	27.4	27.7	26.6

Note : R - revised; B - budget.

Source : Computed from the data available in Indian Public Finance Statistics, Ministry of Finance, GOI, various issues.

education for the States is the same, but there has been an increase in Central Government expenditure after 1995-96. The education expenditure of the Centre increased from 0.25 per cent of GDP in 1994-95 to 0.31 per cent in 1995-96 to 0.36 per cent in 1998-99. The increase is almost due to increases in spending on elementary education, and to a large extent (but not completely) related to the introduction and expansion of the mid-day meal programme. The intra-sectoral allocations also show that there has been a shift towards elementary education in the 1990s.

Table 8.3 gives the combined expenditures on the various heads as a proportion of aggregate expenditure. The shares for education, housing and urban development, social security and welfare and other social services recorded a rise since the mid-1990s. There was no increase in the share of social sector as a percentage of GDP because the shares were calculated as percentage of aggregate expenditures. Table 8.4 shows the changes in the composition of total social sector expenditure. Education is the major head. In 1990-91, 45 per cent of total social sector expenditure was spent on education. This declined to around 43 per cent in the course of the 1990s. The share of health and water supply has been around 17 per cent throughout the 1990s.

In most states, social sector expenditure has not increased very much in the first half of the 1990s, but in the second half there has been an increase, in terms of per capita real expenditure. The rich and middle income states have done better than the poor states, but there are also huge variations within income groups. Within the group of rich states, social sector spending is highest in Goa. Within the group of middle income states, West Bengal's social spending has increased much less than that of the other middle-income countries, while the absolute level is also not very high. Within the group of poor states, the performance (in terms of spending) of Madhya Pradesh, Orissa and Rajasthan has increased considerably, especially after the mid-1990s, while Bihar and Uttar Pradesh did much less well. In general, the situation of three states (Bihar, Uttar Pradesh and West Bengal) is worrying because both levels and growth of expenditure on social services are lower in these states. In the case of Madhya Pradesh, Orissa and Rajasthan, levels are lower in spite of reasonable growth in social service expenditures (Table 8.5).

Table 8.4 : Changes in the Composition of Combined Social Sector Expenditure of Centre and States (per cent)

Major Heads	*1990-91*	*1995-96*	*1998-99*
1. Education, art and culture	45.1	42.5	43.2
2. Health, water supply	17.0	16.4	16.9
3. Family welfare	2.4	2.4	1.8
4. Housing and urban development	4.0	4.0	5.5
5. Broadcasting	1.6	1.1	1.0
6. Social security and welfare	10.0	11.7	10.2
7. Labour and employment	1.9	1.6	1.5
8. Other social services	4.6	4.5	4.5
9. Social and community services	86.7	84.3	84.3
10. Rural development	13.3	15.7	12.7
11. Basic minimum services	-	-	-
Total Social Sector	100.0	100.0	100.0

Source: Same as Table 8.3.

Table 8.5 : Per Capita Expenditure in Total Social Services in 1998-99

States	*Per Capita Expenditure (Rs.)*
Andhra Pradesh	973
Bihar	476
Goa	3069
Gujarat	1211
Haryana	1111
Karnataka	1001
Kerala	1096
Madhya Pradesh	942
Maharashtra	1045
Orissa	782
Punjab	1157
Rajasthan	1037
Tamil Nadu	1205
Uttar Pradesh	571
West Bengal	740
Weight average of 15 states	879

Source : Planning Commission, Government of India, 2000.

Social sector expenditure in India in the 1990s is low. It is low compared to what India spent in the 1980s; it is low compared to other developing countries, and certainly compared to East Asian countries, and compared to the UNDP recommended ratios. However, since the mid-1990s, a higher proportion of government expenditure has been allocated to the social sector.

Table 8.6 : Index of Per Capita Real Expenditure on Social Services and Rural Development (at 1993-94 Prices)

(at State Level)

States	*Health & Family Welfare*			*Social Services*			*Rural Development*		
	1990-91	*1995-96*	*1998-99*	*1990-91*	*1995-96*	*1998-99*	*1990-91*	*1995-96*	*1998-99*
Goa	100	86	105	100	94	125	100	58	77
Gujarat	100	102	155	100	106	157	100	71	101
Haryana	100	103	152	100	135	143	100	55	39
Maharashtra	100	100	106	100	116	137	100	137	99
Punjab	100	85	139	100	100	135	100	95	93
Rich sub-total	100	98	127	100	113	142	100	108	94
Andhra Pradesh	100	104	149	100	124	157	100	70	148
Karnataka	100	115	151	100	120	152	100	73	73
Kerala	100	109	126	100	105	127	100	90	378
Tamil Nadu	100	106	144	100	103	139	100	58	84
West Bengal	100	76	115	100	81	112	100	86	92
Middle sub-total	100	99	135	100	105	136	100	73	127
Bihar	100	126	98	100	103	107	100	81	221
Madhya Pradesh	100	108	170	100	114	165	100	126	138
Orissa	100	106	135	100	120	146	100	56	82
Rajasthan	100	119	143	100	117	148	100	79	63
U.P.	100	87	87	100	90	118	100	46	59
Poor sub-total	100	105	116	100	104	133	100	70	98
TOTAL	100	101	127	100	107	137	100	79	107

Source : Planning Commission, Government of India, 2000.

In this table, the states are clustered according to their per capita SDP, and divided into three categories—rich, middle and poor states. Here, 1990-91 is taken as a base year. Generally, the increase in per capita expenditure is much more in the second half of the 1990s than in the first half and it is higher for social services than for rural development. Comparing 1998-99 with 1990-91, the richer states did slightly better (in terms of percentage increase) than middle-income or poorer states in education and social sector generally. The middle-income states performed better in health and rural development. The intra-group variation is, however, considerable, which makes it difficult to draw groupwise conclusions. West Bengal, for instance, has done much worse in education than the other middle-income states. With regard to health, Bihar and U.P. do much worse than the other poor states. In the case of rural development, all except five states recorded decline in the index in 1998-99 compared to that of 1990-91. There has been an unprecedented increase in expenditure on rural development in Kerala and Bihar in 1998-99. On the other hand, there has been a significant decline in rural development expenditures in Haryana.

An Assessment of Beneficiaries' Participation in Social Development

This analysis is to corroborate the findings in the previous chapter. As already mentioned, the four alternative rankings for each indicator A : Access and benefit assessment, B: Community organization and activity assessment, and C: Community self-reliance and empowerment assessment, provides judgements on the level of participation existing within the project. Scoring on various criteria enables the community to agree on where there are problems, where decisions need to be taken to alter the current working practices and to assist in identification of new aims and criteria. This exercise not only gives an understanding of participation in the project but also helps the communities assess their own position and define their roles within the programme.

Scores for different groups (NGO and corporate sector beneficiaries) have been recorded for assessing participation. A comparison between the group scores on different indicators helped assess the strengths and weaknesses of participation at various levels of the programme. Overall, this process acts as a self-educating tool for the community organizations, individuals

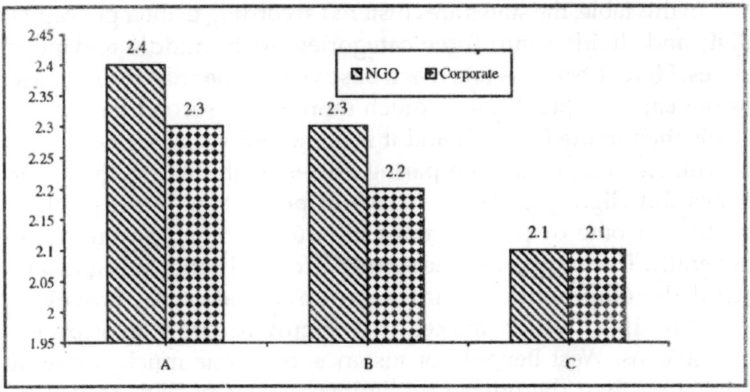

Fig. 8.6 : Comparative Assessment of Participation

and the project staff, apart from a mere assessment of participation in a development project. The following figure presents the mean scores of all the three indicators (A, B and C) in case of both NGO and corporate beneficiaries.

The mean scores for each indicator have been calculated from Tables 7.12 and 7.13 in Chapter 7. The average of the individual components of each three indicators (A: A1; B: B1, B2, B3, B4, B5, B6; C : C1, C2, C3, C4, C5) has been calculated to compare the results between the NGO beneficiaries and the corporate sector beneficiaries. The above figure clearly shows that NGOs have been successful in working closely with the local people. NGOs have better understanding of local people's problems and difficulties. This result provides strong support to the argument that NGO-corporate sector partnership would lead to proper and efficient implementation of social developmental programmes initiated by the corporate sector. Various studies have shown how the wholehearted support of some NGOs has also been an important contributing factor to some of the success stories of the people's planning programme. They contributed by mobilizing people, conducting seminars and camps, organizing training programmes, drawing up projects and development report and publishing a large number of books, manuals and guidelines. Now the positive role of NGOs is widely recognized in decentralized planning.

Conclusion

This chapter has given a picture that how various players in social development in the economy are involved in social development. For the purpose of social developmental planning, all the stakeholders (corportes, NGOs, the government, multilateral and bilateral agencies) have identified the areas, namely, education, health, women's development, agriculture, irrigation, animal husbandry, infrastructure, community development, environment, rural developments , etc. The analysis reveals that the government's spending in social sectors has remained more or less stagnant, but still in terms of the amount of money spent, the government is the dominant player in social development. The NGO and the corporate sectors are emerging as significant partners in social development in the light of not-so-rosy picture of external assistance. The need of the hour is to support innovative forms of partnerships in the triangle of Governments (National, State), businesses, and civil society (communities, NGOs, CBOs). There is a spectrum of possible relationships between public and private actors for the provision of social services.

9 Conclusion and Suggestions

Introduction

Over Fifty years of independence and planned development have taken India several steps forward in various areas of human concern. The increase in food production, the diversity of our energy, industrial and commercial sectors and the breadth of our scientific endeavour are widely and justifiably held up as examples of achievement unparalleled in history.

In these fifty years, the official figures show the literacy has gone up from 17 per cent to 55 per cent, steel production from 1.5 to 25 million tonnes, electricity generation from 3.5 to 90 million MW. Some 10 million Indians can today consider themselves a part of the global elite, holding there own on every front: material possessions, energy consumption, physical comfort, mobility, wealth and world-wide influence. Another 100 million people live in relatively comfortable economic circumstances, comparable to those in middle income countries. Yet another 200 million manage a passable existence, with access to television, telephones and modern transport, if not privately, at least through public facilities.

As the nation is progressing towards becoming a modern technological economy, we have something to be proud of. The flip side of development coin is, however, not so pretty. A large majority of our people, especially in rural India, are still on a never ending treadmill of poverty and deprivation.

The remaining 600 millions of our fellow citizens live in conditions that vary from the sub-human to the abysmal, comparable to those in other least developed economies on earth. Almost none of these people have drinking water sources or toilets in their homes, let alone electricity connections or other modern amenities for their most basic day-to-day needs.

Many among the last 300 million, a population greater than that of North America or Europe, do not even have proper homes or safe drinking water within reasonable distance of their dwelling. They have access to virtually no product or service resulting from modern science and industry beyond safety matches, kerosene lamps, bicycles and of course the ubiquitous transistor radio. The kerosene or batteries are often too costly or difficult for them to get. This situation is more visible across the vast expanse of rural India, which further leads to migration and burgeoning of urban slums.

A careful analysis indicates that the constraints or bottlenecks of one type of institutional stakeholder are in reality, the strengths of another. While government has the reach and ability to make initial public investments; industry has the products, services and ability to garner private entrepreneurship and investments. On the other hand, NGOs have the capability to mobilize local communities and also adapt products and services such that they meaningfully reach the last mile. At the same time, the innovation capability of the scientific community is essential to foresee and design for current and future challenges.

Over the years indian Industry graduated from shaky raw material procurement to addressing business needs based primarily on their own perception of the felt need! Now the issue is, what Indian industry was directed towards its goal and what it has delivered in relevance to 'development' cause, the existing dissimilarity within the system. Understanding the pros and cons of responsibility to do something rather address it as a development issue. Looking at this as an evolving system that would impact quality in totality rather than addressing it disjointedly. Based on this, a comprehensive model could be developed towards growth and sustainability for society at large.

In recent global scenario, often industrial sector assuming threat of uneven competition and coincidentally India has embraced the *mantra* of the market, this can be looked at very optimistically and considering as an opportunity for this phase of 'transition'.

What is lacking, however, is the institutional mechanism for meaningful cooperation. There is an urgent need to establish platforms for Public-Private Partnerships (PPP) where different stakeholders in society are able to contribute their might towards accelerated rural development. The vision of transforming India into a developed nation by 2020 is dependent on several such partnerships and platforms.

Coining an example to justify the present government stand, in the 15th Indian Economic Summit jointly organised by the Confederation of Indian Industry (CII) and World Economic Forum on November 26, 2000, the then Prime Minister, Mr. Atal Behari Vajpayee said the 'rapid changes brought about by technology and globalisation has to be addressed with care and caution and the process of change has to be managed with sensitivity. In this regard, corporate participation in social development for better governance, which will enhance the peoples' confidence in the private sector'.

Conclusion

After the onslaught of liberalisation, privatisation and globalisation (LPG), a small picture has been presented in the study about the government's standing for the social development programmes, which have remained, fluid and unstandardised. There is a multiplicity of schemes that undergo constant repackaging and shifting by governments, as they try to make their agenda more vote oriented. There is a good deal of confusion regarding the actual head of accounts under which the expenditure is made in various government departments. Moreover, allocations are transferred to different states who often reallocate them across different sub-sectors. Thus the transparency of actual flow of funds to the poor is greatly impaired. Another chronic feature is that actual expenditure lags behind the allocations made. A comparative look at the actual spending reveals that there has been significant increase only in two years, i.e. 1993-94 and 1995-96 by 37 per cent and 22 per cent respectively over the previous years in constant terms. Increases in other years are nominal while there has been 18 per cent decline during 1996-97. Considering the objectives of increasing actual spending to the proximity of 20 per cent of allocation in the respective years, the actual expenditure remains far too low. A recent survey conducted by Indian Market Research Bureau (IMRB) suggests positive mood of the corporate sector. The survey covered 500 companies with sales between Rs. 200 crores to Rs. 500 crores. It was found from the survey findings that about 85 per cent of companies apparently showed interest in contributing to social development. The study found that companies viewed their projects as a form of strategic investment[71]. Rather than seen as a return on investment they are viewed as being charitable gifts. But neither are they mere extensions of the firms commercial activities, since they are expected to aid the entire community and not just the company and its shareholders. Community development efforts are oriented to growth rather than Zero-sum game[72] redistribution[73]; their objective is not to divide the pie more equitably, but to grow more pies. Corporate social investment helps the company because the company is a part of the community where the investment is being made. Returns on investment are thus seen as a public good that benefits a company by making its home community a more desirable place to live and work.

The recent estimates released by Associate Chamber of Commerce and Industry in India reveals that the share of private corporate sector in total investment in the economy was 36 per cent in 1999-2000. This investment is equal to 131531 crores. The gross investment by the private sector for the same year has been calculated to be about 8.4 per cent of the GDP. If we assume a situation where 85 per cent of the companies annually invest mere 1 per cent (of their total amount of Profit after Tax) in social development, the total corporate investment will be about Rs. 1 lakh crore, this sum is much more than what people of India expect from the Indian corporate sector.

As noted above in the previous chapters that corporate social development is mainly confined with business-link sponsorship output or they participated in capacity building[74] activities. Joint activities of corporates, NGOs and the government went beyond welfare-based approaches to development. It has been found that NGOs are trying to involve more corporates into social development, and building more and more partnerships. Its a major paradigm shift in the recent trend and contemporary history of social development—for both sectors.

The recent years have witnessed a growing shift in the corporate involvement in social development. However, there is the need for increasing cross-sector collaborations at both ends of the spectrum. Corporate partnerships must be seen as strategic, serving the long-term interests of the company and of the stakeholders in the partnership venture, including both the partners—NGOs and the community beneficiaries. Large and medium-large business houses have come forward realizing their social responsibilities. There are a large number of NGOs that are doing very crucial work in generating awareness, mobilization and organization of the poor and the vulnerable, increasing the access of the poor to various state programmes and working on citizen empowerment.

This 'coming together for social development' within which all stakeholders contribute individually and collectively will ensure allocations of essential means for a viable and sustainable human future. This inter-sectoral approach accesses resources unique to each organisation or each sector to be productive and creates new options that neither sector or organisation can develop on its own. It has been well established in the study. If each sector puts its best only then the emergent effort will be effective for sustainable development. This is possible while each sector can implement its own strategy based on its strengths, whereby giving satisfaction of achievement to all.

This study outlines a correlation between the direction of economic growth and poverty reduction. In the reform period, it is clear that the proportional plan and budgetary allocation for the social sector spending on health, housing, nutrition, water supply, sanitation, education, roads and electrification has come down from 39.32 per cent in 1985-90 (pre-reforms) to 35.95 per cent in 1991-97 (post-reforms). Except for SC/ST welfare, the expenditure on all other sub-sectors under social services showed a declining trend.

While establishing the rationale in favour of the objectives and hypothesis of the study, it has been firmly reflected that the policies cannot succeed unless a degree of stabilization has been brought about. The reform programmes must be tailored to the socio-economic framework prevailing in the Indian economy and must take into account the political feasibility of the measures contained in them. Therefore, it is essential to promote shared growth[75]. In context with this, the corporate participation in social development is the only solution to achieve the real meaning of sustainability.

Most of the activities of the corporate sector have been specific to development at micro-level[76] often overlooking the larger societal issues and concerns related to ecology, natural resources, liberalization, privatization, structural adjustments and issues of rights and justice, citizen organization and empowerment.

The future partnerships can come together as a joint force on larger issues of development on a formal and sustained basis and also can form formidable alliances for advocacy with the government, bilateral and other international development agencies. These partnerships need to see that funds, supports and efforts do not get concentrated for only one type of development approach and ideology and one type of NGOs.

NGOs have developed greater insight into the social and economic relationships and power patterns that exist in our highly hierarchical social structure. Corporates have benefited by partnering the NGOs on many of the dimensions of development. Social development requires a process-based approach to development interventions. There has been a growing recognition in the corporate sector that the way to work towards sustainable development is to reduce the social and economic inequalities. There is also increased understanding at the grassroots level of the resources and expertise required for development. The corporate sector has begun to view their business in the context of the socio-political environment, thereby broadening their perspectives of development beyond GNP and per capita income. There is also a marked shift from charity to social development. More and more businesses, either through their own foundations or in partnerships with NGOs, are now increasingly getting involved in development activities and somewhat more on sustained basis.

Many business corporations today accept that it is in their interest to be more socially aware and to engage in programmes for the benefit of the community. However, the number of corporations actually undertaking social development programmes is still very small. Mostly, companies prefer to undertake development project themselves or to contribute cash on request. There are fewer instances of companies building up sustained relationships with NGOs. For many, the lack of motivation is partly due to a lack of information about and exposure to community problems and social development projects. Corporate support has gradually moved from one time charitable giving to a more long a-term relationship based on a perception of mutual relevance and benefit. The cases selected for the study profile some creative and diverse approaches to corporate social development. As noted above, businesses sponsored or participated in capacity-building activities. Joint activities of corporates, NGOs and the government went beyond welfare-based[77] approaches to development. It has been found that NGOs are trying to involve more corporates into social development, and building more and more partnerships. There exists spectrum of possible relationships between public and private actors for the provision of social development and these need to be exploited.

Limitations

With the onset of the process of 'liberalization, privatisation and globalization' (LPG) since the early nineties, the approach and attitude towards business have changed dramatically. Gone are the days when 'standards' were centred on only the material aspects of the product. Today we are talking of 'social standards' to be achieved by an enterprise if it is to participate in the field of global trade. In recent global scenario, often industrial sector assuming threat of uneven competition and coincidentally India has adopted the mantra of the market, we look at it optimistically and considering as an opportunity to prepare us for this phase of 'transition'. Thus arises the concept of ranking enterprises in terms of their roles in fulfilling 'Social Audit'.[78] Unfortunately, the Indian corporate world is still to take this issue seriously. We, in India, are yet to develop a mechanism to take care of this concern. 'Social Audit' can fill the existing vacuum and identify the extent of 'social responsibility' being borne by the organisation in question. This process has not yet been started and therefore it is one of the major limitations towards developing a conducive environment for sustainable corporate social development practice.

In the current situation, the concept of corporate social responsibility is in between infancy and middle stage in India, though it was existent in different forms, e.g. charity and philanthropy[79] since the last fifty years or so. To what extent corporates are effectively pursuing social development works is not a well-established phenomena in the culture of Indian society. And even in this direction very few studies have been done in India so far. It is observed that most of the corporates (about 95 per cent) do not disclose the amount they spend on social developmental activities. Even in many cases they do not have a planned strategy for their involvement in social development. They spend simply through miscellaneous fund.

Due to the lack of transparency, the future partnerships cannot come together as a joint force on larger issues of development on a formal and sustained basis and also it can be hurdled to form formidable alliances for advocacy with bilateral and other international development agencies.

This study has covered 16 corporates from five respective zones of India and the 16 NGOs, and with systematic case studies and structured volume of data, this intervention categorically gives essence of a national character. To obtain significance of correlation, simple and comprehensive statistical operation was administered rather than in-depth statistical operation. Only descriptive statistical tools have been used for the purpose of arriving at the conclusion. The state-wise coverage of corporate sector and NGOs would have produced a better version of the issue.

Suggestions

1. An institutional linkage that is very much required towards institutionalising the corporate social development.
2. The true meaning of convergence and synergy with diverse stockholders, viz. corporate sector, NGO and government needs to be spelt out more practically at the policy level which could facilitate the themes into reality.
3. In the contemporary stages, especially on this subject, academic researches are very less in Indian context, therefore and thereby systematic research needs to be carried out with the perspective of social work, management and development institutes.
4. During the course of this research it has been observed that for Corporate Social Development a totally different knowledge based professional is required. It needs a professional groomed to understand and analyze both the sector, i.e. corporate and social development at a time with the same value. Therefore, to fill up the existing vacuum a fresh research at the national level is need of the hour.
5. After the package of liberalisation, privatisation and globalisation the international funds are declining for the social sector and State Governments are running out of money. Contrary to this, still there are tremendous in-house untapped resources are existing. So in this juncture corporate associations could play a vital role to collect resources from their respective members and develop a mechanism to channellise this money for social development with a transparent and accountable manner.

6. Mastering the cultural differences between corporate executives and community activists remains one of the most important challenges in making community redevelopment work. To build (or rebuild) bridges, companies need to cultivate relationship with non-profit groups and community leaders who enjoy credibility and stature with local residents. As important as these relationships are, corporate liaison staff should also make a point of maintaining visibility and contact at the grassroots level, so that they are not relying solely on peer-level meetings with local leaders for their impressions of community opinions, concerns and priorities.
7. Private public partnership such as Government-Local People or Local Institutions and Corporate Sector for wasteland development (CII's Study) could generate huge employment and save Rs.10,000 crores imports and leads the country towards sustainable growth.
8. The ISO 9000 and ISO 14000 are essential ingredients to enter into the international market but these are not abiding by the land of the law for the corporate sector. In the same manner and fashion social audit is one of the essential requirements for the corporate sector. In the light of LPG, this has been proved that social auditing is a must for the corporate sector. Therefore, through the knowledge base on corporate social development, social development institutes could play facilitator role for the corporate sector. This is a new emerging area where both the sectors could get benefit. This also covers to get non-compliance but essential certificates.
9. In micro-finance, social marketing and marketing of handloom and handicraft products corporate sector and its respective associations can act as a facilitator for their broader and extended business to empower the people, artisans, producers groups and NGOs towards sustainability.

The Future Challenger

This study has attempted to generate and analyse data on substantial part of corporate and social sector relationship. A trend of tentative estimate on corporate investment in social development has been rationally found. Hitherto, no such study is available on corporate financing of social development. The sectoral secondary data from both sectors are available in various forms. But in absence of applicable enlightenment in regard to the type of relationships between these two sectors, these data cannot be correlated. Corporations need to make a serious commitment to set aside atleast 1/2 per cent of profit after tax (PAT) for social betterment. A part of it could be spent on local community safety nets which could include making provision for vocational skills, colleges, schools, adult education, creation of community assets like water tanks, toilets, creches, and preservation of local art and culture. The balance be given to NGOs or individuals working at any level—State, National or Regional—to promote innovative and experimental research and action, preferably in emerging and underfunded areas. At the macro level, business needs to support more research and action on corporate community involvement, through a long term investment strategy. To have better reflections on the transition from corporate philanthropy to corporate social development, an attempt is made in this study to reveal this transition in the Indian context. It is highly anticipated that in the near future a fresh study will be able to facilitate in-depth impression for future relationships between these two sectors and thus an exemplary new avenue will be open for planners and implementers to incorporate'corporate funds' in their future planning for social development to reconstruct the nation. This study obviously establishes mutually beneficial relationship between these two sectors. Apart from the above, there could be an intervention which would attempt to explore a possible solution for such a huge fund management problem.

Rather than advocating for creation of different agencies for corporate funding in social development, future study can explore very positive and effective roles of corporate associations. But in near future a systematic research intervention is required to strengthen the efforts to exploration to pooling of the unexplored potential fund from different companies (rather than individual investment) and using it through professional bodies of corporate and non-corporate sectors (Non-Government Organizations) that ultimately will help us a lot in our fight against poverty; with an introspect on business towards self-sustained sustainability!

REFERENCES

71. Resources employed to the achievement of a comprehensive set of goals and plans (Mohanty, M. & Singh, A.K., 2001; Voluntarism and Government: Policy, programme and assistance; New Delhi : Voluntary Action Network India - VANI).
72. Where one player's loss is the other players gain [Ball, C. & Dunn, L. (1995); Non-government organizations: Guidelines for good policy and practice; London: The Commonwealth Foundation].
73. Distributing again (Mittal, L. N., 1997; Economic growth vs. social well-being; *Social Welfare*, May, 18-20).
74. A state of betterment brought about in entire community or in all directions (Singh, S., 1996 ; Economic reforms with a human face. Economic Growth and Social Change, March, 90-92.)
75. At the lowest level of operation; At a small scale; [Bhattacharya, D. (1999): Political parties need to make commitments on social development. Equinox, Vol. I, issue I, 3-5].
76. Something that aids or promotes well-being (Singh, K.A.N., 1999 ; Defining the voluntary organizations in India : Some reflections; Institutional Development, Vol. 6, No. 2,10-25).
77. A systematic review of the groups and communities affected by a project, and how the costs and benefits of the project impact on each of them. It assesses the likely impact of the project on their way of life, which may also include cultural considerations (Sampradan, 2001; Giving and Fund Raising in India : New Delhi: Indian Centre for Philanthropy).
78. Voluntary promotion of human welfare; (Nayyar, D., 1996; Globalization: The past in our present. Economic Growth and Social Change, March, 11-16).

APPENDICES

Appendix I

QUESTIONNAIRE SCHEDULE FOR CORPORATES

1. General information:
   - Name of the Organization:
   - Address:

   - Name of Contact Person:
   - Sales Turnover and Profit after Tax year-wise

Rank	Year	Sales Turnover (STO)	Profit After Tax (PAT)

- Details of Projects Taken:
-
-
-
-
-
-

2. (a) Ongoing Projects

-
-
-
-

(b) Selection criteria for project selection:

-
-
-
-

(c) Objective of organization:

-
-
-
-

3. Process of Implementation:
   - As guided by the organisation [Y] [N]
   - Modified for organizational purpose [Y] [N]
   - Modified for the sake of beneficiaries [Y] [N]
   - Participatory approach all through [Y] [N]

4 Achievements:

-
-
-
-

5. Problems faced and

-
-
-
-

6. Strategies to overcome the problems

-
-
-
-

7. Sustainability of the projects/programmes:

-
-
-
-

7A. Qualitative Aspects: Some observations

____

____

____

____

QUESTIONNAIRE SCHEDULE FOR NGOS

1. General Information:
   - Name of the Organization:
   - Address:
   - Year of Registration:
   - Name of Contact Person:
   - Details of Projects Taken:

2. (a) Ongoing Projects/Programmes:
   -
   -
   -
   -

   (b) Selection criteria for project selection:
   -
   -
   -
   -

   (c) Objective of organization:
   -
   -
   -
   -

(d) Demand of the beneficiaries:

-
-
-
-

(e) Availability of fund:

-
-
-
-

3. Sources of Funding:

Government	Foreign	Matching Grant	Raising Fund From Corporate	Asking for Donations	Others

4. Process of Implementation:
   - As guided by the funder [Y] [N]
   - Modified for organizational purpose [Y] [N]
   - Modified for the sake of beneficiaries [Y] [N]
   - Participatory approach all through [Y] [N]

5. Beneficiaries (Methods used):

-
-
-
-

6. Achievements:

-
-
-
-

7. Problems faced and Strategies to overcome the problems:
   -
   -
   -
   -
8. Sustainability of the projects/programmes:
   -
   -
   -
   -

QUESTIONNAIRES ON ASSESSING PARTICIPATION VIZ. SUSTAINABILITY IN THE EYES OF BENEFICIARY

Name :
Gender :
Age :
Place :

A. Access/benefit assessment

01. How many people are utilising project services and benefiting from the programme?
    3 = Entire community in the programme area.
    2 = Most of the community in the programme area.
    1 = Some of the community in the programme area.
    0 = Only few members of the community in the programme area.

B. Community organisation and activity assessment

01. Who are the representative (social groups) in the community based village organisation?
    3 = Representatives from all the social groups and castes.
    2 = Representatives from prominent social groups and castes.
    1 = Rich and influential people with some members from dominant castes.
    0 = Only rich and influential people.
02. What is the representation of women and lower/backward classes in the community organisation
    3 = Equal representation of women, lower/backward class.

2 = Organisation has women, lower/backward class representation but lacks equal representation.
1 = Women, lower/backward class representatives are very few.
0 = There are no women, lower/backward class representatives.

03. What is the frequency of meetings of the village organisation?
3 = Very frequent
2 = Not too frequent but not very irregular as well
1 = Not very frequent
0 = Meet occasionally when need arises

04 What is the contribution (in cash or kind) of the people in group activities?
3 = All contribute willingly and enthusiastically.
2 = Most of them contribute, depending on their situation and capacity.
1 = Some of them contribute and some do not.
0 = No one contributes for group activities.

05. How dependent is the community organisation on the Project Implementing Agency (PIA) and the programme?
3 = Group can now or very soon operate essentially on its own with only minimal assistance from PIA and programme.
2 = Group can within 6-12 months operate on its own with minimal assistance from PIA and the programme.
I = Group can within 12 - 2 = 4 months operate on its own with minimal assistance from PIA and the programme.
0 = Group cannot within foreseeable future operate on its own.

06. How much understanding and support have the group created within the community?
3 = Group enjoys strong and enthusiastic support from the community at large for its activities and continuation.
2 = Group has good understanding and support from parts of the community, such as village heads and village administration.
1 = Group has a little understanding and support from the community.
0 = Group has no understanding and support from the community.

C. Community self-reliance and empowerment assessment

01. How well does the community carry on its meetings without the PAs?
    3 = The community is able to meet regularly and effectively without the PAs.
    2 = The community can meet without the PAs but, PAs occasional attendance in meetings necessary for regular and effective meetings.
    1 = Community can from time to time meet without PAs.
    0 = Community cannot meet without PAs present.
02. Do the community members help each other apart from the group activities?
    3 = Community members frequently help each other with loans and other services.
    2 = Community members sometimes help each others.
    1 = Community members once in a while help each others.
    0 = Community members never help each other.
03. Do the community members show increased self-confidence as a result of group activities?
    3 = All the community members have gained much self-confidence as a result of group activities.
    2 = Most of the community members have gained some self-confidence from group activities.
    1 = Some of the community members have gained some self-confidence from group activities.
    0 = Community members have not gained any self-confidence as a result of group activities.
04. How does the community get and ensure feedback on its performance?
    3 = Community has well established procedures for monitoring and evaluating its performance.
    2 = The community has periodic monitoring and evaluation of its performance.
    1 = The community has occasional monitoring and evaluation of its performance.
    0 = The community has no provision for monitoring and evaluating its performance.
05. How confident is the community that it can maintain itself after the development programme is withdrawn?
    3 = The community is quite confident that it can maintain itself on its own.

2 = The community is somewhat confident that it can maintain itself on its own.
1 = The community thinks it might be able to maintain itself on its own.
0 = The community lacks confidence that it can maintain itself on its own.

QUESTIONNAIRE FOR MULTILATERAL ORGANIZATION (Non-Profit Organization)

1. General Information:
   -
   -
   -
   -
2. Objectives/Aims:

   ____

   ____

   ____

3. Manner of Function:
   -
   -
   -
   -
4. Sector-wise Assistance in the Past:
   -
   -
   -
   -
5. Present Sector-wise Funding:
   -
   -
   -
   -
6. Conditions for Assistance (India *vis-a-vis* regional and global):
   -
   -
   -
   -

QUESTIONNAIRE FOR BILATERAL ORGANIZATION
(Non-Profit Organization)

1. General Information:
   -
   -
   -
   -
2. Aims and Objectives of Subsector Funding:
   -
   -
   -
   -
3. Funding Criteria and Pattern in the Past and the Present:
   -
   -
   -
   -
4. Change of Policy Strategy:

   ____

   ____

   ____

   ____

   ____

   ____
5. Special Comments (if any)
   -
   -
   -
   -

E-mail Questions:

1. Is your company involved in any kind of social development activities? Y N
2. What kind of social developmental activities your company is performing?
   -
   -
   -
   -
   -
   -
3. What kind of people should be given social developmental support?
   -
   -
   -
   -
   -
   -
4. Is your company pursuing sustainable kind of development programmes? Y N
5. What is the mode of your company's involvement in social development?
   -
   -
   -
   -
   -
   -
6. Do you think that taking up social development work will add human aspect to your company's image? Y N
7. Do you think your social developmental participation will provide great boost to the smooth functioning of the Government? Y N

Appendix II

Names of the companies Responded to E-MAIL Questions

Company	*Sales (Rs. Cr.)*	*Sales Rank*	*PAT (Rs. Cr.)*	*PAT Rank*	*NFA (Rs. Cr.)*	*RANK*	*M.CAP (Rs. Cr.)*	*M.CAP Rank*	*ROCE %*	*ROCE Rank*	*Total*
Hindustan Lever	10,604	8	1,310	7	1,204	46	42,691	1	52.01	5	38
Indian Oil Corporation	106,739	1	2,720	2	22,089	2	9,200	8	20.73	72	47
Videsh San-char Nigam	7,298	12	1,681	4	2,413	24	5,619	12	25.51	42	59
ITC	4,204	21	1,006	10	1,961	31	15,015	6	29.39	28	61.5
ONGC	23,369	6	5,229	1	23,844	1	18,894	4	16.85	106	64
BPCL	45,932	2	820	12	5,166	13	4,259	15	19.71	77	68
Reliance Petroleum	30,963	4	1,464	6	14,384	5	13,476	7	16.73	110	71.5
Reliance Industries	25,429	5	2,646	3	15,448	4	23,146	3	15.85	124	73.5
HPCL	44,589	3	1,088	9	6,515	9	3,673	20	18.45	89	76.5
GAIL	9,826	9	1,126	8	7,101	7	4,034	16	17.00	100	82.5
WIPRO	3,054	27	666	15	603	76	24,744	2	33.84	17	83
MTNL	5,785	18	1,557	5	5,028	15	6,993	10	17.51	93	84.5
Infosys Techonologies	1,901	44	623	17	558	80	15,893	5	44.85	8	101.5
Hero Honda Motors	3,171	24	261	26	454	93	3,656	21	43.32	9	109
TISCO	6,839	14	839	11	2,538	6	2,671	27	15.90	121	110

Contd...

Contd...

Company	*Sales (Rs. Cr.)*	*Sales Rank*	*PAT (Rs. Cr.)*	*PAT Rank*	*NFA (Rs. Cr.)*	*RANK*	*M.CAP (Rs. Cr.)*	*M.CAP Rank*	*ROCE %*	*ROCE Rank*	*Total*
National Aluminium	2,406	33	654	16	3,192	22	2,713	26	19.53	78	117
IPCL	4,987	19	249	30	6,144	10	871	49	16.77	107	141.5
BHEL	6,129	17	469	18	1,204	45	3,108	23	13.88	152	147.5
Grasim Industries	4,822	20	378	21	3,321	21	2,286	30	13.40	160	151
Nestle India	1,582	55	191	53	418	102	4,966	14	39.61	11	152
Nirma	2,052	41	250	29	1,902	32	2,314	29	16.87	105	153
Larsen & Toubro	7,379	11	269	25	4,671	16	3,997	17	10.65	210	153.5
Hindalco Industries	2,275	34	678	14	3,439	20	3,803	18	11.72	192	165
Tata Power	3,360	23	403	19	3,600	19	2,044	33	11.62	195	172.5
Satyam Computer	1,220	78	316	24	369	110	3,442	22	36.89	13	173.5
Ranbaxy Lab.	1,689	51	182	36	644	69	7,121	9	15.85	123	174
BSES	2,683	31	321	23	2,109	27	2,344	28	11.97	187	177.5
Shipping Corporation	3,064	26	383	20	2,999	23	610	65	14.19	144	184.5
Bajaj Auto	3,026	28	343	22	1,362	42	2,990	25	11.38	202	186
Indo Gulf Corporation	2,199	36	252	28	1,807	35	654	62	16.29	115	187
Neyveli Lignite Corporation	2,198	37	729	13	4,130	17	1,367	42	11.89	189	188.5
TATA Chemicals	1,382	65	255	27	1,884	33	667	61	16.62	111	211.5
Container Corporation	1,075	89	217	34	608	75	871	50	26.57	37	212

Contd...

Contd...

Company	*Sales (Rs. Cr.)*	*Sales Rank*	*PAT (Rs. Cr.)*	*PAT Rank*	*NFA (Rs. Cr.)*	*RANK*	*M.CAP (Rs. Cr.)*	*M.CAP Rank*	*ROCE %*	*ROCE Rank*	*Total*
Dr. Reddy's Laboratories	913	105	145	43	331	120	5,449	13	30.60	25	212
IBP Co.	8,507	10	54	102	639	70	596	67	16.89	103	214.5
Castrol India	1,238	76	134	45	173	171	3,084	24	35.08	16	216
Asian Paints	1,197	80	106	61	376	108	1,683	38	24.94	45	225
Chambal Fertilizers	1,795	48	116	55	2,050	28	406	85	16.99	101	225
Gujarat Ambuja Cements	1,269	71	186	35	1,963	30	2,064	32	11.96	188	229.5
Ashok Leyland	2,252	35	92	70	961	52	673	60	13.95	150	231
CIPLA	967	98	179	37	187	162	6,650	11	24.66	50	233.5
Hindustan Zinc	1,613	54	169	39	648	68	549	71	16.21	116	236.5
ACC	2,610	32	47	114	2,298	25	1,808	34	9.94	223	247
Bharat Electronics	1,667	52	155	40	201	156	480	76	25.49	43	247.5
Mahindra & Mahindra	3,521	22	127	49	1,483	41	581	69	8.81	232	252
Motor Industries Company	1,472	57	96	68	320	123	597	66	19.33	79	258
Chennai Petroleum	6,957	13	122	51	1,288	44	296	105	11.66	194	262.5
Colgate Pamolive	1,123	83	63	93	201	158	2,169	31	24.90	46	262.5
Smithkline Beecham	753	125	12	57	340	117	1,719	37	29.21	29	263.5
Dabur India	1,107	85	78	74	243	142	1,626	39	21.56	66	265
Kochi Refineries	6,229	16	94	69	1,531	39	410	82	9.84	226	265

Contd...

Contd...

Company	*Sales (Rs. Cr.)*	*Sales Rank*	*PAT (Rs. Cr.)*	*PAT Rank*	*NFA (Rs. Cr.)*	*RANK*	*M.CAP (Rs. Cr.)*	*M.CAP Rank*	*ROCE %*	*ROCE Rank*	*Total*
Indian Aluminum Company	1,227	77	130	48	753	60	540	73	14.12	145	276.5
Britannia Industries	1,286	70	71	80	159	184	1,397	41	21.47	68	277
Sterliute Optical Tech.	748	127	226	32	292	127	567	70	58.39	3	278
Great Eastern Shipping	1,007	92	177	38	1,615	38	546	72	13.13	167	285.5
Siemens	1,083	88	69	84	245	140	693	59	23.79	54	286
Century Textiles	1,712	50	74	77	1,833	34	232	117	14.95	134	289.5
Gujarat Narmada Valley	1,339	66	106	62	955	54	314	100	15.17	131	289.5
Punjab Tractors	965	99	113	56	163	180	788	54	26.33	38	290
Sail	14,277	7	731	290	16,398	3	1,735	36	8.74	233	306
Ballatpur Industries	1,446	60	100	64	1,678	37	279	107	12.43	180	307.5
Escorts	1,291	68	107	60	662	67	350	92	13.02	168	307.5
Cummins India	860	109	109	58	172	174	992	46	18.77	86	314
Videocon International	3,076	25	155	41	2,013	29	128	152	10.41	215	319.5
Indian Rayon	1,416	61	69	83	808	59	414	81	10.04	221	323.5
TVS-Suzuki	1,812	47	63	91	436	98	204	124	15.74	125	328
GTL	815	116	243	31	508	88	243	114	18.95	83	331
Lupin	831	112	60	97	437	97	278	109	30.23	26	331
RCF	2,052	40	61	95	990	51	279	108	9.80	227	334.5
India Cements	1,257	72	48	111	1,491	40	408	83	10.54	212	336.5

Contd...

Contd...

Company	*Sales (Rs. Cr.)*	*Sales Rank*	*PAT (Rs. Cr.)*	*PAT Rank*	*NFA (Rs. Cr.)*	*RANK*	*M.CAP (Rs. Cr.)*	*M.CAP Rank*	*ROCE %*	*ROCE Rank*	*Total*
Adani Exports	3,014	29	118	54	38	270	236	116	23.00	60	337
Glaxo India	851	111	71	82	101	217	1,508	40	20.48	74	337.5
Telco	6,688	15	430	289	3,824	18	1,747	35	1.56	270	338.5
MRF	1,873	45	64	88	440	96	205	122	13.32	163	340.5
NIIT	750	126	224	33	114	211	368	91	36.69	14	346
Aurobindo Pharma	942	102	68	85	172	175	304	104	30.69	24	348
Indian Hotels	688	132	120	52	664	66	530	74	13.21	166	348
Tata Tea	810	117	100	65	333	119	722	58	12.09	185	359.5
Cadbury India	571	146	52	106	140	194	1,315	43	23.68	56	367
Madras Fertilizers	1,404	63	30	146	622	72	89	181	27.10	35	370.5
Jaiprakash Industries	1,615	53	99	67	1,095	47	107	164	11.56	196	372
Engineers India	973	97	126	50	56	253	385	89	17.63	92	383.5
Nicholas Piramal India	506	170	67	86	228	146	765	55	18.65	87	384.5
Finolex Industries	654	137	56	100	596	78	327	94	15.40	130	385
P & G Hygine & Health Care	408	192	78	75	124	200	864	51	42.38	10	385.5
ITI	2,185	38	25	158	321	122	69	199	33.38	19	386.5
Asea Brown Boveri	793	118	54	103	143	191	789	53	14.40	141	388.5
HFCL	1,252	74	131	47	344	115	247	113	7.01	248	392
Mangalore Refinery	2,889	30	-185	287	5,844	11	469	78	1.09	272	393
Madras Cements	618	140	48	110	956	53	513	75	11.55	197	395

Contd...

Contd...

Company	*Sales (Rs. Cr.)*	*Sales Rank*	*PAT (Rs. Cr.)*	*PAT Rank*	*NFA (Rs. Cr.)*	*RANK*	*M.CAP (Rs. Cr.)*	*M.CAP Rank*	*ROCE %*	*ROCE Rank*	*Total*
Eid-Parry	1,318	67	45	121	531	84	109	162	15.10	133	398
Indo Rama Synthetics	1,749	49	19	176	1,725	36	116	158	12.81	171	398.5
EIH	477	180	99	66	1,084	48	1,205	45	8.01	239	401.5
BPL	1,559	56	81	73	537	82	111	161	10.16	217	403
Century Enka	764	123	71	81	581	79	159	137	15.16	132	406
ITC Bhadrachalam	534	160	35	137	668	65	328	93	16.88	104	406
Marico Industries	658	135	46	117	127	199	317	97	28.66	32	406
Resoram Industries	1,109	84	46	116	608	74	108	163	14.81	135	409.5
Jindal Strips	1,447	59	53	104	689	62	82	187	12.49	178	418
Whirlpool of India	918	104	20	174	421	101	160	136	19.20	81	418
Hind Lever Chemicals	1,092	87	32	142	168	179	184	131	17.03	99	428
Apollo Tyres	1,142	82	25	157	430	100	147	142	13.66	155	430
Hoechst Marion Roussel	380	203	39	130	171	176	912	48	24.16	52	430
Godrej Industries	782	120	75	76	338	118	79	192	24.63	51	434.5
Candila Healthcare	478	178	65	87	263	133	595	68	13.50	158	435
Novartis India	432	189	42	123	119	205	647	63	25.57	41	436.5
SPIC	2,167	39	16	187	1,317	43	55	215	14.56	140	439

Contd...

Contd...

Company	*Sales (Rs. Cr.)*	*Sales Rank*	*PAT (Rs. Cr.)*	*PAT Rank*	*NFA (Rs. Cr.)*	*RANK*	*M.CAP (Rs. Cr.)*	*M.CAP Rank*	*ROCE %*	*ROCE Rank*	*Total*
Exide Industries	770	121	45	119	524	86	163	133	12.74	173	443
Finolex Cables	513	168	73	78	205	154	470	77	13.27	165	443.5
Balrampur Chini Mills	556	152	48	113	328	121	144	143	21.52	67	445.5
Pidilite Industries	438	188	48	112	152	187	404	86	24.80	48	447.5
Raymond	1,287	69	-6	247	371	109	443	80	7.61	243	448.5
Gillette India	477	179	26	153	261	136	817	52	13.99	147	449
Gujarat Gas Company	295	236	49	109	162	181	726	57	28.33	33	454.5
Coromondal Fertilizers	596	142	53	105	250	139	101	171	25.36	44	457
Ahmedabad Electricity	956	100	24	160	848	57	177	132	8.11	237	459
Jindal Vijaynagar Steel	1,161	81	-50	275	5,568	12	290	106	3.06	263	462
CMC	534	161	25	159	57	252	391	88	33.70	18	463.5
Tube Investments India	990	93	36	135	267	131	129	151	12.42	181	467.5
Bharat Forge	458	185	33	141	441	95	198	125	19.30	80	468
Godfrey Philips India	549	157	47	115	70	244	315	98	21.27	69	469
Usha Beltron	945	101	49	108	926	55	61	206	13.32	164	470.5
Pentamedia Graphics	552	155	154	42	236	144	142	145	13.49	159	472.5

Contd...

Contd...

Company	*Sales (Rs. Cr.)*	*Sales Rank*	*PAT (Rs. Cr.)*	*PAT Rank*	*NFA (Rs. Cr.)*	*RANK*	*M.CAP (Rs. Cr.)*	*M.CAP Rank*	*ROCE %*	*ROCE Rank*	*Total*
GSFC	2,051	42	4	229	2,112	26	82	189	9.67	229	473
DCM Shriram	976	96	41	126	485	89	80	191	13.35	162	475.5
Zee Teleflims	385	199	138	44	110	214	3,781	19	3.81	262	478
Tamilnadu Petroprodct	623	139	51	107	631	71	133	149	11.04	205	479.5
Pfizer	330	220	38	132	37	272	953	47	29.02	31	484.5
Reckitt Benckiser India Ltd.	549	158	21	172	80	241	635	64	16.49	114	485.5
Deepak Fertilizers	473	181	63	92	356	112	111	160	17.72	90	488
Titan Industries	639	138	24	163	211	150	127	153	18.87	84	489.5
Knoll Pharmaceuticals	316	224	58	99	43	268	407	84	60.22	2	492.5
HEG	553	153	40	129	289	128	121	156	16.57	113	494
Mahavir Spinning Mills	715	130	58	98	393	105	84	184	13.50	157	494
SRF	693	131	40	128	534	83	93	177	13.01	169	498
Jindal Iron & Steel Company	1,412	62	-97	283	601	77	189	130	5.83	255	499.5
E. Merick (India)	311	226	39	131	81	237	453	79	30.96	22	500
Bombay Dyeing	821	114	18	179	347	114	157	138	10.94	206	501.5
Electro Steel Casting	489	176	63	89	190	161	131	150	16.93	102	502
McDowell & Company	821	115	22	170	226	147	148	141	12.49	177	503
Voltas	765	122	70	181	142	192	140	148	17.35	96	504.5
MIRC	655	136	30	145	143	190	103	169	22.22	65	505

Contd...

Contd...

Company	Sales (Rs. Cr.)	Sales Rank	PAT (Rs. Cr.)	PAT Rank	NFA (Rs. Cr.)	RANK	M.CAP (Rs. Cr.)	M.CAP Rank	ROCE %	ROCE Rank	Total
Electronics											
Samtel Colour	569	147	41	127	360	111	62	205	20.06	75	508.5
CESC	1,821	46	-98	284	5,127	14	75	194	7.18	247	512.5
Rolta India	253	258	91	71	149	188	242	115	29.95	27	516
Philips India	1,454	58	-34	267	174	169	314	101	-4.40	282	518
Berger Paints India	490	175	29	149	77	243	215	121	23.02	58	521
Kodak India	667	134	34	139	58	251	190	129	15.68	126	521
Torrent Pharmaceuticals	356	212	41	125	174	170	216	120	18.86	85	522
Essar Shipping	466	183	100	63	1,003	50	102	170	8.84	231	525
ICI India	731	128	23	167	214	149	224	118	7.65	242	525
Videocon Appliances	902	106	35	138	517	87	20	262	17.48	94	527.5
Wockhardt	521	163	72	79	173	172	47	226	29.03	30	529.5
OTIS Elevator Co. (India)	309	228	33	140	44	267	326	96	48.60	6	530.5
Aptech	466	182	82	72	205	153	116	159	13.51	156	531.5
Bhusan Steel	924	103	46	118	743	61	43	233	10.43	213	532
Hindustan Motors	1,389	64	-19	260	406	103	50	224	15.60	127	533
Ispat Industries	1,969	43	-312	288	6,575	8	59	210	0.75	274	538
Digital Global Soft	184	288	54	101	19	286	762	56	54.50	4	539.5
Tata Infotech	515	167	27	152	53	257	217	119	16.75	109	545
Kirloskar Oil Engines	791	119	41	124	153	185	53	219	16.76	108	546.5

Contd...

Contd...

Company	*Sales (Rs. Cr.)*	*Sales Rank*	*PAT (Rs. Cr.)*	*PAT Rank*	*NFA (Rs. Cr.)*	*RANK*	*M.CAP (Rs. Cr.)*	*M.CAP Rank*	*ROCE %*	*ROCE Rank*	*Total*
Zuari Industries	1,204	79	24	161	220	148	54	217	10.75	209	555
Bata India	719	129	16	189	208	151	162	134	6.58	251	558.5
Shree Cement	556	151	26	156	611	73	89	182	9.97	222	558.5
Orchild Chemicals	360	210	36	136	476	91	190	128	10.10	220	561.5
Polaris Software Lab.	266	249	60	96	52	259	194	126	31.24	21	563
Eveready Industries India	874	107	12	199	836	58	46	228	11.43	200	563.5
Smithkline Beecham India	324	222	30	143	48	262	369	90	17.28	98	563.5
Sundaram Fastners	373	204	29	147	174	168	153	139	15.44	128	564.5
Huges Software Systems	199	287	63	90	61	248	314	99	31.48	20	565
Crompton Greaves	1,253	73	-73	281	451	94	99	172	2.46	266	565.5
Essel Packaging	228	270	43	122	160	183	400	87	16.17	118	568.5
Silverline Technologies	273	246	132	46	200	159	205	123	11.05	203	573
VST Industries	325	221	28	151	34	274	249	112	22.57	63	577
Gujarat Alkalies	979	95	-33	265	1,083	49	52	220	10.15	218	581
Bayer (India)	553	154	7	215	124	201	97	174	17.28	97	584.5
Blue Star	503	173	24	164	95	226	67	201	25.84	40	589
Goodlass Nerolac Paints	567	148	23	168	97	223	122	154	11.75	191	593
Birla Corporation	869	108	-13	254	353	113	90	180	7.48	245	594
Bongaigaon Refinery	1,094	86	-57	277	470	92	88	183	-7.29	284	595.5

Contd...

Contd...

Company	*Sales (Rs. Cr.)*	*Sales Rank*	*PAT (Rs. Cr.)*	*PAT Rank*	*NFA (Rs. Cr.)*	*RANK*	*M.CAP (Rs. Cr.)*	*M.CAP Rank*	*ROCE %*	*ROCE Rank*	*Total*
Madura Coats	763	124	-13	252	234	145	161	135	-1.41	276	595.5
Alembic	421	190	30	144	185	163	46	229	23.00	59	602
CEAT	985	94	-14	255	525	85	53	218	7.75	240	602
Basf India	368	206	22	169	133	198	192	127	12.68	174	603.5
Dalmia Cement	363	209	29	148	286	129	104	167	11.83	190	609.5
Mukund	824	113	-41	269	688	63	18	264	13.97	149	617.5
Jagatjit Industries	302	232	13	197	393	104	277	110	6.03	253	619
Bharat Earth Movers	1,251	75	6	218	172	173	50	223	4.50	260	623.5
Shree Rama Multi-Tech	205	285	45	120	285	130	143	144	13.83	153	630.5
Chemplast Sanmar	385	198	16	184	265	132	64	204	13.97	148	634
Rallis India	1,028	91	-28	264	174	167	37	239	12.10	184	637.5
Tata SSL	565	149	0	243	175	166	82	188	11.52	198	640.5
Wochardt Lifesciences	246	262	-18	259	240	143	1,308	44	2.31	267	640.5
Wartsila India	321	223	16	183	34	273	140	147	17.38	95	645.5
Bajaj Tempo	516	166	-17	258	98	222	310	102	-1.50	277	646.5
Birla 3M Ltd.	209	282	11	203	38	271	305	103	24.69	49	646.5
Gammon India	504	171	15	190	178	164	51	222	13.82	154	647
Gujarat Mineral Development	218	275	62	94	152	186	118	157	13.91	151	647.5
Orient Paper	552	156	-13	253	379	107	17	267	17.71	91	648.5
Eicher Motors	392	195	24	162	95	225	37	240	24.84	47	652

Bibliography

ADITHI (1996) : Integration of Women in the Key Economic Sectors : A Report (mimeo.) Patna : ADITHI.

Annual Report (1993-94) : Receipt of Foreign Contributions by Voluntary Associations; New Delhi : Ministry of Home Affairs, Foreigners Division, GOI.

Annual Report (2000-2001) : SDCA. Confederation of Indian Industry (CII).

Anshen, M. (1980) : *Corporate strategies for social performance;* New York : Macmillan.

Asian Development Bank (1995) : Guidance note on how to do stockholder analysis of aid projects and programs; Overseas Development, Social Development Division.

Asian Development Bank (1999) : *Reducing poverty : Major findings and implications;* ADB Publications.

Asian Development Bank (1999) : *Polity on indigenous people;* Manila, Philippines : ADB Publications.

Aswathappa, K. (2001) : *Essential of business environment;* New Delhi : Himalaya Publishing House.

Amber, T. and Wilson A. (1995) : "Problems of a stakeholder theory," *Business Ethics,* 4 (1) : pp. 30-35.

APSO-Agency for Personal Service Overseas (1998) : Annual Report 1998, Dublin, Ireland.

Arkin, A. (1996) : "Open business is good for business"; *People Management,* 2(1).

Ball, C. & Dunn, L. (1995) : *Non-government organizations : Guidelines for good policy and practice;* London : The Commonwealth Foundation.

Beteille, A. (1999) : *Economic and Political Weekly,* Vol. 34, Nos. 10 & 11, 589-597.

Bhat, R. (2000) : Issues in Health : Public-Private Partnership; *Economic and Political Weekly,* December 30, 4720-4716.

Bhattacharaya, D. (1999) : Political parties need to make commitments on social development; *Equinox*, Vol. 1, issue 1, 3-5.

Brooks, L.J. (1980) : "An attitude survey approach in the social audit : The Southern Press Accounting, *Organisations and Society*, 5(3).

Buchholz, R. (1982) : *Business Environment and Public Policy*, Prentice-Hall, Englewood Cliffs, NJ.

Chauhan, U. & Lal, N. (1999) : Public-private partnerships for urban poor in Ahmedabad : A slum project, *Economic and Political Weekly*, Vol. 34, Nos. 10 & 11, 636-642.

Cherunilam, F. (2001) : *Global economy and business environment;* New Delhi : Himalaya Publishing House.

Chowdhry, K. (1994) : *Gandhi and agenda* 21; New Delhi : Vikram Sarabhai Foundation.

Clarkson, M.B.E. (1995) : A stakeholder framework for analyzing and evaluating corporate social performance; *Academy of Management Studies*, Vol. 20, No. 1, 92-117.

Confederation of Indian Industry (1995) , *A New India—The New Indian Industry*, New Delhi : CII.

Cotton, P., I. A.M. Fraser and W.Y. Hill (1998) : The Social Audit Agenda—Primary healthcare in a stakeholder society, Working paper, Faculty of Business, Glasgow Caledonian University.

Coy, D. and Pratt, M. (1998) : "An insight into accountability and politics in universities : a case, *Accounting, Auditing and Accountability Journal*, 11(5), pp. 540-561.

Cernea, M. M. (1991) : The building blocks of participation : testing bottom-up planning; World Bank Discussion Paper No. 166.

Davis, K. (1973) : The case for and agains business assumption of social responsibilities. *Academy of Management Journal*, Vol. 16, No. 2, 312-22.

Dev, S.M. & Mooij, J. (2002) : Social sector expenditures in the 1990s : Analysis of central and state budgets, *Economic and Political Weekly*, Vol. 37, No. 9, 853-866.

Dawson, E. (1998) : "The relevance of social audit for Oxfam GB", *Journal of Business Ethics*, 17(13), pp. 1456-69.

Dennis, B., Evans, R. and R.H. Gray (1995) : "Towards social information systems and bookkeeping : a note on developing the mechanisms for social accounting and audit", *Journal of Applied, Accounting Research*, 2 (3), pp. 36-69.

Dierkes, M. and A. Berthoin (1986) : "Whither corporate social reporting : is it time to legislate?" *California Management Review,* 28 (3), pp. 106-21.

Epstein, E.M. (1987) : The corporate social policy process : Beyond business ethics, corporate social responsibility, and corporate social responsiveness, *California Management Review,* Vol. 29, No. 3, 99-114.

Filios, V.P. (1984) : "Corporate social responsibility and public accountability", *Journal of Business Ethics,* 3(4), pp. 153-173.

Filios, V.P. (1985b) : "Social process auditing : a survey and some suggestions", *Journal of Business Ethics,* 4(6), pp. 477-85.

Filios, V.P. (1986) : "Review and analysis of the empirical research in corporate social : *Journal of Business Ethics,* 5(4), pp. 291-306.

Fredrick, W., J. Post and K. Davis (1992) : *Bussiness and Society,* New York : McGraw Hill.

Gandhi, P. J. (2001) : Dynamics of global economy : Its diagnosis and prognosis, *Sourthern Economist,* May 1, 11-14.

Garain, S. (2001) : Corporate citizenship and corporate volunteering, *Yojana,* December, 12-14.

Government of India (1996-97) : *Statistical Outline of India,* 1996-97, p. 14.

Goyder, G. (1951) : *The future of private enterprise : A study in resopnsibility,* Oxford : Basil Blackwell.

Guruswamy, M. (2001) : How good is our liberalization? *Seminar,* November, 39-44.

Gray, R., C. Dey, D. Owen, R. Evans and S. Zadek (1997): "Struggling with the praxis of social accounting: stakeholders, accountability, audits and procedures", *Accounting, Auditing and Accountability Journal,* 10(3), pp. 325-364.

Haq, M.U. (1996) *Reflections on human development,* New Delhi: Oxford University Press.

Holliday, C. (2001): Sustainable growth : The DuPont way, *Harvard Business Review,* September, 129-134.

Heard, J.E. and W.J. Boice (1981) : "The Political significance of corporate social reporting, *Accounting, Organisations and Society* 6(3), pp. 247-55.

Hill, W.Y., I.A.M. Fraser and P. Cotton (1998) : "Patients" voices, rights and responsibilities—on implementing social audit in primary healthcare, *Journal of Business Ethics,* 17(13), pp. 1481-1497.

Humphrey, C. and D. Owen (2000) : 'Debating the Power of audit", *International Journal of Auditing*, 4(1), forthcoming.

India : Planning Commission (1969) : Fourth Five Year Plan, 1969-74, Draft, New Delhi.

India : Planning Commission (1976) : Fifth Five Year Plan, 1974-79, Draft, New Delhi.

India : Planning Commission 1980 : Sixth Five Year Plan, 1980-85, Draft, New Delhi.

India : Planning Commission (1980) : Seventh Five Year Plan, 1985-90, Draft, New Delhi.

India : Planning Commission (1992) : Eighth Five Year Plan, 1992-97, Draft, New Delhi.

India : Planning Commission (1997) : Ninth Five Year Plan, 1997-2002, Draft, New Delhi.

J. Bhagyalakshmi (2001) : New initatives for poverty alleviation, *Yajana*, November, 12-13.

Jain, N. (2001) : Globalization : Indian business scenario, *Southern Economist*, May 1, 15-18.

Jalan, B. (1991) : *India's Economic Crisis*, New Delhi : OUP.

Jha, S. & Swaroop, V. (1999) : Foreign aid to India : What does it finance? *Economic and Political Weekly*, May 8, 1142-1146.

Kabra, K. N. (1995) : Social development : Elements of an alternative agenda, *Economic Growth and Social Change*, March, 91-92.

Kerby, D. (2001) : Government and corporate social responsibility : An overview of selected Canadian, European, and International Practices, Canada : Canadian Business for Social Responsibility.

Khan, A.M. (1997) : *Shaping policy : Do NGOs matter?* New Delhi : Society for Participatory Research in Asia.

Kulkarni, P.D. (1997) : Integrating social development, In P.D. Kulkarni and M.C. Nanavatty (Eds.), *Social Issues in Development*; New Delhi : Uppal Publishing House.

Kurain, T. (2001) : Rethinking on globalization and development : A view, *Southern Economist*, May 1, p. 19.

Macchiwalla, T. (1997) : Perspectives on sustainable development, *Search Bulletin*, Vol. 12, No. 2, 15-22.

Mitra, A. (2001) : Civil society, globalization and sustainable development, *Seminar*, 507, 47-52.

Mittal, L.N. (1997) : Economic growth vs. social well-being, *Social Welfare*, May 18-20.

Mohanty, M. & Singh, A.K. (1996) : *Foreign Aid and NGOs,* New Delhi : Voluntary Action Network India (VANI).

Mohanty, M. & Singh, A.K. (2001) : *Voluntarism and Government : Policy, programme and assistance,* New Delhi : Voluntary Action Network India (VANI).

Moen Mathiot, E. (1998) : *NGOs and Grassroots Development Work in South India,* Lanham : University Press of America.

Mukherjee, K. K. (1994) : *Emerging Societal Challenges and Voluntary Organizations : Challenges and Responses,* Ghaziabad : Gram Niyojan Kendra.

Mackenzie, C. (1998) : "Ethical auditing and ethical knowledge", *Journal of Business Ethics,* 17(13), pp. 1395-1402.

Marx, T.G. (1998) : "Corporate social performance reporting", *Public Relations Quarterly,* 37(4).

Murphy, P.E. and Burton, E.J. (1980) : "Accountants assess the social audit", *Business,* 30(5).

Narayan, J. (2001) : Good governance is the key to prosperity, *Economic Times,* August 18, 2001.

Nayyar, D. (1996) : Globalization : The past in our present, *Economic Growth and Social Change,* March, 11-16.

Norgaard, R.B. (1999) : Beyond growth and globalization, *Economic and Political Weekly,* Vol. 34, No. 36, 2570-2574.

Natale, S.M. and J.W. Ford (1994) : "The social audit and ethics", *Managerial Auditing Journal,* 9(1), pp. 29-36.

New Economics Foundation (NEF) (1996) : Value-based Organisation-Organising NGOs for Value-based Effectiveness, London.

New Economics Foundation (NEF) (1998) : Briefing Paper on Social Auditing, London : The New Economics Foundation.

Overseas Development Institute (1996) : The Impact of NGO Development Projects, Briefing Paper 2/96.

Ostapski, S.A. and C.N. Isaacs (1992) : "Corporate moral responsibility and the moral audit : Challenges for Refuse Relief Inc.", *Journal of Business Ethics,* 11 (3).

Ostapski, S.A. and D.G. Pressley (1992) : "Moral audit for Diabco corp.", *Journal of Business Ethics,* 11 (1).

Qizilbash, M. (2001) : Sustainable development : Concept and rankings, *The Journal of Development Studies,* Vol. 37, No. 3, 134-161.

Pearce, J. (1996) : Measuring Social Wealth, A Study of Social Audit Practice for Community and Co-operative Enterprises, New Econimics Foundation, London.

Pearce, J., P. Raynard and S. Zadek (1997) : Social Auditing from Small Organisations, New Economics Foundation, London.

Pearce, J.P. (1997) : " Auditing and corporate governance—a look forward into the 21st century", *International Journal of Auditing,* 1 (1), pp. 3-12.

Perumalsamy, S. & Manickavasagam, S. (1996) : Strategy for sustainable development, *Economic Growth and Social Change,* March, 75-76.

Pongsapich, A. & Kataleeradabhan, N. (1997) : *Thailand nonprofit sectior and social development,* Bangkok : Chulalongkorn University Social Research Institute.

Pomeranz, F. (1978) : "Social measurement : a primer for implementation," *Journal of Accounting, Auditing and Finance,* 1(4).

Puxty, A.G. (1991) : "Coming together. A review of contemporary approaches to social accounting, auditing and reporting in non-profit organisations", *Journal of Business Strategy,* 20(6), pp. 39-43.

Ramachandran, V. (1996) : NGOs in the time of globalization, *Seminar,* 447, November, 54-59.

Rao, K.S. (1997) : *Financing of primary healthcare in Andhra Pradesh,* Report prepared for World Health Organization.

Reich, R.B. (1998) : The new meaning of corporate social responsibility, *The California Management Review,* Winter, 8-17.

Sampradan, (2001) : *Giving and Fund Raising in India,* New Delhi : Indian Centre for Philanthropy.

Sethi, S.P. (1987) : Models of business and society interaction, In S.P. Sethi & C.M. Falbe (eds.), *Business and society : Dimensions of conflict and cooperation,* Lexington, MA : Lexington Books.

Shiva, V. (1998) : Globalization, Gandhi and Swadeshi, *Mainstream,* May 23, 13-23.

Shoney, M. (1998) : The right cure : Will the industry initiative in improving Tamil Nadu's primary health centres succeed? *Business World,* November.

Singh, B.P. (2001) : 5th Dr. Rajendra Prasad Memorial Lecture, *Hindustan Times,* 28 the November.

Singh, K.A.N. (1999) : Defining the voluntary organizations in India: Some reflections, *Institutional Development,* Vol. 6, No. 2, 10-25.

Singh, M. (1995) : Development—the human angle. *Economic Growth the Social Change,* September, 71-72.

Singh, S. (1996) : Economic reforms with a human face, *Economic Growth and Social Change,* March, 90-92.

Singh, S. (1999) : Paradigm shifts in social development in India : A critique, *The Indian Journal of Social Work,* Vol. 60, Issue 1, 141-152.

Singhania, H.S. (1980) : The pace setters, *The Economic Times,* August 3.

SRI (1992) : *Survey on Corporate Philanthropy,* New Delhi : Action Aid.

SRI (1997) : *Report on Survey on Corporate Involvement in Social Development in India,* New Delhi : Partners in Change.

SRI (2000) : *Report on Survey on Corporate Involvement in Social Development in India.* New Delhi : Partners in Change.

Srivastava, J. (2000) : Emerging role of NGOs in the WTO, *Mainstream,* July 8, 11-15.

Srivenkataramana, T. & Narayan Raj, N. (1997), NGOs are vital to social development, *Social Welfare,* July, 15-17.

Stephen, F. (1997) : Sustainable development : A paradoxical paradigm, *Search Bulletin,* Vol. 12, No. 2, 3-14.

Suman Chandra, K. (1998) : Social justice and development, *Social Welfare,* March '98, 21-26.

Sundra, P. (2000) : *Beyond business : From merchant charity to corporate citizenship,* New Delhi : Tata McGraw-Hill.

Swanson, D.L. (1999) : Towards an integrated theory of business and society : A research strategy for corporate social performance, *Academy of Management Review,* Vol. 24, No. 3, 506-21.

Sillanpaa, M. (1998) : "The Boby values report— Towards integrated stakeholder auditing," *Journal of Business Ethics,* 17 (13), pp. 1443-56.

Spicer, B.H. (1978) : "Accounting for corporate social performance : Some problems and issues", *Journal of Contemporary Business,* 7 (1).

Spreckley, F. (1997) : *Social Audit Toolkit,* Willenhall, UK : Social Enterprise Partnership.

Steiner, G. and J. Steiner (1991) : *Business, Government and Society,* New York : McGraw-Hill.

Tandon, R. & Mohanty, R. (2000) : *Civil society and governance :*

A research study in India, New Delhi : Society for Participatory Research in Asia (PRIA).

The Prince of Wales International Business Leaders Forum (2000) : Corporate Social Responsibility in Central and Eastern Europe : Business sense or business burden? London, United Kingdom : IBLF.

The Economist (2001) : Giving Something Back, June 16, 2001.

Trapp, R. (2001) : Virtue and reality, *People Management*, October, 28-34.

Traidcraft Exchange : Social Accounts 1995-96. Gateshead, Traidcraft Exchange.

Traidcraft plc. Social Audit Report 1992-93; Social Audit Report 1993-94; Social Accounts 1994-95; Social Accounts 1995-96, Gateshead, Traidcraft.

Turnbull, S. (1995) : "The need for stakeholder councils in social audit", *Social and Environmental Accounting*, 15 (2), pp. 10-13.

United Nations Development Programme (UNDP) (1997) : *Human Development Report* 1997, New York : Oxford University Press.

United Nations Development Programme (UNDP) (1997) : *India : The Road to Human Development*, pp. 5-7. New York : Oxford University Press.

United Nations Development Programme (UNDP) (2001) : *Human Development Report 2001*, New York : Oxford University Press.

Venkateshwaran, S. (1999) : Can NGOs and corporates meet? *Sampradan*, No. 11, December.

Vinten, G. (1990) "The social auditor", *Indernational Journal of Value-Based Management*, 3 (2), pp. 125-36.

Wartick, S.L. & Cochran, P.L. (1985) : The evolution of the corporate social performance model, *Academy of Management Review*, Vol. 10, No. 4, 758-69.

Wartick, S.L. & Wood, D.J. (1998) : *International Business and Society*, Oxford : Blackwell.

Weisbrod, B. (1975) : Towards a theory of the voluntary non-profit sector in a three-sector ecnonomy, In Edmund Phelps (ed.), *Altuism, Morality and Economic Theory*, pp. 175-195. New York : Russell Sage Foundation.

Wood, D.J. (1991) : Corporate social performance revisited, *Academy of Management Review*, Vol. 16, No. 4, 691-718.

Wood, D.J. & Jones, R.E. (1996) : Research in corporate social performance : What have we learned, In D.F. Burlingame &

D.R. Young (eds.), *Corporate philanthropy at the crossroads*, Bloomington : Indiana University Press.

Wokutch, R.E. and L. Fahey (1986) : "A value explicit approach for evaluating corporate social, *Journal of Accounting and Public Policy*, 5 (3), pp. 191-214.

Woodward, D.G. (1998) : "An attempt at the classification of the quarter of a century of (non-critical), Paper presented at the British Accounting Association Annual Conference, April, Manchester.

Zadek, S. (1993) : "The social audit of Traidcraft plc." *Social and Environment Accounting*, 13(2), pp. 5-6.

Zadek, S. (1998) : "Blancing performance, ethics, and accountability", *Journal of Business Ethics*, 17 (13), pp. 1421-41.

Zadek, S. and R. Evan (1993) : *Auditing the Market*, (NEF) Traidcraft, Gateshead.

Zadek, S. and P. Raynard (1995) : "Accounting works : a comparative review of contemporary approaches to social and ethical accounting", *Accounting Forum*, 19 (2/3), pp. 164-75.

Index